BEYOND THE BASICS

Excelling at
BADMINTON

BEYOND THE BASICS

Excelling at
BADMINTON

A Practical Reference Manual for Players and Coaches

JAKE DOWNEY
Director of Coaching
Badminton Association of England

Hodder & Stoughton
LONDON SYDNEY AUCKLAND

Cover photographs courtesy of Louis Ross and AllSport Photolibrary

British Library Cataloguing in Publication Data

Downey, Jake
Excelling at Badminton – (Beyond the Basics Series)
I. Title II. Series
796.34

ISBN 0-340-57664-2
Copyright © Jake Downey 1993
Photographs © Louis Ross
First published in Great Britain 1993

Published by Hodder and Stoughton,
a division of Hodder and Stoughton Ltd,
Mill Road, Dunton Green, Sevenoaks, Kent TN13 2YA
Editorial Office: 47 Bedford Square, London WC1B 3DP

Set and designed by John Youé
with drawings by Ethan Danielson

Printed and bound in Great Britain by
BPCC Hazell Books Ltd
Member of BPCC Ltd

Contents

Plan Your Journey   8

Introduction   11

1   KNOW THE GAME   13
    Principle of attack – logical structure of the game – situations in the game –
    basic tactical moves – rallies and action phrases – parts of an action phrase –
    body movements – stroke moves used – complete action phrases and rallies

2   KNOW YOUR CRAFT   20
    Technical skill practices – tactical skill practices – individual specific skill practices –
    informal competition – formal competition – studies – fitness training and diet –
    mental training – summary

3   WHAT DO YOU WANT TO ACHIEVE?   24
    Competition goals – tournament goals – team goals – performance goals – intrinsic
    and extrinsic goals – are your goals realistic?

4   PLAN TO ACHIEVE YOUR GOALS   27
    Procedure in planning an action programme

5   MAKE THE MOST OF YOUR PRACTICE   29
    What is practice – types of practice – technical and tactical practices – practice and
    routines – learn how to practise – stages in practices – how much should you
    practise – so you don't feel like practising – practice partners – from the practice
    court to the match court – bridging the gap – conditioned games – informal
    competition – formal competition – a positive approach to practice

6   YOUR COMPLETE REFERENCE LIST OF TECHNICAL SKILLS   39

7   LEARN HOW TO IMPROVE YOUR RACKET SKILL   42
    The grips – hitting techniques – control your racket head – control of the racket face –
    practices to improve your racket skill

Contents

8   LEARN HOW TO IMPROVE YOUR BODY SKILL   50
    Body skill components – posture and balance – starting and stopping – travelling –
    transitions – lunge and recovery – jumping and landing – specific practices for
    body skill

9   KNOW YOUR STROKES, CORRECT YOUR FAULTS AND PRACTISE TO IMPROVE   60
    Body skill faults and corrections – your strokes, common faults, causes, corrections
    and practices – description of the stroke-move analysis headings – overhead
    rearcourt stroke-moves – low rearcourt strokes-moves – midcourt stroke-moves –
    serves – forecourt stroke-moves

10 ANALYSING AND CORRECTING YOUR TECHNICAL FAULTS   109
    Identify the problem – diagnosis – correction – practices

11 CREATE YOUR OWN PRACTICE PROGRAMME   111
    Practise your stroke and action phrases – from single to combination stroke
    practices – make use of the practice procedure – practice aims and standards –
    set practice targets and measure your success in practice – develop your technical
    practice – fitness – mental attitude – devise your own practice routines –
    stroke practice form – technical practice programme form

12 LEARN HOW TO PRACTISE YOUR TECHNICAL SKILLS UNDER PRESSURE   118
    What are the purposes of practices – zone practices – action phrase practices –
    continuous rally practice – multifeed practice

13 GET YOURSELF FIT FOR BADMINTON   126
    What you need to know – am I in good health – what is fitness – what do I need
    to do to get fit – how fit do I need to be – how do I maintain my fitness –
    how do I get fit – training – preparation – warm up and cool down – flexibility –
    slow stretching exercises – developing your endurance – develop your strength,
    power and speed – find out how fit you are – diet – rest – plan your own training
    programme

14 INJURIES AND HOW YOU CAN TRY TO PREVENT THEM   146
    Physical injuries – forms of injury – overuse injuries – traumatic injuries –
    overload injuries – treating an injury

15 **DEVELOP A WINNING ATTITUDE AND EXPLOIT YOUR OPPONENT'S ATTITUDE** 149
What is a mental attitude – attitudes you need for competition – how do I develop
such attitudes – how do I exploit my opponents' attitudes – what do you do with
players who try to exploit your attitude – confidence, character and the will to win

16 **IMPROVE YOUR DEFENCE** 153
Passive and active defence – how to learn it – how to practise it

17 **LEARN TO DECEIVE YOUR OPPONENT** 156
Body language – how do I learn and improve my deception –
some ways in which you can be deceptive

18 **LEARN TO ANALYSE AND ASSESS YOUR PERFORMANCE IN COMPETITION** 158
How should I record information – questionnaire – how shall I use this information –
performance analysis report form

19 **PREPARE AND COMPETE TO WIN AT SINGLES** 163
The qualities of a good player – technical skill – tactical skill – percentage play –
strategies – fitness – attitude – preparation and competition

20 **PREPARE AND COMPETE TO WIN AT LEVEL AND MIXED DOUBLES** 173
Your role in the team – your functions – hit- and set-up players – playing as a team –
how to become a better performer – getting into the right positions –
playing as a team in attack and defence – general advice on attacking play

Recommended Reading 191

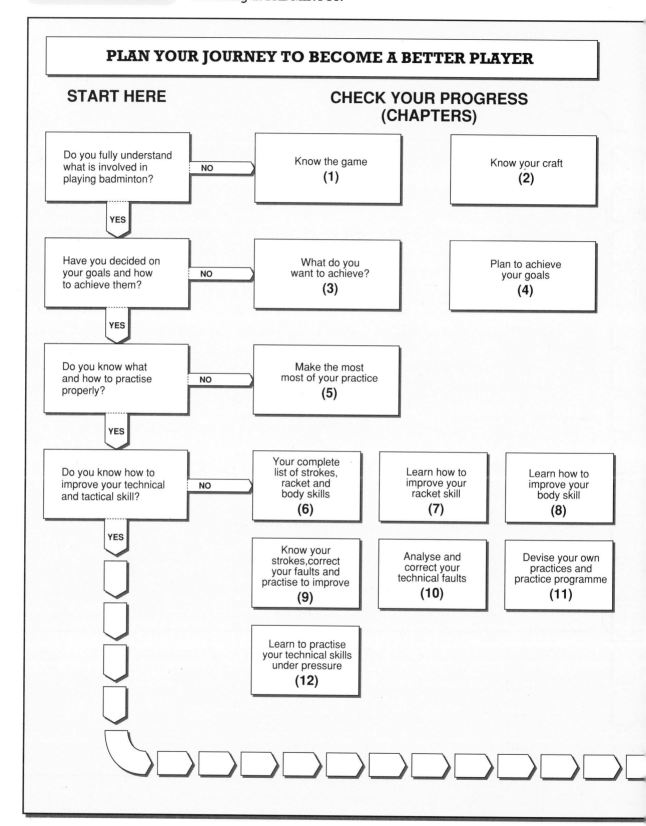

PLAN YOUR JOURNEY TO BECOME A BETTER PLAYER

START HERE

CHECK YOUR PROGRESS (CHAPTERS)

Do you fully understand what is involved in playing badminton? — NO →

Know the game **(1)**

Know your craft **(2)**

YES ↓

Have you decided on your goals and how to achieve them? — NO →

What do you want to achieve? **(3)**

Plan to achieve your goals **(4)**

YES ↓

Do you know what and how to practise properly? — NO →

Make the most most of your practice **(5)**

YES ↓

Do you know how to improve your technical and tactical skill? — NO →

Your complete list of strokes, racket and body skills **(6)**

Learn how to improve your racket skill **(7)**

Learn how to improve your body skill **(8)**

YES ↓

Know your strokes, correct your faults and practise to improve **(9)**

Analyse and correct your technical faults **(10)**

Devise your own practices and practice programme **(11)**

Learn to practise your technical skills under pressure **(12)**

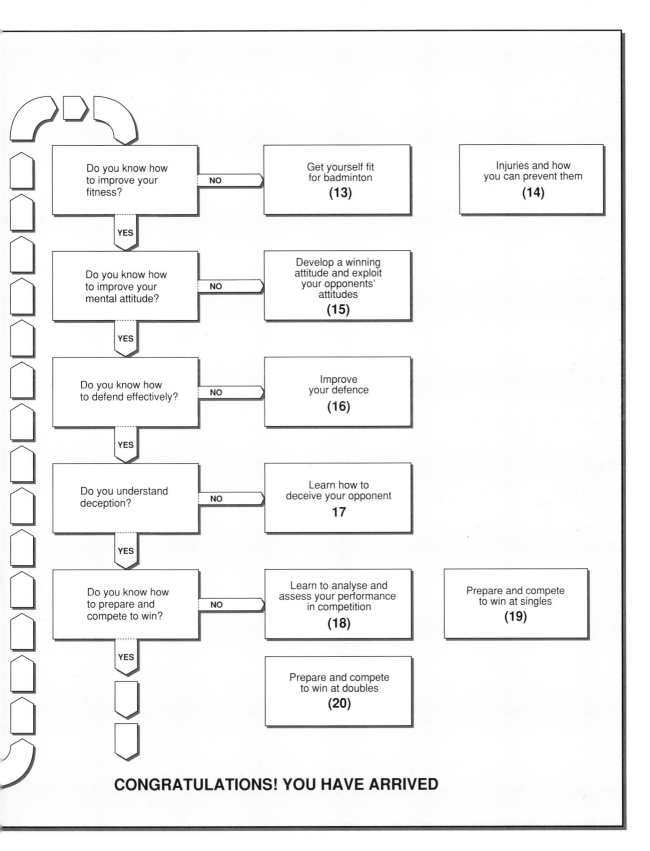

Do you know how to improve your fitness?

NO → Get yourself fit for badminton **(13)**

Injuries and how you can prevent them **(14)**

YES ↓

Do you know how to improve your mental attitude?

NO → Develop a winning attitude and exploit your opponents' attitudes **(15)**

YES ↓

Do you know how to defend effectively?

NO → Improve your defence **(16)**

YES ↓

Do you understand deception?

NO → Learn how to deceive your opponent **17**

YES ↓

Do you know how to prepare and compete to win?

NO → Learn to analyse and assess your performance in competition **(18)**

Prepare and compete to win at singles **(19)**

YES ↓

Prepare and compete to win at doubles **(20)**

CONGRATULATIONS! YOU HAVE ARRIVED

Introduction

EXCELLING AT BADMINTON

My intention in writing this book has been to provide a practical reference manual for you to refer to on any aspects of the game of badminton so that it will act as a self-help guide whenever you are in need of some form of tuition. I have assumed that you are an experienced player and know quite a lot about the game already. This book has therefore been designed to allow you to refer only to those areas of the game that you want to learn more about.

As a coach I believe that all players can benefit from a deeper study of the game they play. Badminton is a fascinating game, full of interest and challenges for any player but to appreciate the game fully and play it well you must understand it. Obviously, if you are reading this book you are curious to learn more about badminton and perhaps would like to become a better player. I hope that I will manage to satisfy your curiosity and help you to improve your game.

It is a common feature of most sports that players and coaches often recommend a return to the basics in order to improve their play. The simple fact is that to go beyond the basics you must first master them. This is what all good players work so hard to do in order to become even better players of the game.

You will be familiar with the usual basics in badminton. No doubt when you first started to play the game you learned how to hit the shuttle; how to hold the racket (the grips); achieve the ready position; how to perform the strokes and rally; how to start and stop quickly and travel to the various parts of the court: and how to play singles, doubles and mixed games. All the basic things required to play and enjoy the game.

If you can do all these things then you are ready

to go beyond the basics and work to become even more skilful at doing them. You should then become a better player.

You will know if you are becoming a better and more skilful player by how you perform in competition. You will need to play other players to test yourself and to measure your progress. In testing yourself you should give 100 per cent effort to try to win. Only then will you obtain an accurate measure of your progress.

It doesn't follow, however, that you must win to become a better player. You can lose and still consider that you have made some progress. You may for example be making fewer errors than before; the rallies may be longer; you may win more easily against regular opponents; you may gain more points than usual and even a game against a better player. You might begin to use the backhand clear under pressure rather than try to play your usual forehand round the head shot. When these things happen you will find it most rewarding because you know that the hard work is paying off and the effort to become a better player has been worthwhile.

Surprisingly you will be in good company in your ambitions. Most top-class players continually work to become better players. If they did not they would risk lowering their standards and being overtaken by others.

You must decide just how much better you want to become or are capable of becoming. Whatever you do decide this book should help you to improve and to achieve your particular goals as a player.

The book is very easy to use. First read the Route Map on page 8 and start at the areas of the game you wish to improve.

**When using this book, please remember
these points:**

1 I have assumed that you are a right-handed
   player. If you are left handed then reverse the
   descriptions where appropriate.

2 The noun 'man' and the pronoun 'he' are used
   for general discussion. All the comments about
   'he' and 'man' apply equally to women unless
   specific reference is made to male or female
   players, e.g. as in mixed doubles.

3 The symbols shown right have been used in
   the diagrams to designate the players and the
   shuttlecock.

(P) ⟶   The player doing the practice

(F) ⟶   the 'feeder', practice partner
         or opponent
         (as in a tactical practice)

● ⟶   the attacking player

○ ⟶   the defending player

⟶   the arrow represents the
         direction a player travels
         in the court

⟶   the length of the arrow indicates
         the distance a player travels

✗   shuttle position in the court

– ⟶🏸– – direction of shuttle pathway

RC   rearcourt
MC   midcourt
FC   forecourt
fh   forehand
bh   backhand

Example of players travelling
whilst adjusting their positions in
the court

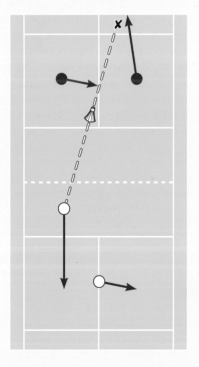

Jake Dawey

Know the Game

I have literally been through two tennis lives. The first was a totally instinctive, spontaneous approach to the game. The one I'm living now, at thirty-two, is a much more intellectual and professional one, and it's definitely more satisfying. I've learned that it is not enough to do something well. You have to know how you did it to fully appreciate the accomplishment. Especially if you have any hope of ever re-creating it.
Virginia Wade on winning Wimbledon

A good player is like a craftsman; a great player is like an artist. Common to both is that they are masters of their craft and they control what they do. Artists are special people – they usually have that something extra, something unique, which makes them stand out. You may not become an artist but you can certainly become a craftsman at the game of badminton. But to achieve this you must know and understand all the various aspects of your craft.

In some respects playing badminton is similar to playing chess. Both games involve trying to defeat your opponent(s) by playing tactical moves. For example, whenever you hit the shuttle over the net you are making a tactical move in the game. It is tactical because it obtains a certain response from your opponent(s). For instance, your opponent will respond differently if you clear from your rearcourt than if you play a dropshot. If you clear he will be forced to travel backwards to his rearcourt. Alternatively he would respond differently to a straight dropshot than to a cross-court dropshot. As the game is a contest the purpose of your tactical moves is to win the rallies and ultimately the game. To play in this way is to play in accordance with the *principle of attack*.

THE PRINCIPLE OF ATTACK

There are two ways of applying this principle – a positive one and a negative one.

The positive one is:

● At all times try to create a situation to increase your chances of eventually winning the rally.

If you cannot do this then apply the negative one, which is:

● Whenever necessary try to create a situation to reduce your opponent's chances of winning the rally.

As your strokes are the means by which you make your tactical moves then if you apply the *principle of attack* in your play, your strokes cease to be just actions and become *stroke-moves*. Your strokes and tactics, therefore, should be inseparable.

It is these features which provide the logical structure of the game, i.e. the game is a contest, in which the strokes are used as tactical moves in accordance with the principle of attack.

The Logical Structure of the Game
See Fig 1 *below.*

SITUATIONS

moves
(strokes)

an appropriate
stroke-move
if played in
accordance
with the
principle
of attack

stroke-moves
logically
possible

stroke-moves
actually possible

stroke-move
actually played

In any game you will find yourself in different situations – as shown at the top of Fig 1. In each situation there will be a number of tactical moves which are *logically possible*. These will be the total of *stroke-moves* that can possibly be played from any situation in the court. Although there will be a number of logically possible moves in any given situation it might be the case that you do not know how to play them all. What stroke-moves are *actually possible* therefore will depend on what you can do. If you cannot play all the stroke-moves you will have fewer options available. This will, of course, be an advantage to an opponent who has studied your game and knows what you can and cannot do in certain situations.

You can, however, only play one stroke-move at a time, although you should always be able to play at least two tactical moves from any situation. In this instance let's assume that you can perform several stroke-moves, which makes it difficult for your opponent to anticipate which one you will choose.

You play your stroke-move, but is the stroke-move you *actually played* a good tactical move and was it appropriate in the circumstances? This is where we can refer to the principle of attack for guidance. If the move helped to create a situation which improved your chances and reduced your opponent's chances of winning the rally then it was an appropriate tactical move. We could even describe it as a good move – intelligent, clever, shrewd, etc. – all implying that it was played in accordance with the principle of attack.

The logical structure of the game is quite easy to understand. Its value is that it gives purpose to all your actions providing that you apply the principle of attack as you play. You can use it to judge whether your stroke-moves are effective or not in helping to win the game. The structure should also draw your attention to the various situations you will encounter in the game and should help you to consider all the stroke-moves that can be played in each situation. Above all it helps to focus attention on your opponent, in that everything you do is aimed at defeating your opponent.

THE SITUATIONS IN THE GAME

There are three major situations in the game. These are the rearcourt (RC), midcourt (MC), and forecourt (FC). *See* Fig 2. The stroke-moves are played from high or low positions in each situation: high, if above net height; low, if below net height. It is a simple exercise to work out all the stroke-moves logically possible in a situation, e.g. high in the forehand rearcourt. *See* Fig 3.

Fig 2
Shows the court and the situations.

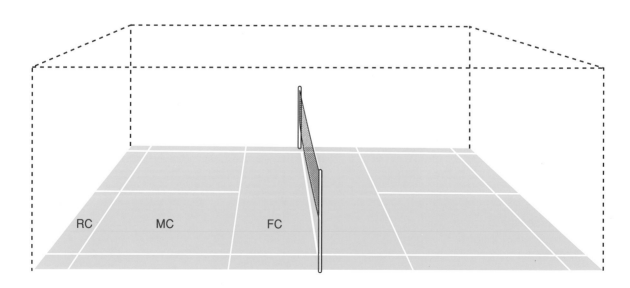

THE BASIC TACTICAL MOVES

Although there are many stroke-moves which are logically possible within the various situations in singles, level and mixed doubles, they can all be reduced to four basic tactical moves.

1 There are stroke-moves used to send the opponent to the rearcourt. These are: the overhead clear, the lob, the drive, the high serve and the flick serve.

The reasons for playing this move are:
a) To draw the opponent out of position away from the centre of the court and as far away from the net as possible.
b) To reduce the effectiveness of the opponent. He cannot do much damage from the back of the court.
c) To create space.

2 There are stroke-moves used to send the opponent into the forecourt. These are: the overhead dropshot, the block to the smash, the net reply (of which there are several) and the low serve.

The reasons for playing this move are:
a) To draw the opponent out of position away from the centre.
b) To create space.
c) To force the opponent to hit the shuttle upwards (a lift).

3 There are stroke-moves used to send the opponent to the sides of the court, i.e. rearcourt, midcourt or forecourt. All the strokes can be used to create this type of situation.

The reasons for playing this move are:
a) To draw the opponent out of position away from the centre.
b) To create space.

4 There are the stroke-moves used to exploit the opponent in the midcourt. These are: the smash, the long dropshot, the drive, the push and the kill from the net.

The reasons for playing this move are:
a) To attempt a winning shot.

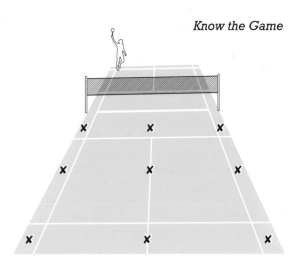

Fig 3
Shows the range of stroke-moves logically possible from the forehand rearcourt.

b) To create space.
c) To force an upward hit (a lift).
d) To force a weak reply.
e) To force an error.

What is common to these basic moves is that several strokes can be used to play them. They are all used to create situations to increase your chances of winning the rallies and eventually the game. The first, second and third basic moves are slightly different in purpose to the fourth, the intention behind the first three being to use the strokes mainly as **building shots**, while the intention behind the fourth is to use some of the stronger strokes as **attempted winning shots** as well as building shots, e.g. the smash. Obviously all the strokes used to play the basic moves may be used as building shots or attempted winning shots; some are just more effective as one or the other in a particular situation.

RALLIES AND ACTION PHRASES

The fact that you and your opponent(s) use your strokes as tactical moves to try to create situations, which will eventually lead to a winning shot, causes a great deal of activity on the court. The building shots and attempted winning shots that you both play will cause you both to travel to and fro between the rearcourt, midcourt and forecourt. You will play short or long rallies depending on how many shots you will have to play before the rally ends.

A game is made up of rallies. In winning a rally you will win a point or the serve. Your obvious task is to win more rallies than your opponent when you are serving and to make sure that you win a rally as quickly as possible when your opponent is serving. To do this you must become a skilful and fit player. A closer look at what goes on in a rally will indicate in what aspects of the game you must become skilful.

Rallies are made up of *action phrases*, so called because everything you do on the court when in practice, training and competition will take place within an action phrase. You will perform the strokes, body movements and tactical moves within an action phrase. To inspect a complete action phrase take a look at Fig 7 on page 19. To make it easier to understand I will explain how it is built up.

THE PARTS OF AN ACTION PHRASE
See Fig 4 *below*

Court Starting Position This is the start of the action phrase. Here you are in position in a rearcourt, midcourt or forecourt situation ready to cover your opponent's most probable tactical moves.

Approach Travel Phase Once your opponent hits the shuttle he will create a new situation so that you must now travel into position to hit the shuttle and play your tactical move – unless of course the

shuttle is hit straight towards you and there is no need to travel anywhere except for a slight adjustment to your stance as you get into a hitting position.

Hitting Position Having travelled towards the shuttle you get into position to hit it effectively. This is the position on the court from which you perform the stroke-move.

Recovery Travel Phase Having hit the shuttle and played your tactical move you will need to travel into position to cover your opponent's most probable replies in the new situation that you have created.

THE BODY MOVEMENTS USED IN AN ACTION PHRASE
See Fig 5 on page 17
Good posture and balance should be maintained throughout.

Posture and Balance It helps to have a good posture and balance at all times during an action phrase since this contributes to good body movement and control when hitting the shuttle.

Start From the court starting position you will need to accelerate very quickly from the spot you are standing in – an explosive start. The quickness of the first few steps is very important in travelling towards and away from the shuttle. There is a

Fig 4

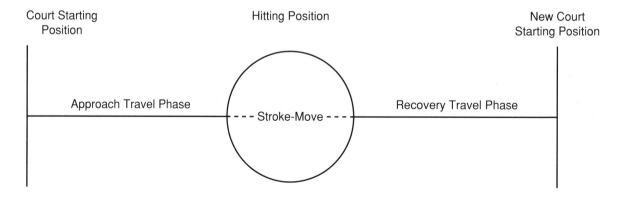

Court Starting Position · Hitting Position · New Court Starting Position

Approach Travel Phase · Stroke-Move · Recovery Travel Phase

Present Situation · Create New Situation · New Situation

special technique for this which is described on pages 51–2.

Step Patterns There are several ways of travelling to and from the hitting position. These include walking, running, and chasséing forwards, backwards and sideways. You should use the most effective method for you in a given situation. Whatever method you do use it is most important that you travel lightly and quietly over the floor. We usually describe this as travelling with '**soft feet**'.

Stop Just as you should be able to start quickly so should you be able to stop quickly and in balance when the occasion demands it. This is usually prior to or just after hitting the shuttle and when you arrive into position to cover the opponent's probable replies.

Transitions These refer to the 'changes of direction' you will perform in the action phrase. You will usually perform these during the travel phases, for instance when your opponent plays a tactical move before you have completed your recovery travel phase; or immediately after hitting the shuttle, e.g. on landing after a jump smash in the rearcourt.

Lunge and Recovery Though these usually take place in the forecourt you will also perform them in the midcourt and rearcourt. You will need to practise the various approaches to the half lunge and full lunge in the different parts of the court so you

will be able to perform them at speed and in good balance prior to or while you are hitting the shuttle. You should practise the various ways of recovering from the lunge in order to get into position to cover the opponent's replies.

Jumps and Landings You will need to practise the various jumps into a hitting position in different parts of the court. Then after hitting the shuttle you will need to learn to land lightly and to stop in balance before starting off quickly, or to perform a transition on landing in order to begin the recovery travel phase.

THE STROKE-MOVES USED IN AN ACTION PHRASE
See Fig 6

The stroke-moves include all the strokes logically possible in the game, played from the rearcourt, midcourt and forecourt. Most players use their stroke-moves in three ways in order to create a situation which will increase their chances of winning the rally (the principle of attack). These are: building shots, attempted winning shots and 'hit and hope' shots.

Building Shots You could play a number of tactical moves as building shots to create a situation from which you can attempt a winning shot. They can be well or poorly performed. Well-performed building shots should be consistently accurate, and

Fig 5

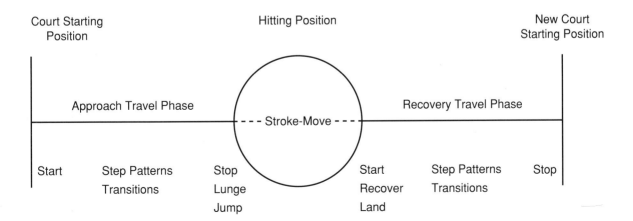

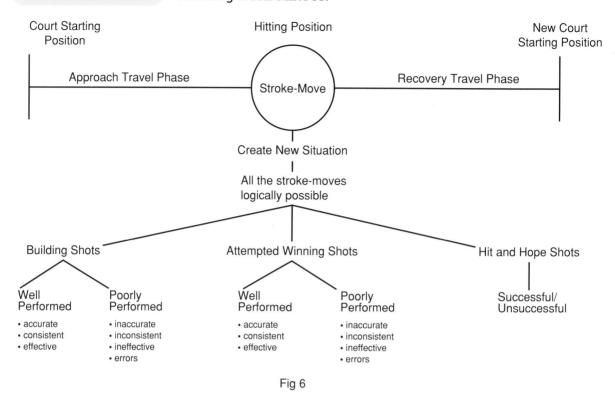

Fig 6

achieve the desired effect on your opponent. Poorly performed shots will be quite the opposite and most probably give the advantage to your opponent.

Attempted Winning Shots You should always consider these shots as *attempts* to hit a winner. If you do this you will always be ready for a reply if the shot is returned. If it does succeed then all the better. Well-performed shots will be consistently accurate and more likely to be effective. Poorly performed shots may give the advantage to your opponent or result in an error from you and the loss of the rally.

Hit and Hope Shots These are precisely as described. Shots played when you are caught out and simply *hit* the shuttle as best as you can and *hope* that it will go somewhere over the net to your advantage. Sometimes you will be successful and may learn a new stroke-move which you can use again in a similar situation. More often than not you will be unsuccessful and either give your opponent the advantage or make an error and lose the rally.

THE COMPLETE ACTION PHRASE
Fig 7 illustrates the action phrase with all its parts included. This will give you some indication of the total sum of things you must be able to do to be a good player of badminton. What it does not show is how fit you must become to perform many action phrases in one rally and to play many rallies in a game. In a singles or doubles match of three games, which could last up to an hour or longer, you may have to play many long rallies. In addition you need to consider the mental attitude you should develop for such a contest, e.g. your concentration, determination and perseverance. These mental attitudes would also be reflected in your behaviour during the action phrase.

Rallies
Rallies are made up of continuous complementary and overlapping action phrases. As you begin one action phrase your opponent will be completing one and so on. Examine Fig 8. You will see that whenever player A or B is in position to hit the shuttle the other is in position ready to cover the probable shots. As long as one player keeps synchronised with the opponent in this way the rally

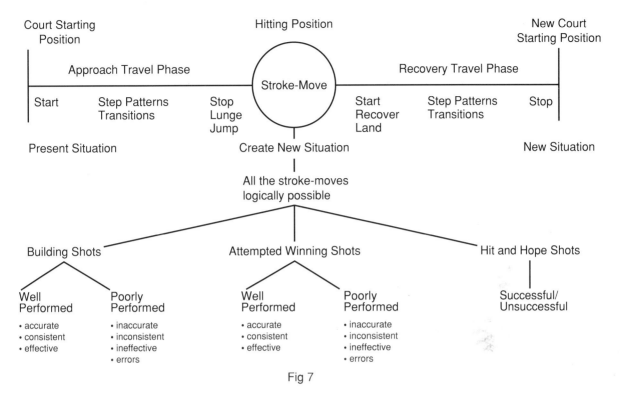

Fig 7

will continue. It is almost like a dance with perfect harmony being maintained between the two players except that to win the rally one player must try to create disharmony and put the other player out of synchronisation.

This is shown in Fig 8. Look closely at B's third action phrase and you will see a dotted vertical line to indicate where B actually is when A hit the shuttle. B has not recovered into position to cover A's probable shots and therefore will be out of synchronisation and at a disadvantage. He will have allowed A more space to hit the shuttle into and consequently he will have to work extremely hard to establish the harmony again.

For another example look at B's fifth action

phrase and you will see a dotted circle. This shows B has not arrived into position to hit the shuttle and could be late playing his shot, if he can actually do so before the shuttle hits the ground.

A rally may contain as few as two action phrases, e.g. A serves, B hits a winning shot; or as many as 100. When Morten Frost defeated Sugiarto, the Indonesian player, in the 1987 All England Men's Singles final there were several long rallies of upwards of ninety shots, e.g. ninety-eight action phrases. To perform rallies as long as these requires much fitness, skill and concentration.

These are the things that you must develop if you want to learn your craft.

Fig 8

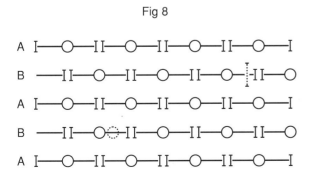

I Shows the court position where players should be to cover the opponent's replies.

O Shows hitting position players should be in.

⋮ Shows the court position where B actually was when A played his shot.

⊙ Shows the actual hitting position from which B played his shot.

Harmony

Disharmony

Know Your Craft

*It is well known that when you do anything, unless you understand its actual circumstance,
its nature and its relations to other things, you will not know the laws governing it,
or know how to do it or be able to do it well.*
Mao Tse-tung*

Like any interesting craft badminton is made up of a number of parts. All players must learn them and become competent in them all if they seriously want to become good players of the game.

They are:

- technical skill practices
- tactical skill practices
- individual specific skill practices
- informal competition
- formal competition
- studies
- fitness training
- mental training.

Most of what there is to learn and master in these parts and the ways in which they are learned has been developed and handed down over the years as part of badminton tradition. These traditional practices may be changed or added to as new ways of playing are introduced which, if successful, become the conventional practices of the day. Thus the game continues to develop and the store of knowledge and practices that must be learned by the players grows.

This chapter will provide you with a simple explanation of these parts. They will also be examined in greater detail in later chapters. The explanation of each part will include a brief description of the **content**, what the part contains, the recom-

mended **procedure** in learning the part, and the mental **attitude** required by the player in learning and mastering the part.

TECHNICAL SKILL PRACTICES

These practices should be learned and performed by all players, from beginners to world champions. They are the essential means for you to learn, improve and maintain the technical skill required to play badminton. In these practices the focus should always be on your SELF and **how** you do **what** you do.

CONTENT

- Racket skill.
- Body skill.
- The strokes.

PROCEDURE

FIRST PHASE, you should learn *what* the technical skill is, its *function* in the game and *how* to perform it.

SECOND PHASE, you should practise each skill to attain the desired standard of performance; then, to raise the standard and, finally, to maintain the standard.

MENTAL ATTITUDE

Your attitude in the first phase should be one of *interest* in how to perform the technical skill; you should apply yourself to the task and show *perseverance and patience*; adopt an enquiring mind and be prepared to discuss and explore ways of performing and using the skill. Above all do not expect to achieve too much while you are still learning how to perform the skill.

---

*Quotations from *Chairman Mao Tse Tung*, Foreign Languages Press, Peking, 1972.

Your attitude in the second phase will be different in several ways. You will have learned the skill and will want to improve your standard of performance. So now you should concentrate on the task, show determination to do it well and persevere until you do so. This is where more self-discipline is required. It should hurt your pride to get it wrong or not achieve the standard you are working to attain or maintain. The quality of your performance in practice should be game-like, i.e. demanding the same degree of commitment, effort and skill as you would give in competition.

TACTICAL SKILL PRACTICES

CONTENT

These practice routines should also be learned and performed by all players from beginners to world champions. They refer to the conventional tactical situations that emerge in the game. In these practices your emphasis should be first on trying to control, and second on trying to outwit, the OTHER PLAYERS in singles and level and mixed doubles.

PROCEDURE

First, you should determine the stroke-move and the game situation, e.g. you will lob from the forecourt.

Second, you should determine the action phrase you will perform, e.g. travelling forwards to play a lob from below the net in the forecourt with the opponent ready to attack.

Third, you should practise the action phrase with the focus on your reply and its effect on the *other* player.

Fourth, you should develop the practice and add more action phrases to re-create the situation as it might have occurred in a game.

Fifth, you should make it more 'game-like' by introducing the elements of uncertainty and competition, thus making it more difficult and challenging to perform.

MENTAL ATTITUDE

Your attitude should be one of interest, concentration, self-discipline, determination, perseverance and patience, as you question and discuss the situation and explore possible ways to improve your performance in game-like practices.

INDIVIDUAL SPECIFIC SKILL PRACTICES

CONTENT

These practice routines may be selected from the conventional practices in the game or some variations devised especially for you or your doubles team. They will be devised to correct and to improve particular weaknesses that have been exposed in competition.

PROCEDURE

First, you should determine what you need to improve by analysing your performance in formal competition.

Second, you should devise and develop a technical and/or tactical skill practice.

Third, you should practise until the required standard is attained.

MENTAL ATTITUDE

Your attitude should be one of interest, concentration, discipline, determination, perseverance, patience, as you question and discuss the situation and explore possible ways to improve your performance in game-like practices.

INFORMAL COMPETITION

CONTENT

When you have learned or improved some aspect of your performance you should test your competence in competition. This is best done initially in informal competition when **the score is not so important** and when the main focus can be on trying to implement the practice work in the game. Informal competition in club nights and practice games is the ideal setting for new ideas and skills to be tried out. On these occasions you can focus on your own game and try out ideas or new skills without being too concerned about winning or losing the game.

If, unfortunately, the results do matter to you it is unlikely that you will take the risk of using the strokes or tactics that you are still working on, and may be unsure about, just in case you should lose the contest. And if you do not use them in informal competition you will be unlikely to include these new skills in formal competition. Consequently you will slow down or restrict your progress in becoming a better player. Players who have the good sense and sometimes the courage to try out new ideas will assess their performance not on the score at the end of the game but on how often and how successfully they used their improved or new technical or tactical skill in the game.

MENTAL ATTITUDE

Your attitude should be one of concentration, perseverance, patience, discipline, and determination. You should not be concerned about the score and the result of the game but that the practice work is implemented. You should be prepared to lose games in informal competition in order to win them, eventually, in formal competition.

FORMAL COMPETITION

CONTENT

Here the results do matter – they are all-important, as is your attitude. You should give 100 per cent effort in trying to win. Only by doing so will you provide a true *test* of your current competence and gain an accurate measure of your progress as a player. You will also establish the areas of performance you are improving or lacking. You will learn what to work on to become a better player.

MENTAL ATTITUDE

Your attitude should be one of concentration, determination, adventure, perseverance, care, patience, fairness and a 100 per cent commitment to trying to win the game.

STUDIES

Over the years new ideas and ways of playing the game have been added to our conventional knowledge of badminton. The idea of spinning the shuttle at the net developed in the 1970s; new doubles formations developed with the increase in speed and power that came with racket technology. The game will continue to develop by accident or design as the equipment improves or the players introduce new innovations. Rather than wait for new ideas to develop it is possible to explore and to create new ways of doing things ourselves. Studies are not part of badminton convention but they are an essential part in learning the craft.

Their purpose will be to help you to experiment, to explore ideas and new or different ways of doing things, e.g. hitting techniques, develop-

ing skill in moving, deception, tactical moves and positional play. Studies will be a means of helping you to develop your imagination, to be innovative and creative. They will help to increase your practical knowledge and to raise your skill levels.

CONTENT

The content will include tasks to tackle, problems to solve, and questions to answer with respect to any part of the game.

MENTAL ATTITUDE

Your attitude should be one of interest and curiosity in trying out new ideas and developing your technical and tactical skill. You should remain open-minded and be willing to explore various ways of doing things in different game situations.

FITNESS TRAINING AND DIET

CONTENT

You must be fit enough to do the work required at the levels at which you play. A balanced programme of fitness training, diet and rest will make this possible.

MENTAL ATTITUDE

Your attitude should be one of determination, patience, self-discipline, perseverance, care and commitment.

MENTAL TRAINING

Mental training is the means by which you will learn to adopt the appropriate mental attitude to perform the craft of playing badminton. Adopt the recommended mental attitude for any part of your craft and you will train yourself through regular practice to respond appropriately and effectively in any situation in badminton. It is an on-going part of your development as a player.

Think about what you want to achieve and then focus solely on that. If you are not clear in your *purpose* you will not express the appropriate mental attitude and train yourself to respond effectively.

SUMMARY

The following diagram illustrates the parts of the craft you must master if you want to become a better player.

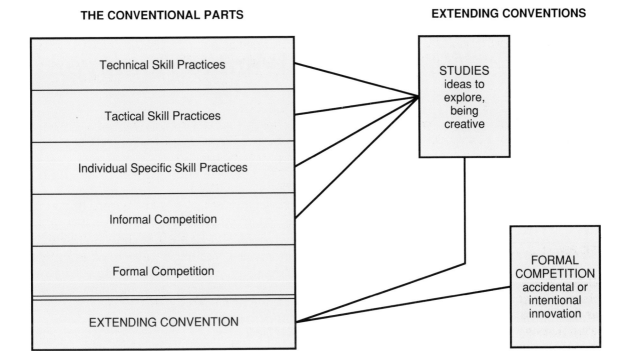

chapter 3

What Do You Want to Achieve?

It is important that you know what you want to achieve. Until you decide this and do something about it you will drift along aimlessly. You may, of course, be quite happy with doing that and expect nothing more than you get. You enjoy playing games and having a good workout. Sometimes you win and sometimes you lose. It is not important, the main thing is that you are having a good time. If, however, you do want to achieve something in badminton you must decide what that is. This book should then help you to achieve your particular ambitions. There are a number of goals you might set as targets. They fall within two groups, *competition goals* and *personal performance goals*.

COMPETITION GOALS

If you are a talented player you might, for example, aspire to becoming the World or Olympic Champion, or you may want to play for your country in the Thomas or Uber Cup. Alternatively, you may be happy playing for the club team, winning the club tournament or beating a particular player or doubles team. These are all examples of what we call *competition goals*.

You can see that to achieve your competition goals you must be successful in winning. Your main task will be to beat other players although this does, of course, depend on who they are. You will compete against players who may be of a lower, the same, or a higher standard than you.

Under normal circumstances, and providing that you have been doing regular practice, training and competition, you should defeat the lower standard opponents and be holding your own and perhaps beginning to edge ahead of players of the same standard. With players of a higher standard

you should not expect to win. Though again, if you have been working hard to improve your personal performance, you might begin to close the gap between the two of you by winning a few more points or the occasional game each time you meet.

TOURNAMENT GOALS

Your success in tournaments will depend on the practice and training you do to improve some or all aspects of your personal performance, and on the players you will compete against. Your main task in tournaments will be to win or to reach a certain stage in the tournament. This will of course depend very much on your opponents' 'operational' standard of play at the time. You should not forget that your opponents may also be working to become better players and may also have made progress. Never go on court predicting the result before you start or during the match. Your opponents may 'operate' at a higher standard than you expected and you may 'operate' at a lower standard than usual. This is a problem you will have to overcome on the court if you want to win. Do not make your task more difficult by getting upset with frustration or fear because things aren't going as you expected or you risk losing the match. Your mental attitude is as important a part of your performance as your technical skill or fitness so make sure that it works in your favour. I will explain more about this in chapter 15.

TEAM GOALS

In order to achieve your team goals and be selected for a team you will obviously have to be successful in individual competition. Your 'operational' standard of play in such competitions will increase your chances of being selected for the team if that is what you desire. Unfortunately you will have less control over your progress here as generally you will have little say, if any, in the selection of the team. Your place will be dependent on those doing the selecting. Selectors, as you will undoubtedly experience, will not always hold the same opinions as you do about your value to the team.

If you do find that you are not selected for a team when you believe that you should be there are several courses of action you can take.

First, you could ask the selectors, courteously I should advise, why you have not been selected and what is required of you to gain selection. It would be reasonable to expect an explanation and advice. Do not argue if you disagree because that will not help your case and usually it will make the selectors hold to their decision more firmly. If you do obtain an acceptable answer and advice then, providing it makes sense, follow it and do what is required of you.

Second, if you do not obtain an acceptable answer then you could do what some players do. They work harder to improve their personal performance and try that much harder to win competitions, making it impossible for selectors not to select them.

PERSONAL PERFORMANCE GOALS

These are goals in which you aim to improve some aspect of your performance regardless of whether you win or lose in competition. Your aims here will be to raise your standards of performance in your technical and tactical skill, fitness and attitude. Of course, by becoming a better performer you should usually increase your chances of achieving your competition goals.

For example, if you train to get slightly fitter by improving your endurance and practise getting more height and length on your overhead clear, you might just beat your main rival and win that singles tournament you keep losing each year. Or, if you improve your defence, you might make the doubles team.

You should aim to be in complete control over what you want to and what you actually achieve in your performance goals. You can practise and train as much or as little as you want to, or even not at all. If you do nothing about your personal performance you should not expect to make progress.

You should expect to be inconsistent, make errors, lack accuracy and experience frustration and irritation on occasions when you play poorly.

If, however, you do practise and train you can measure your progress in practice and competition. In practice you can work to improve a stroke-move or your quickness off the mark and you will be able to assess your progress by what you do, how it feels and the outcome, e.g. you can now accelerate quickly off the spot to get to the rearcourt and your clear now goes high and deep to the back of the opponent's rearcourt.

In competition you can do the same thing and show a 25 per cent improvement in getting into the hitting position in the rearcourt or greater accuracy and consistency in playing the clear as a building shot. In this area of the game you can be in complete control and totally responsible for what you achieve.

INTRINSIC AND EXTRINSIC GOALS

So far, in discussing competition and personal performance goals, I have described the types of goals you may want to achieve in badminton. These are the *intrinsic* goals which are logically built into and essential to the game.

You will also be aware that some players may have *extrinsic* goals which logically have little to do with badminton but which in reality have a lot to do with their interest in the game. They include such ambitions as wanting to travel, to earn money, to be a somebody, to be popular and to gain a public status. We call these extrinsic goals, in the sense that they are not a part of the game in the way that competition and performance goals are. You could not become a better player or a winning player without achieving your intrinsic goals but you could do so without achieving your extrinsic goals. You will, however, usually need your on-court successes in order to achieve your extrinsic goals.

If someone were to ask you for the main reasons why you play badminton you would probably answer by mentioning both your intrinsic and extrinsic goals and as long as your intrinsic goals remain the most important then it can be quite beneficial having extrinsic goals. They can help to motivate you when you do not feel like doing the practice and training necessary to become a better player. If, however, your extrinsic goals become the more important then you could affect your progress because you may settle for less than you are capable of, and you could stop working to improve, or adopt unfair means to achieve them. The players who never seem to accept that they have been beaten by a better player on the day and are full of excuses, the cheats, the drug-takers, the rule-breakers, are players whose goals are mainly extrinsic. What other reasons could be provided for their behaviour? All need to be successful in competition to achieve their extrinsic goals and adopt whatever means they can to ensure that they do win. I am sure that you can think of many other similar examples of players behaving in particular ways due to their extrinsic goals. So try not to become one of them!

Try instead to be honest with yourself about why you play the game. I hope that primarily it will be because you want to become a better player which you want for its own sake; and that it gives you satisfaction to master your craft. By all means recognise the importance of such extrinsic goals as money, travel, status and popularity but not at the expense of the game's intrinsic goals. Get your priorities and values right and you will be on the way to achieving your intrinsic goals.

ARE YOUR GOALS REALISTIC?

Most players usually only set themselves competition goals. They all too frequently base their achievements solely on whether they have won or lost. Consequently they seldom progress into higher levels of play. Such progress can only come if they have personal performance goals and work constantly towards becoming better players.

If you want to achieve success in competition against players of a similar operational standard to you and, eventually, of a higher operational standard, then you will have to do the necessary practice, training and competition.

It may be too soon to decide accurately whether your goals are realistic but you will know this in time. You can, however, set about making a reasonable assessment by asking yourself a number of questions.

- How good are you now as compared with how good you want to be?

- Do you realistically have the ability to achieve your desired goals?
- How much practice and training and competition will you need to do and can you do it?
- Do you have the facilities and opportunities to enable you to reach your goals?
- How much time will it take and can you put in that time?
  How much will it cost and can you afford it?
- Have you considered your other commitments and responsibilities, if any, e.g. education, work, family, social life?
- If necessary, will you be prepared to sacrifice some of these other things?

When you have seriously considered these questions then you can decide whether your goals seem realistic or not. If they are not or you are uncertain about them, then set new ones, which should be both challenging and attainable. Lower or raise your sights accordingly, choose more realistic goals and see how you get on.

In this respect be cautious and slightly sceptical about people who tell you that you can be the best player in your league; that you can play for your country; that you can be the next All England or World Champion. Or, alternatively, that you will never be any good. This caution should apply particularly if you are a keen young talented player. Beware of the coach or official who makes these claims. Do not let the flattery or criticism warp your judgment or, if you are a junior, that of your parents. Question the reality of the claim and ask the person on what basis they believe this. Ask them about their track record in developing such outstanding players and if necessary obtain a second opinion. If you do not receive accurate judgment you may end up paying a lot of money, giving up a lot of time, neglecting your education and social life, achieving little, feeling that you have failed, and you will probably not be enjoying the game. I have seen too many players in badminton end up like this.

Assuming that you have given some thought to the questions above and set some realistic goals you will need to plan and design a programme to achieve them. In the next chapter I will explain how to do this.

Plan to Achieve Your Goals

My career goal is to be the best tennis player that I can. I don't want to look back with any regrets. I never want to say what if I'd done this or that.
Jim Courier*

Once you have set some realistic goals you are more likely to achieve them if you plan an *action programme*. This is quite easy to do and no more difficult than planning to go on a journey for your holidays. Some plans may, however, be more complex than others, depending on the starting point for the journey and how far away your goals are at the destination.

If, for example, you want to plan to become the Olympic Champion your action programme could be very detailed and complex with a time-scale of four to five years, if not longer. Alternatively, if all you want to do is to learn a backhand clear for use in competition, your programme could be quite simple with a short time-scale of three months.

If you plan a long-term programme to achieve some distant goals, you will find that there will be a number of short-term goals which you will need to achieve in order to reach your final long-term goal. To become an Olympic Champion you may, for example, aim to get into the national side or to increase your position in the world rankings by beating higher-ranked opponents. To achieve this you may in the first year decide to improve your fitness and technical skill and to enter specific tournaments in order to improve your results against certain opponents. Your short-term goals will therefore be to improve your fitness, technical skill and competition performance.

If you are a club player you may decide that your long-term goal will be to get into the club team next season. You decide that your short-term goals will be to improve your serve and return of serve, and your defence and positional play in level and mixed doubles. To do this you decide to

set a time-scale of one year.

There are as many goals as there are things to learn and to achieve. Only you will be able to decide what you want to achieve. Your plan will provide you with a positive means to attain them. Although other players' plans may differ from yours with regard to their action programme, the particular journey they will travel to reach their short- and long-term goals will usually follow the same procedure described below. Use it to plan your own journey.

Remember, however, that when you plan something you are actually trying to predict what will happen in the future. You will know from your own experience that sometimes things do not always work out as you had planned no matter how carefully you mapped them out. My advice, therefore, is to be prepared to adapt and change your plans as you go along and to remain flexible. To be flexible you will need to make periodic checks to see how things are progressing. If you decide that things are going well then carry on. If not, make the necessary changes. What is exciting about planning to become a better player is that you are entering into unknown territory which should make your journey quite an adventure. I know you will enjoy your travels.

PROCEDURE IN PLANNING AN ACTION PROGRAMME

1 ESTABLISH YOUR STARTING POINTS

You should already have some idea of how good you are, what you can do and what your weaknesses are. If you do not know this then now is the time to find out. You have two options in establishing your starting point. You can give yourself a

---

* *Guardian*, May 26th, 1992.

complete badminton check-up – a thorough examination of *all* parts of your play – or a *partial check-up* – a thorough examination of *some* part of your play.

If your ambitions are high you will need a complete badminton check-up – you cannot afford to have any weaknesses so you must ensure that everything is checked over and improved as necessary. If you want to make the club team and you have decided that your defence needs putting right then you will need a partial check-up only and improvements will be made as required.

2   ORGANISE YOUR BADMINTON CHECK-UP

You will need to examine your performance in every aspect of your game (*see* chapter 2 and the diagram on page 22). You should examine your play in practice and in competition and decide how good or not you are. Please refer to the following for specific areas of your game.

- your technical skill – refer to chapters 7, 8, 9, 10, 11, 12,
- your tactical skill – refer to chapters 9, 19, 20
- your fitness – refer to chapter 13
- your mental attitude – refer to chapter 15

Ultimately it is your performance when playing in competition that is all-important. In order to check your performance in the game you should have a good understanding of how to play good standard badminton even if you cannot do so yet. Refer to chapters 19 and 20 for a detailed explanation of how to play singles, doubles and mixed doubles.

3   ANALYSE YOUR PERFORMANCE

You will need to obtain information about your performance then analyse it to decide what and how you need to improve. Read chapter 18 for advice on how to do this.

4   RECONSIDER YOUR GOALS!

You know what goals you want to achieve and you have now worked out what you need to do to achieve them. Before you go ahead and plan your action programme just think whether your goals are realistic. Read through pages 24–7 again to make sure. If they are not then alter them; if they are then go ahead and plan your programme.

5   PLAN YOUR ACTION PROGRAMME

It will be relatively easy to plan a short-term programme with a single goal, e.g. to make the club team. It will be more difficult to plan a long-term programme including a number of short-term programmes. This will need some careful planning.

6   DECIDE ON THE CONTENT OF THE PROGRAMME

Decide what the programme will include and then write down what you will do in each area of your performance. A long-term comprehensive programme should include the following parts:

- technical skill practices
- tactical skill practices
- individual specific practices
- studies
- fitness training
- mental training
- informal competition
- formal competition
- competition results
- self-analysis forms
- opponent analysis forms
- programme evaluation.

7   WORK OUT HOW YOU WILL ORGANISE THE PROGRAMME

You cannot do everything at once so work out in what order you will achieve your goals. You may decide for example that you will concentrate mainly on improving your fitness first. When your fitness levels improve you could then switch the emphasis to your skill improvement.

8   DECIDE ON THE TIME-SCALE

How long will you allow to achieve the shorter-term goals? Make a calculated guess and be prepared to adapt the programme slightly if your guess is wrong. Your journey should be an adventure so be flexible in your planning.

9   WRITE OUT THE PROGRAMME

Keep a logbook to record the programme.

10 EVALUATE YOUR ACTION PROGRAMME

Check your action programme periodically and decide whether it is effective in achieving your goals. If it is not then alter it as necessary.

chapter 5

Make the Most of Your Practice

*If you want to add new dimensions to your game or correct old habits that
lose you matches, stop playing sets and return to the practice court. That's what I do.*
Martina Navratilova*

WHAT IS PRACTICE?

The main purpose of practice is to improve some parts of your craft. The idea is to repeat these until you get them right and up to the required standard. There are as many practices as there are parts you might want to put right. These include your grips, racket control, strokes, movement, tactics and mental attitude.

You will have heard the saying 'practice makes perfect', which it will if you do things properly. But there is another saying you should also be aware of, 'Practice makes permanent'. You could be practising the wrong techniques and end up a worse player than when you began. To avoid this you should understand exactly what it is you are trying to improve. If you do this you will correct parts of your game as you practise. Doing the right things then becomes a habit so that you will do them automatically when you play. Ultimately, this is what you should be trying to achieve – *to play well without conscious thought.*

TYPES OF PRACTICE

There are generally two types of skill practice: technical and tactical skill practice.

Technical skill is to do with how you use your racket and body while playing. It includes all the different strokes and parts of a stroke; the different ways of using your body as you start and stop, travel, retain balance, change direction, lunge and recover, jump and land; all these features are illustrated in the action phrase on page 16.

Tactical skill is to do with the use of strokes as

tactical moves when you play *building shots* and *attempted winning shots* in accordance with the principle of attack.

Of course technical and tactical skill are interrelated. If you want to be able to play a variety of stroke-moves to outwit your opponent in any situation, i.e. have good tactical skill, then you must have the technical skill to achieve this.

It is important to know how to do each type of practice and to recognise the difference between them. Technical and tactical skills differ mainly in what you **focus on** when doing one or the other. For example, let us imagine that you are practising your cross-court forehand sliced smash, first in a technical practice and second in a tactical practice. In the technical practice your focus will be on your SELF and how you perform the actions in order to become more fluent, accurate or consistent. In the tactical practice your focus will be on the OTHER player and how you can make him respond to your smash. Look at the following examples to see the difference.

TECHNICAL PRACTICE

(*See* Figs 9(a), (b) *overleaf.*)
Aim of practice: to improve accuracy in using the forehand sliced smash.

TACTICAL PRACTICE.

(*See* Figs 10 (a), (b) *overleaf.*)
Aim of practice: to manoeuvre F out of position and force him to travel forwards to the side of the MC and hit the shuttle upwards from near the floor.

You can see in these examples that though the same sliced smash actions are being used in both practices, the aim of each practice is different.

---

*Martina Navratilova, *Tennis My Way*, Allan Lane, 1984.

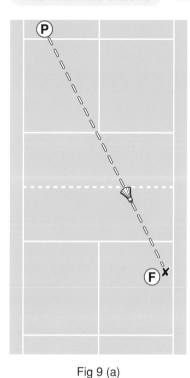

Fig 9 (a)

Fig 9(a) *left*
P practises the smash.
F feeds the shuttle.
P stays in the hitting position in the RC and practises aiming the shuttle to land at the side of the MC as shown.
F stands at the side of the MC as shown and hits the shuttle back to P each time until P chooses to stop.
P pauses to work on corrections as necessary.
P develops the practice further by adding the approach travel phase and the recovery travel phase.
See Fig 9(b) *right*.

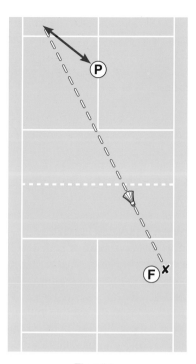

Fig 9(b).

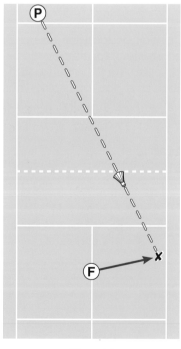

Fig 10(a)

Fig 10(a) *left*
P remains in the hitting position in the RC as shown.
F starts in the MC and serves high to P and gets ready to defend against a possible smash. P can hit a straight smash as well as the sliced smash he is using to manipulate F.
P plays a sliced fh smash and looks to see if he has succeeded in manoeuvring F out of position and made F hit the shuttle from near the floor.
F lobs the shuttle high to P and recovers into position to defend again. If F cannot lob to P then F begins with a high serve again and P practises again.

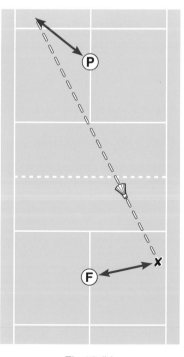

Fig 10 (b)

If you do not understand the aim of the practice, then don't do it. You won't know what you are doing. It will be meaningless and you could be wasting your time and not make any improvements.

Getting things right is crucial when you are learning something new or trying to raise or maintain your standards.

PRACTICE AND ROUTINES

Coaches and players often ask me for routines (drills) for various aspects of the game. I always refuse because I believe that, in general, the way most players and coaches use routines makes them completely meaningless and often a prime cause of why many players fail to become better players in competition. The courts are often full of good, energetic 'routines' players who unfortunately are poor competition players. This is because they do routines without really practising anything. You must make sure that you are not one of them.

There are routines for all the strokes and court situations but unfortunately doing a routine will not necessarily improve your performance as a player.

This is because a routine has no purpose to it. You have to give it a purpose and use it for the specific practice of some part of your game.

All practices involve the use of routines but routines need not involve the practice of anything.

A routine is simply part of an action phrase, i.e. the strokes and the movement in the approach or recovery travel phases. Let us examine a typical one.
See Fig 11. Player A clears and drops from the rearcourt and player B clears from the rearcourt and lobs from the forecourt.

What do you think the players are practising in doing this routine?

Most players and coaches will answer that they are practising clears, lobs and dropshots. But that tells us very little. We can see that they are doing clears, lobs and drops, but what are they really practising? We want to know what they are trying to improve in doing these strokes. Are they doing a technical practice and trying to improve their ability to start and stop quickly, correct their timing in the clear or getting into the correct hitting position?

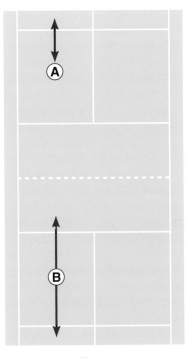

Fig10(b) *left*
P develops the practice by adding the approach travel phase and recovery travel phase to the practice. P now does a complete action phrase. *See* Fig 7, page 19

Fig 11 *left*
B lobs and recovers to the MC.
A travels to the RC, clears and recovers to the MC.
B travels to the RC, clears and recovers to the MC.
A travels to the RC, drops and recovers to the MC.
B travels to the FC and lobs.
The rally continues.

Fig 11

Are they doing a tactical practice and trying to force each other out of position with building shots and make time to recover into position to cover the opponent's replies? What we need to know is in what ways doing this routine will help them to improve. **Unless the players know and can tell us then they are wasting their time**.

Make sure that you do not waste your time. Decide first what you want to improve and then select or make up a routine to practise it.

LEARN HOW TO PRACTISE

There are a number of stages you may need to go through when you practise. Your skill level and what you want to improve will suggest whether you need to go through them all, begin at a later stage or just work on one stage. Each stage is described so that you can decide which one you will start at whenever there is something you want to improve by practice. Remember, how you practise will depend on what you are trying to achieve in either a technical practice or a tactical practice.

TECHNICAL PRACTICE

There are always three main aims in a technical practice. These are: **fluency** in performing the stroke, **accuracy** in hitting the shuttle and **consistency** in doing both successfully.

Let us assume that you are learning the backhand clear and want to improve your standard in using it in competition. Remember that in this technical practice your focus will be on your SELF and how you perform the actions.

Stages – the Backhand Clear

1st Stage: the feel of the stroke
Your aim is to develop **the feel of the stroke** so that it feels *comfortable* and *fluent*. This might involve miming the stroke, going through the actions slowly and then speeding them up to develop the correct *feel*.

Then, from the hitting position in the rearcourt, you should practise hitting backhand clears with the focus still on getting the feel of the stroke. Don't be too concerned about hitting the shuttle to the other rearcourt just yet. Once you get the *feel* of the stroke you can begin to try to increase the distance you hit the shuttle by increasing the racket head

speed. If you lose the *feel* of the stroke then hit with less effort until you get the *feel* again.

A good general rule to follow is: begin from the hitting position when you are working on your strokes (*see* Fig 4, page 16) and ignore the travel phases at this stage.

2nd Stage: accuracy
Now, from the hitting position, practise hitting the shuttle accurately to the opposite rearcourt. Take pauses, if necessary, between each attempt while you consider how you are doing and make any corrections.

3rd Stage: consistency
If you think you are hitting accurately, practise to develop **consistency**. Remain in the hitting position and hit a number of clears continuously as single shuttles are served to you or as you rally with your 'feeder'. In this way you will train your muscles in a particular movement pattern and so 'groove' the stroke.

You might set a target of ten clears to test your score out of ten. In this way you can measure your progress.

4th Stage: the travel phases
Add the travel phases with the body movements required in the approach travel phase and the recovery travel phase. (Fig 5, page 17.) In doing this you will still be trying to maintain your standards of accuracy and consistency.

You may decide to make your court starting position near the rearcourt so that, at first, you don't have to travel so far. Once you feel comfortable with a travel and recovery phase then start from the centre midcourt and recover there. You must decide what is best for you. *See* Figs 12(a) and (b) *opposite*.

5th Stage: uncertainty
Introduce an element of uncertainty in your practice so that you will not know when your feeder will hit the shuttle to your backhand rearcourt. Ask the feeder to play the occasional dropshot or clear to your forehand rearcourt. In this way you will learn to react and to start quickly under 'game-like' conditions. In fact you may find that doing this exposes a weakness in your body skill, e.g. your start or footwork in the approach travel phase. You

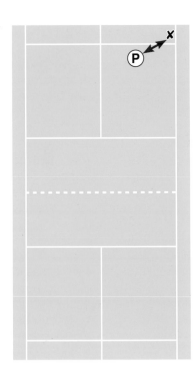

Fig 12 (a) *left*
Partial travel phases

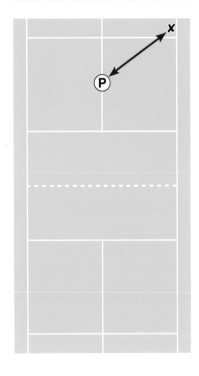

Fig 12(b) *right*
Full travel phases

would then need to make your corrections and practise to improve that part of the travel phase.

Take your time in practice

It is important that you take your time when practising. The main task is to get the feel of the stroke and then build up your practice until you can perform the stroke under game-like conditions. To do this you might want to pause and go back a stage before progressing forwards again. Once you feel happy with the stroke then you can develop your consistency by increasing the number of repetitions you perform in practice to maintain or raise your standards in performing it.

TACTICAL PRACTICE

There are two main aims in a tactical practice. These are: *effectiveness* in achieving the intended outcome with your building shots or attempted winning shots, and *consistency* in your play. Remember that the focus will now be on the *other* player, your 'opponent', and how you make him respond to your clear.

How will you want him to respond to your backhand clear?

Let us assume that your 'opponent' has hit the shuttle to your backhand rearcourt and that he has positioned himself in the centre midcourt to cover your possible replies. He will not know whether you intend to play a clear or a backhand dropshot so he must cover both tactical moves.

You decide that you will use the backhand clear as a building shot. You intend therefore to move your 'opponent' out of position to his forehand rearcourt as far away from the net as possible and hit the shuttle high enough to give you time to recover to your centre midcourt to cover his probable replies.

The response that you want to see is your 'opponent' having to travel the full distance to the rearcourt, in order to get into a hitting position on the rear line, with you in waiting in a midcourt position before he hits the shuttle. It would count as an effective building shot if you could create this situation.

Stages – the Backhand Clear

1st Stage: *game situation and action phrase*
Decide on the game situation and the action phrase.
Game Situation: You are positioned in the midcourt covering a possible smash and your opponent has hit the shuttle to your backhand rearcourt.
Action Phrase: You will travel to the backhand

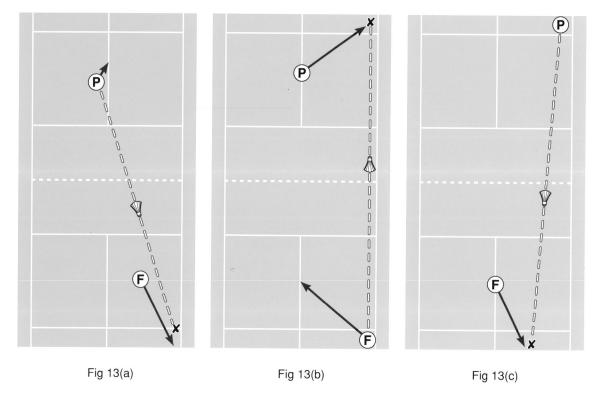

Fig 13(a)   Fig 13(b)   Fig 13(c)

rearcourt and play a backhand clear as a building shot and recover to the midcourt to cover the replies.

2ND STAGE: *start and end of practice*

Decide how you will commence the practice and end it.

Example: You will start the practice with a high serve from the midcourt. Your 'opponent' will travel to his rearcourt and hit a clear to your backhand rearcourt to create the game situation. When he does so you will perform your action phrase. *See* Figs 13(a), (b) and (c).

The practice will end with your opponent making any reply to your backhand clear. Your task is to check that you succeeded in making him travel to the rearcourt to make a reply.

3RD STAGE: *development*

Develop the practice by adding more action phrases before and after the actual action phrase you are practising.

4TH STAGE: *increase difficulty*

Make it more difficult to perform the backhand clear in an action phrase by altering the action phrase slightly. You could increase the speed at which you practise by reducing the time you allow to perform a stroke or by increasing the distance you have to travel into the hitting position. For example you may decide that your court starting position will be in the forecourt. *See* Fig 13(d).

5TH STAGE: *uncertainty and competition*

Allow the 'opponent' to use other stroke-moves to make it more competitive and to try to catch you out before he hits the shuttle to your backhand rearcourt. The more competitive game-like situations you can practise the better you will be in formal competition.

HOW MUCH SHOULD YOU PRACTISE?

You will know from experience that there are several factors, apart from lack of facilities and time, which can affect how much you will practise. These are:

- the standard you are already at or want to reach
- whether you are learning something new or simply making a few corrections
- the meaningfulness and importance of the practice to improve your game

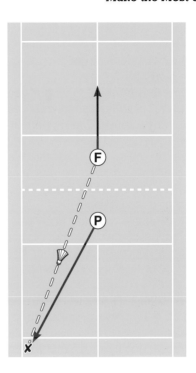

Fig 13(d) *right*
F lobs the shuttle to P's bh RC
during a net rally.
P travels to the RC while F
travels to the centre MC to
cover the replies.

● the interest and enjoyment value

These factors will determine whether you do a lot of practice at a time or regular small amounts. With experience you will soon decide what is best for you.

In general you must always practise regularly, even daily if you are a national-level player, to maintain your standard. If you want to improve then you must practise to raise your standard and then continue to practise regularly to maintain it. This is the only way you will succeed.

SO YOU DON'T FEEL LIKE PRACTISING?

Sometimes before you start or during practice you may begin to feel that you don't want to practise. This could be for several reasons. You might have lost interest, feel bored, tired, frustrated at lack of success, can't see the point of the practice, do not know how to do it properly, or it could be too difficult and complex.

When you are in this state you have several choices.

First, you could apply some willpower and self-discipline and just get on with it. The need for practice will not go away so you have got to do it at some point – why not now? Such self-discipline will stand you in good stead when you have to apply yourself to the task of winning in competition. So you could take this opportunity to practise self-discipline as well as whatever else you should be practising at the time.

Second, you could take a rest and do something else for a while and then try again later when you may be in a better mood.

Third, you could think about the practice and what it is you are trying to improve then work through slowly until you understand it and get the feel of it.

Not all practices are interesting and enjoyable. Sometimes they require a lot of self-discipline and effort to get them right. But you will feel rightly satisfied when you do get them right.

PRACTICE PARTNER(S)

For most practices you will need a practice partner. He will usually act as a *feeder* or an 'opponent', depending on what you are practising. When he acts as a *feeder* he needn't be the same standard as you just so long as he can hit the shuttle accurately to a specific part of your court as required. This will be expected from your feeder in both technical and tactical skill practices. Just to emphasise the point we sometimes call such practices *co-operative practices*.

When your partner is to act as an 'opponent' you will expect him to play at a higher standard and be able to put you under pressure. The 'opponent' will not be co-operating fully with you now, he will be competing against you to some extent. We usually call such practices *competitive practices* and as you might expect these mainly occur when you are improving your tactical skill.

There is usually an element of uncertainty built into competitive practice as your 'opponent' is not going to make the practice easy for you. For example, you may be practising your defence in doubles – your lob to the rearcourt to keep your 'opponent' on the back line. His task will be to hit a winning smash so he will work to create an opening. He will use building shots to get a weak reply so that he can attempt a winning shot. What will he do? He will vary his smash, aim it at your body or at the sides; he will slice it to make it fall short; he will play a dropshot. If you do not lob accurately to the rearcourt you will provide him with a chance to hit a winning smash. The practice will end when he has hit three winning smashes. *See* Fig 14.

FROM THE PRACTICE COURT TO THE MATCH COURT

A most difficult task is to make the transfer from practice to formal competition. If you are one of those players who just does routines (drills) to develop your technical skill then you may find it difficult to make the transfer. The game is full of players who appear great in practice but never seem to perform to the same standard in formal competition where it really matters. They have only learned to focus on themselves in their technical practices whereas they should also learn to focus on their opponents. If you have been doing tactical practices you will have learned to do this, in which case you will already be partly prepared to make the transition to the match court.

There are however a few other hurdles to overcome. It takes *confidence* to try out the newly practised skill in formal competition. It doesn't follow that because you can do it in practice you can immediately do it in a game. You may have doubts whether it will stand up to the test of a good opponent, particularly when the point of the game is to try to win. It would not be unusual, therefore, if you played safe and kept to your old trusted skills.

Your confidence will increase, however, as your

Fig 14
Aim of practice:
P must keep opponent (F) in RC.
Players play in half court only.
P must lob all shots to RC.
Opponent (F) can smash and drop.
Practice ends when F has hit three winning shots.

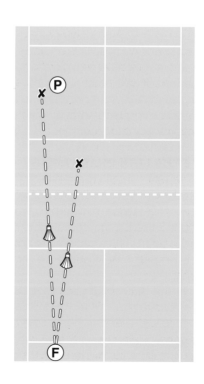

new skills become an automatic part of your game, when you don't have to give any thought as to whether you can do them. You just know that your backhand clear, which you have been practising, has become as reliable as your forehand clear – even against the strongest opponent.

BRIDGING THE GAP
Fortunately you don't have to jump immediately from the practice court to the match court. There are a few ways of bridging the gap. If you have been working hard to improve some part of your game then you can put it to the test. I have already suggested one method which is to set a target to see how consistent you are out of ten attempts. You should test yourself in this sort of way whenever you are practising. If your score improves over a period of time you will know that you are improving.

CONDITIONED GAMES
Another useful test is to play a *conditioned game*. If you can show an improvement in a game then your practice work really will be showing dividends. Conditioned games also provide an effective way of making sure that you really do use the practised part in a game. *See* page 172.

For example, let's take the backhand clear you have been practising. You now play a game but add an extra rule, i.e. 'You must always use the backhand clear from your backhand rearcourt.' If you break the rule then you lose the rally. Just to make sure you ask your 'opponent' to play 75 per cent of his lobs and clears to that corner.

Or assume that you have been practising your replies from your forecourt to the opponent's forecourt. It requires much courage and skill to take on an opponent at the net in a match. So we make you do it. Simply add an extra rule to the game: 'You must return the shuttle to the forecourt when it is in your forecourt', i.e. play net replies from your forecourt. If your opponent also knows the rule he will simply play a shot into your forecourt and then wait to attack any poor replies. I can assure you that you will quickly improve.

In either case you should keep a mental note of how many times you have played the strokes and how many were successful. *Success breeds success* and with it grows self-confidence in your ability to play the strokes in competition. You will

be well on your way then to doing so in a real competition when you play according to the normal rules.

INFORMAL COMPETITION
This is where informal competition can be of value. Here you can and should try out new ideas and strokes as the score should not be important. Games at the local club, practice games in squad sessions and with regular practice partners provide the perfect opportunity to do this. You can use your newly practised skills as much as possible, even at times when you may be uncertain and they may cause you to lose a rally or the game.

This is when you should be forward-looking. Realise that the more you try out a particular skill in informal competition, when the results do not matter, the easier it will be to do in formal competition when the results do matter.

Once again try to keep a mental record of your successes in using your practised skill. For example, assess your success in using the backhand clear which your are trying to develop. Let's assume that it goes into your backhand rearcourt twelve times. You use the backhand clear ten times, out of which you hit seven successfully to the rearcourt. This would be a success rate of 70 per cent. That is a good basis for using it with confidence in formal competition. Keep working on it and try to increase that score to 80-90 per cent.

FORMAL COMPETITION
In formal competition the emphasis should be on trying to win. Even though this will be a serious business there is still the opportunity to practise in play. But to do so can be risky so you must be sensible about how you practise.

A number of years ago I was working with one of England's world-class singles players, Paul Whetnall. We agreed that Paul would use the earlier rounds of a tournament to practise parts of his game. He did this in several ways. If he was playing a weaker opponent and stood a good chance of winning, he took every opportunity to practise a new stroke-move in certain situations even to the extent of giving the opponent the advantage. For example he would hit a short-length clear or lob to allow his opponent the chance to attempt a winning smash, so that he could practise his speed and control in defence. Another time he would play a drop to the forecourt, stay back near the rearcourt to invite his opponent to play a net reply, and then travel forwards at speed to take the shuttle late near the ground and make a net reply with his opponent waiting there ready to attack.

If Paul began to lose too many points and the opponent began to become a threat then he would revert to his normal 'winning' game against that opponent. He would continue in this way with different opponents until he met a respected strong opponent and then concentrate on trying to win in his usual efficient way. With continuous play in this way the practised part soon became an automatic part of his total game.

You should try some of these methods of bridging the gap between the practice court and the match court and perhaps develop some of your own. The more you do so the sooner you will master your craft and become a better player.

A POSITIVE APPROACH TO PRACTICE

In most practices you will be working hard to get things right whether it is your speed off the mark, a backhand smash or a kill from the net. In doing so you must expect to make errors. If you don't make any errors there would be no reason to practise to improve.

You will be likely to make more errors when attempting a winning shot than you will when playing a building shot. The reason for this is that the margin for error will usually be smaller, e.g. a kill just off the top of the net from a defensive block to your smash. This is likely to happen in other situations also when you are required to be adventurous and to take risks to attempt a winner.

Do not be put off by making errors in these situations and revert to playing a safer shot. Be adventurous and have a go. With regular practice you will begin to make fewer errors and more winners when the chances arise. Only by attempting something can you learn to do it. You will learn

to be adventurous by being adventurous. The more you succeed the more your confidence will grow until it will become a habit to play in this positive way. You will realise that what was once adventurous play for you and what others may still consider to be adventurous has now become quite normal play for you.

This is another reason why just doing routines can hold you back. Players who spend their time doing numerous repetitions of a routine, no matter how fast, do not necessarily become adventurous and take the chances when they arise in formal competition. They often become play-safe players – dull, mediocre, obvious and boring to watch. You certainly do not want to join the ranks of these players. That is why you should know the aim of any practice and certainly you should practise playing attempted winning shots as much as you practise your building shots.

This is where you can also develop your mental attitude. I often think of the winning shot played by Rudi Hartono when he was four match points down to the Swedish player Sture Johnsson in the 1976 All England singles semi-finals. Johnsson had just played a tight spinning net shot when Hartono leapt forwards and hit a winner from just off the net. The crowd and Johnsson were stunned. Hartono then held his serve to win the match. He continued to beat his next opponent and win his eighth final, an all-time All England Men's Singles record.

Some years later I asked Hartono about this game and that particular shot. I suggested that with regular practice it had become a habit to be adventurous and to go for the chances when they arose. He agreed but also added that both in practice and competition he had always played as if he were playing the match point. His reply draws attention to another feature of being a craftsman – ultimately when all things are equal between you and your opponent it will be the player with the strongest mental attitude who will win. Hartono confirmed for me that you can practise to develop such an attitude on the practice court and in competition.

Your Complete Reference List of Technical Skills

Below is a list of most, if not all, the technical and tactical skills included in this book. The list has been divided into three parts:

● racket skills, skill in controlling the racket head and face

● the strokes, skill in performing the strokes and using them as tactical moves

● body skills, skill in moving.

If your technical skill is below standard then you will usually practise in at least one of these parts to put it right.

Read through the three sections and check which skills you can and cannot do. Then refer to the appropriate pages for information about any skills. This includes an analysis of each technical skill and its tactical use, common faults, their probable causes and corrections, and practices for each stroke.

RACKET SKILLS

		PAGES		
		Analysis ⇩	Technical Practice ⇩	Tactical Practice ⇩
Holding the racket	● the forehand grip	43	46	
	● the backhand grip	43	46	
	● the multipurpose/ universal grip	43	46	
	● changing grip		46, 47	
	● grip tensions		47	
	● long and short grips	43		
Controlling the racket head	● cocking the hand	44	47	
	● tap action	44	47	
	● push action	45	47, 48	
	● whip action	45	48	
Controlling the racket face	● flat face hits	45	49	
	● glancing face hits	45	49	

THE STROKES
(All played from the forehand and backhand sides and used for straight and cross-court shots)

REARCOURT STROKES		Analysis	Technical Practice	Tactical Practice
Overhead rearcourt strokes	● power smash	63	65	66
	● sliced smash	63	65	66
	● standard clear	67	69	69
	● attacking clear	67	69	69
	● defensive clear	67	69	69
	● fast flat drop	70	72	72
	● fast sliced drop	70	72	72
	● long drop	70	72	72
	● slow drop (check smash)	70	72	72
	● backhand clear	73	74	74
	● backhand smash	75	76	76
	● backhand drop	77	77	78
Low rearcourt strokes	● lob	79	80-1	81
	● drive	79	80-1	81
	● drop	79	80-1	81

MIDCOURT STROKES

		Analysis	Technical Practice	Tactical Practice
Overhead midcourt strokes	● power smash			
	● sliced smash	82		
	● fast drop			
	● slow drop			
Net height strokes	● drive	79	83	84
Low midcourt strokes	● block	85	87	87
	● push	85	87	87
	● tap	88	89	89
	● lob	90	91	91
Serves	● low serve	92	93	
	● flick serve	94	95	
	● high serve	95	96	
	● drive serve	96-7	97	

FORECOURT STROKES

		Analysis	Technical Practice	Tactical Practice
Above net	● kill	98	99-100	
	● brush	100	101	
	● push	101	102	
Just below net height	● tumbler	102	103	104
	● push	101	102	

		Analysis ⇩	PAGES Technical Practice ⇩	Tactical Practice ⇩
FORECOURT STROKES *continued*				
Low – near the floor	● hairpin net reply	104	105	
	● lob	106	107-8	108
BODY SKILL				
Posture and balance	● centring the body	50	51	
Starting	● transferring body weight	51	54	
	● bounce start	52		
	● split jump	52		
Stopping	● transferring body weight	54	54	
	● split jump	54	54	
Travelling	● walking			
	● running			
	● chasséing	54	54	
	● cross-over steps			
	● lightness			
Transitions	● forwards to backwards			
	● backwards to forwards			
	● sideways	54	54	
	● diagonals			
	● split jump			
Lunges	● step patterns			
	● half lunge	55	56	
	● full lunge			
Recovery from lunge	● weight transfer	56	56	
Jumping	● vertical jumps			
	● diagonal jumps			
	● spin jumps	56	57-8	
	● scissor jumps			
	● forward jumps			
	● side jumps			
Landings	● deep landing			
	● rebound landing	57	57-8	
	● steps landing			

CHAPTER
7

Learn How to Improve Your Racket Skill

You will improve your racket skill once you know how to control your racket head and face. You will need this control in order to hit the shuttle with more or less force (changing the pace of shuttle speed) in any given direction towards your opponent's court and, most importantly, to be able to perform all the strokes. To get such control you will need to master some basic grips and hitting techniques. First, I will describe them and then give you some practices to help you to master them.

THE GRIPS

Most good players use a number of grips to control the racket for different strokes. They hold the racket handle gently in the fingers and then make minor adjustments to grip the racket differently for different shots. Initially there are three basic grips: the forehand, backhand and multipurpose or universal. *See* plates 1, 2 and 3.

I would advise you to master the basic forehand and backhand grips before you learn the universal grip and other variations. You will then become familiar with the two primary positions of the hand on the handle of the racket, i.e. the palm side, for forehand strokes, and the thumb side, for backhand strokes. When you can change from one side to the other side automatically then you can prac-

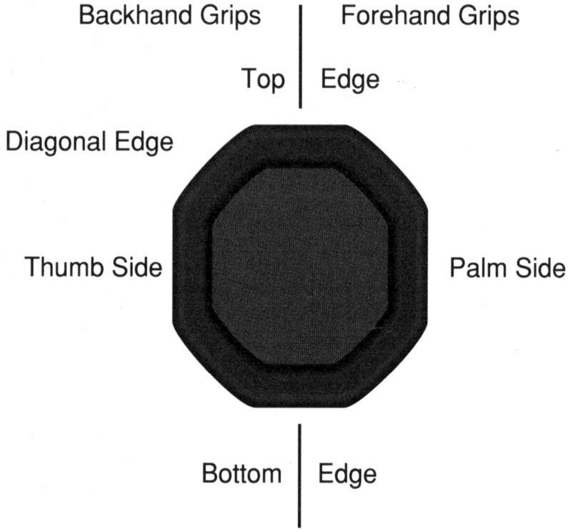

Backhand Grips | Forehand Grips

Top | Edge

Diagonal Edge

Thumb Side | Palm Side

Bottom | Edge

Fig 15

Plate 1 – The Forehand Grip

tise the universal grip, for forehand and backhand strokes, and make slight variations as you need to. Examine the diagram of the racket handle in Fig 15.

THE FOREHAND GRIP

Hold the racket handle gently in your fingers with the palm positioned mainly behind the racket handle. Now you will hit the shuttle as if with the palm of your hand. Make sure that you do not hold the handle in a tight fist grip or you will have less control over your racket and find it difficult to change quickly to another grip.

THE BACKHAND GRIP

Place your whole thumb flat behind the racket handle with your fingers spread out to hold it gently. Your thumb will apply the pressure on your racket handle when you do backhand strokes. The little finger side edge of your hand will point towards the shuttle as you go to hit it, e.g. karate style.

NOTE Some players tend to think that backhand strokes are played as if with the back of the hand and so they develop a weak backhand. If you follow the instructions above and apply thumb pressure on the thumb side of the racket handle, as shown in Fig 15, then it will feel as if you are playing the backhand stroke as if with the side edge of the hand. This is more correct and effective.

THE UNIVERSAL GRIP

Place your thumb flat on the diagonal edge of the racket handle (*see* Fig 15) and spread your fingers to hold the racket handle. This is similar to the backhand grip and is used as the main grip by many top players.

SHORT AND LONG GRIPS

In addition to using these basic grips you can shorten or lengthen your racket by placing your hand at the top or bottom of the top of the handle. The short grip will give you more racket control especially for quick hitting in the midcourt and

Plate 2 – The Backhand Grip

Plate 3 – The Universal Grip

Plate 4 – *(right)*
The Short Grip

Plate 5 – *(below)*
The Long Grip

forecourt. The long grip will be more useful in the rearcourt for playing smashes and clears. *See* plates 4 and 5.

HITTING TECHNIQUES

Every time you hit the shuttle you will use one of three basic hitting techniques to control the **racket head**, and one of two basic hitting techniques to control the **racket face**. I will describe these in turn.

CONTROL YOUR RACKET HEAD

The three techniques used describe the *feeling of the movement* you will experience in your hand and forearm as you hit the shuttle. These are the tap, push and whip actions. However, before you actually hit the shuttle you must get your racket ready.

Cocking the Hand

To do so you should 'cock' your hand to take the racket head back ready to hit the shuttle before impact. Some players and coaches refer to 'cocking the wrist' but it is more accurate to say 'cock the hand'. *See* plates 6 and 7.

Make sure the end of the racket handle points towards the shuttle before you hit it.

The Tap Action

Hold the racket in front of you with your arm slightly flexed at the elbow. Fully cock your hand ready to hit the shuttle. As you hit the shuttle check your racket head speed on impact. You will notice a quick, light rebound action in your hand which will be similar to the experience of *tapping* something, e.g. a downward tap at the net. On the forehand side your experience will be as if the palm is tapping the shuttle; on the backhand side it will be as if your thumb is doing so.

The Push Action

Hold your racket in front of you with your arm slightly flexed at the elbow. Fully cock your hand ready to hit the shuttle. As you hit the shuttle keep your hand fully cocked throughout the action, as if locked at your wrist. You will experience the feeling of *pushing* the shuttle away in a smooth continuous movement, with the racket face following the flight of the shuttle as your arm extends (follows through) before recovering to the racket starting position. On the forehand side it will feel as if your palm is pushing; on the backhand side, as if your thumb is pushing, e.g. the low serve.

The Whip Action

Hold your racket in front of you with your arm slightly flexed at the elbow. Hit the shuttle upwards at speed and allow your hand to 'uncock' fully. You will experience the feeling of *whipping* your hand and racket head through the shuttle as you hit it.

NOTE A common fault is for players to uncock their hand completely when performing a stroke which requires a push or tap action, so losing some control and accuracy, e.g. a low serve, which results in the shuttle being hit too high above the net; or a kill at the net, which results in the shuttle being hit down into the net. Make sure that you use the correct hitting technique in all your strokes.

CONTROL OF THE RACKET FACE

There are only two ways of using the racket face:

Flat Hits

These apply when the racket face meets the shuttle square on and directs the force of the hit through the centre of the shuttle.

Plate 6 –
Cocking the Hand for Forehand Strokes

Plate 7 –
Cocking the Hand for Backhand Strokes

Glancing Hits

These apply when the racket face meets the shuttle at an angle, gives it a glancing hit and directs the force of the hit off-centre which causes the shuttle to rotate. Sliced smashes and net tumblers are typical examples of glancing hits.

NOTE Correct use of your racket face is important. For example, you may find that your clear falls short of the rearcourt simply because you are slicing it and using insufficient force when you should be using a flat racket face to apply the force. A simple racket face adjustment would ensure that the shuttle travels the full distance as intended.

The three ways of controlling the racket head and the two ways of using the racket face apply to any action that can be used to hit the shuttle. They are *fundamental* to all racket skills. You should master them through regular practice if you wish to hit the shuttle accurately.

PRACTICES TO IMPROVE YOUR RACKET SKILL

Racket skill comes from getting the right *feeling of the movement* in using the grips, performing the correct hitting actions and using the racket face effectively. The practices in this section are designed to increase your *awareness* of this feeling. I will assume that you have a practice partner, a 'feeder', for these practices unless I have indicated a solo practice.

These practices should take place mainly in the midcourt and forecourt, as the emphasis is on developing the use of your racket hand and fingers to control the racket. Travel phases will not be included here although some body skill will be required, e.g. posture and balance, bouncy knees and general alertness, and quickness of movement from the sides attack stance. *See* plate 11.

THE GRIPS

Change of Grip Practices

1ST PRACTICE

Hold the handle and slowly change from one grip to the other using your fingers and thumb to move the handle around in your hand, almost like practising finger exercises at the piano. You must get to know your racket handle well so that you know where your hand is positioned on it at all times.

In this practice it helps to *watch how* you

change the grip. You may also decide that the *starting position* of your hand on the racket handle will be either a forehand grip or a backhand grip. Most players start by using a forehand grip as compared with many top players who tend to use a multipurpose or backhand grip between shots. Try both grips and then decide which one feels right for you.

2ND PRACTICE

● Hold the racket handle in your starting grip.
● Practise quickly changing your hand position from the forehand to the backhand grip and back again, i.e. palm or thumb behind the racket handle.
● Do this first looking at your hand and then without looking at it.
● You can develop this action by spinning the handle in your hand and then just stopping the handle in the forehand or backhand grip.
● Do this for at least 5 – 10 minutes each day until you can do it quickly and automatically.

When I was first learning the grips I read somewhere that the racket should be an extension of my hand so I practised changing grip while watching television. It didn't spoil my viewing and worked wonders for my racket skill.

3RD PRACTICE

Play shadow badminton and use different grips to hit imaginary shuttles from different positions around your body.

4TH PRACTICE

● Stand in the centre midcourt with your 'feeder' opposite you and rally at medium pace hitting the shuttle to travel horizontally across the net. *See* Fig 16.
● Rally using the forehand grip and then the backhand grip.
● Hit the shuttle with the racket head above your hand for a number of hits and then with the racket head below your hand.
● Continue rallying until you get the comfortable 'feel' of the grip.

5TH PRACTICE

Rally as in the second practice. This time alternate between the forehand and backhand grips until

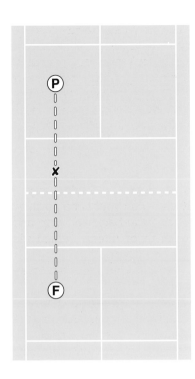

Fig 16 *(left)*

Fig 17 *(right)*

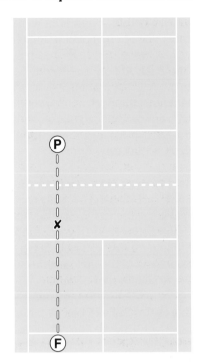

you can change the grips at speed. It may help to hit two forehands and then two backhands before changing alternately for forehand and backhand hits.

Develop this by rallying at speed in the midcourt using the forehand and backhand grips as required and in no particular order.

Grip Tension Practices

If you grip the racket handle too tightly then you will find it difficult to 'cock' the hand easily and to change grip quickly. If this is so then try this practice.

FLOPPY HITTING Hold the racket handle in a short grip with your thumb and first two or three fingers only. Rally with your partner changing grip as necessary.

You will find that your hand will be able to 'cock' completely and the racket head will feel very loose (floppy) in your hand. After some practice hold the racket handle gently in all your fingers and continue to rally, making sure that you cock the hand completely and maintain the gentle grip.

RACKET HEAD CONTROL
The Tap Action

In the following practices you should try to get the feeling of the tap action when hitting the shuttle with the racket head:
a) above your hand
b) below your hand
c) level with your hand.
The shuttle should be hit from in front of you.

1ST PRACTICE

Stand in the midcourt with your feet sideways apart, facing your practice partner across the net. Rally using forehand and backhand tap actions to hit the shuttle quickly across the net.

2ND PRACTICE

Stand in the forecourt in a forward attacking stance (racket foot in front) with your partner positioned in the opposite rearcourt. *See* Fig 17.

Use the tap action to rally to each other with forehand and backhand grips. You should tap the shuttle with your racket head above your hand; your partner should hit the shuttle from the side and below his hand. Make sure that the shuttle skims the net. Practise until you can increase the speed and yet retain control of your racket head. Then change place.

ADVICE Make sure that you use the correct grip and do not try to hit the shuttle too hard. The action should be quick and light with a rebound of the racket head on impact with the shuttle.

The Push Action

In the following practices you should develop the feeling of the push action while hitting the shuttle with the racket head above, at the side and below the hand. In these practices the shuttle is hit from in front of the body.

1st Practice: Midcourt Positions

See Fig 16 on page 47. Rally using the push action, making sure that the shuttle skims the net and falls below net level as it travels to the opposite midcourt. Make sure that you rally using the forehand and backhand grips and follow through in the direction of the shuttle after each hit.

2nd Practice: Forecourt and Midcourt Positions

Stand in the forecourt with your partner in the opposite midcourt. *See* Fig 18.

Rally using pushes from the forecourt and midcourt, making sure that you use both forehand and backhand grips. Change over when you feel satisfied that you can use the push action from near to the net with your racket head above your hand.

Taps and Pushes

You should also practise alternating tap and push actions. This will help to develop your skill in controlling the racket head and it will give you control in changing the pace of the shuttle. A tap action will make the shuttle travel quickly, whereas a push action will make the shuttle travel slowly through the air.

To practise tap and push actions rally with your partner from midcourt to midcourt, and from forecourt to midcourt.

Reminder Your hand will partly uncock for the tap action and remain fully cocked for the push action.

The Whip Action

You will usually only use this action for strong hits when, for example, you completely uncock your hand to hit a clear, a smash or a lob. To experience a whip action simply practise these strokes and focus on letting your hand whip the racket head through at speed as you hit the shuttle.

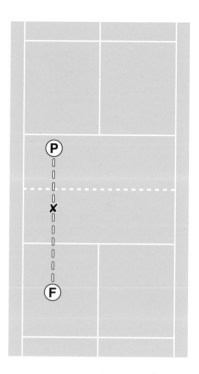

Fig 18

Wall Practices

A flat smooth wall can be very useful for practising your racket skills. The shuttle rebounds quite easily so that you can practise your hitting techniques, grips and change of grip.

1st Practice: Taps and Pushes

Stand 2½ metres from the wall. Facing the wall, begin rallying against it. Regular practice will improve your racket skill and also develop the essential muscular endurance and strength required in your fingers and racket arm.

If the wall is high enough you can also practise backhand clears, clears and smashes.

2nd Practice: Hitting from in Front of the Body

In racket skill practice the shuttle is usually hit from in front of you. Try to take your racket arm behind you to prepare to hit the shuttle instead of keeping it in front of you all the time.

Stand with your back pressed flat against the wall, feet about 15 cm from the wall and knees comfortably bent.

Rally (taps and pushes) with your partner positioned about 8 metres from you. A few knocks on the elbow as you take the racket arm back against the wall should soon help you to begin to hit the shuttle from in front of you.

RACKET FACE CONTROL

Control of the racket face will enable you to play a greater range of strokes, it ensures greater accuracy and, most importantly, makes it easier to exploit your opponent in competition.

For example you may find that your clears are falling short of a good length. You think that you are performing the stroke correctly and hitting the shuttle hard enough to reach the rearcourt but, in fact, instead of hitting the shuttle with a flat racket face you find that you are giving it a glancing hit and reducing some of the force required to hit a full-length clear. If you are aware of the racket face angle then the correction is quite easy – you adjust it to hit the shuttle with a flat face.

You might have a powerful smash gained from hitting the shuttle with a flat racket face but which a particular opponent is successfully defending. To upset the opponent's timing you decide to hit a sliced smash so that the shuttle falls short as it loses speed. Your racket face control should make this quite simple to do.

The tumblers which you play as net replies all depend on your control of the racket face. The more you practise the more control you will gain.

Glancing Hits

1st Practice

Start in the midcourt facing your practice partner and rally using glancing hits. Experiment with different ways of holding the racket using backhand and forehand grips.

2nd Practice

Now practise different strokes using a glancing hit, e.g. sliced dropshots and smashes, replies to the smash, net replies, and serves. Experiment and find out how to use the racket face in this way.

Flat Hits

Rally with your partner using different strokes and practise hitting the shuttle with the flat face of the racket. You should notice a difference in the feel and the sound of the hit which will be more solid than when using a glancing hit.

Flat and Glancing Hits

Rally with your partner using a variety of strokes and practise hitting the shuttle with a flat face or a glancing face. If you can do this effectively you have increased your awareness and with it your control of the racket face.

RACKET HEAD AND RACKET FACE PRACTICES

Now that you have mastered using the racket head and face separately it will be helpful if you combine them.

Practice

Rally with your partner to experiment in using your racket head and face. Try the following:

- Push action + glancing/flat hit
- Tap action + glancing/flat hit
- Whip action + glancing/flat hit.

These practice routines will help you to develop a greater *awareness* and control in using the racket head and face. In this way you should improve your racket skill.

Learn How to Improve Your Body Skill

It would make life much easier on the badminton court if players were always in a comfortable balanced position to hit the shuttle. Good players usually are which is why they always seem to have so much time to play their shots. The secret lies in getting to the shuttle early, for which good body skill is essential.

There is a lot more to body skill than just *footwork and balance* which is how your movement about the court is usually described. There are in fact six components you will need to master:

● posture and balance
● starting and stopping
● travelling
● transitions (changing direction)
● lunge and recovery
● jumping and landing.

Of these posture and balance are common to all the components while the others are interrelated. For example transitions (changes of direction) involve stopping and starting, and a lunge and recovery involves a transition.

I will describe each one in some detail and give you some awareness exercises to help you to master them before providing some on-court practices.

Advice

In all body skill exercises and practices that involve knee bending, and there will be much of that, you should take care to ensure that your knees bend in the correct alignment. The knee joint is a hinge joint, it bends in one direction, and consequently any twisting movements or uneven bending of the knee may cause strain and possible injury. To reduce the risk of injury you should follow the general rule that the centre of your knee-cap bends directly over the centre of your foot. I would advise you to check the position of your knees in relation to your feet to make sure that you do bend your knees correctly when practising your body skills.

THE BODY SKILL COMPONENTS

POSTURE AND BALANCE

Good posture is when you have an awareness and control of your body parts in relation to your body space (the space occupied by your body) to the extent that you feel *centred*, in balance within yourself.

The best way to experience this is to stand tall, evenly centred, and then move parts of your body off centre. For example, let your head and shoulders slump forwards. You will feel your muscles straining at the back of your neck and shoulders until you stand tall and become centred again. It is so easy to develop a poor posture and cause a strain on other muscles and equally easy to develop a good posture if you are aware of this strain.

Good balance requires an awareness and control of the positions of your body parts in relation to gravity. You should feel centred, in balance, in relation to the ground. You could, for example, have a poor posture as described above, and yet have perfect balance. If you didn't then you would always be staggering about to regain balance or falling over.

In play you will experience many occasions when you get out of balance to return the shuttle; with a heightened awareness of balance you will recover more quickly and to your advantage.

Awareness Exercises

POSTURE
Stand tall and centred, as if being pulled upwards by a string on the top of your head. Your shoulders should be relaxed and your abdominal muscles slightly tensed. Now just let parts of your body collapse, e.g. head, shoulders, trunk, so you are not centred and adopt a poor posture.

Hold the position until you feel the muscles straining and then stand tall and centre yourself again into a good posture and the straining feeling will disappear.

BALANCE
SWAYING: stand tall with your feet together and in balance. Simply sway in different directions until you feel you will overbalance and then regain your balance. Try this with your eyes closed for heightened awareness of balance.

TRAVELLING: walk or run forwards, backwards or sideways and then stop suddenly in balance. At first you may overbalance and sway or take an extra step. Practise until you can stop in balance and in complete control of your movements.

You will notice that you usually stop with your knees bent which is the result of lowering your centre of gravity and using your legs as 'shock absorbers and brakes'.

PRACTISING POSTURE AND BALANCE
Select a stroke within an action phrase and practise maintaining good posture and balance while you rally with your partner. Though there are numerous strokes and action phrases in which you can practise your posture and balance it would be sensible to select one where you know you have difficulty in maintaining your balance as you travel or hit the shuttle. For example, when you perform a lunge at speed in the forecourt, or when landing after jumping backwards to smash in the rearcourt.

STARTING AND STOPPING
Your ability to accelerate quickly from a stationary starting position and to stop just as quickly (and in balance) is an essential part of your game. If you could save a tenth of a second with a quick start just think how much earlier you would reach the shuttle and how much less time you would give

your opponent. It could be worth a few points every game.

Examples of starting are: when receiving a serve, in forecourt attack, in midcourt defence. From these positions you may be required to accelerate, forwards, backwards and sideways.

Examples of stopping are: when running or jumping into the forecourt or rearcourt at speed, and when returning quickly to the midcourt to defend.

STARTING
There are several ways of starting:

- By swaying out of balance in the direction you want to go. You must then take a step or you will fall over. This is a slow start, the type we use when we start to walk anywhere. There is no need to practise it for badminton.
- By bending the knees and then swaying out of balance ready to push down into the ground to extend the legs and feet rapidly. This is a faster start, e.g. when receiving the low serve. This

Plate 8 – The Split Jump

Plate 9 – Forward Attacking Stance

Plate 10 – Backward Attacking Stance

would be similar to adopting a standing start for a sprint race.

- By quickly transferring your weight into the direction you want to go and your feet into position ready to push you away in the new direction with a rebound action. Most good players do this by using a **bounce start*** or a **split jump**.

This is often the quickest way to accelerate from a given spot. In the bounce start the effect is gained from pre-tensing your thigh muscles by bending your knees quickly in a 'get ready' movement and then *using your thigh muscles to bounce on them* as you take the weight off your feet so that you can

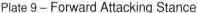

* A quick bend of your knees will 'load' your thigh muscles as they tense (contract eccentrically) causing the muscles' stretch reflexes to activate; which you then use to rebound and push away from the spot by straightening your legs rapidly. It is claimed that you can gain an increase of 30 per cent more force to push you away by doing so and thus increase your acceleration. Read the section on Plyometrics in chapter 13.

transfer them into position ready to push you off the spot. In the split jump you simply perform an astride jump on the spot to transfer your feet into position to push you off the spot. The split jump is most often used when you are travelling towards the midcourt and want to stop or change direction quickly. You can do this by jumping into an astride jump (split your legs) to transfer your feet into position to allow you to stop in balance or to rebound away from the spot quickly on landing from your jump. *See* Plate 8.

Which start you use will depend on your initial stance of which there are several, so let us look at these before I explain how to start quickly.

Court Positions and Stances

- Forecourt — *forward attacking stance* (racket foot forwards). It is used when you prepare to attack an expected net reply from close to the net. *See* Plate 9.
- Front midcourt — *backward attacking stance* (racket foot to the rear). It is used when

Plate 11 – Sides Attacking Stance

Plate 12 – Defensive Stance

expecting an upward hit from the midcourt or forecourt, e.g. a lob or flick serve. *See* Plate 10.

- Central midcourt — *sides attacking stance* (feet about shoulder width apart), upright stance with your knees slightly flexed ready to 'bounce start' and move quickly to counter-hit a smash or drive from the midcourt. *See* Plate 11.

- Central midcourt — *defensive stance*, feet wider apart than in the sides attacking stance. You would use this when ready to defend against a strong smash. *See* Plate 12.

How to Start

How you actually start in a game will depend on the game situation. Let us examine a few of them.

Receiving the Low Serve

Stance: Stand in a backward attacking stance and keep your feet on the ground until the shuttle is hit. Position yourself with your weight forwards and your knees and ankles slightly flexed (muscles charged) ready to thrust you forwards and upwards to attack the serve.

Start: If you do attack the serve your knees should quickly flex further just before you extend your legs and feet rapidly as you push backwards and downwards into the floor to thrust you from the spot.

Receiving the Flick Serve

Stance: As for the low serve.

Start: Keep your knees bent and sway backwards to transfer your weight on to your rear foot before thrusting away from the spot.

Waiting to Attack a Net Reply

Stance: Stand in a forward attacking stance ready to stop or jump forward to attack a net reply.

Start: You should find that you will be slightly bouncing on your knees (keeping the muscles charged) in a state of readiness to jump or step forwards (or backwards) quickly.

Counter-Attacking in the Midcourt

Stance: Stand in a sides attack stance. Keep your knees slightly bent as you bounce on them (keep-

ing the muscles charged) ready to move quickly.
Start: Use a jump or bounce start.

DEFENDING IN THE MIDCOURT

Stance: Stand in a sides defence stance. Bend your knees ready to move quickly to defend against the smash or to travel to the rearcourt or forecourt to return the shuttle.
Start: Bounce start.

Awareness Exercises

Take up each of these stances and experiment with the different ways of starting to accelerate forwards, backwards or sideways.

Attitude: You will need to concentrate on getting to the shuttle quickly in order to apply a strong explosive force to accelerate you from the spot. It might help if you imagine that you are in a race with the shuttle. Thus if you are receiving the low serve the question is can you beat the shuttle to the net. Try this exercise and you will find that your posture, stance, general alertness, concentration and determination all improve. This same attitude should apply whenever you have to race against the shuttle to any place in the court.

STOPPING

You should already have developed some awareness of stopping if you have tried out the awareness exercises for balance. There are two methods of stopping quickly.

1ST METHOD

To stop quickly in balance after travelling at speed you should transfer your centre of gravity into the opposite direction of travel. For example, if you are running forwards your centre of gravity will be more to the front so you will simply transfer it backwards by bringing your feet and legs to your front.

By doing this you will experience three sensations:

● a preparatory checking step and a lowering of your centre of gravity, immediately prior to stopping on the next step
● an extended step ahead of your body
● your body weight being 'thrown' or held back in the opposite direction to that in which you are travelling.

2ND METHOD: SPLIT JUMP

This time you can transfer your body weight into the opposite direction by travelling and jumping on to the spot where you want to stop. To do this you would simply change your run into an astride jump and rebound on the spot with feet wide apart, i.e. a 'split jump'.

Awareness Exercises
1ST METHOD

Sprint forwards and stop suddenly by using a preparatory checking step. Now do this in different directions. Make sure that all parts of your body stop simultaneously, i.e. 'freeze' while you stop in balance. You will know if you are doing this effectively from the sound of your steps. As you stop you should hear the sound of the checking step (to slow you down) and then the final step to stop you, i.e. check step, stop step sounds.

2ND METHOD

Walk or run forwards and backwards and use a *split jump* to stop.

TRAVELLING

This is the aspect of your movement which is usually referred to as 'footwork' and involves different types of step patterns, e.g. walking, running, sprinting, side-stepping. You should use quality of movement for each step pattern: fluent, smooth, lightness and softness of foot. In fact I often refer to this quality as travelling with **soft feet**.

Awareness Exercises
1ST EXERCISE

Travel round freely using different step patterns but without making any sound, i.e. with *soft feet*.

2ND EXERCISE

Choose a court starting position and stance and then perform a **shadow** action phrase. Experiment with different step patterns in the approach and recovery travel phases using soft feet.

TRANSITIONS

This term refers to your ability to change direction quickly and smoothly from:

● side to side
● forwards and backwards and vice versa

- forwards and sideways
- backwards and sideways.

Most changes of direction, as you will know, take place in the central midcourt which is where you return to stop or pass through after playing a shot from the rearcourt, forecourt or midcourt sides.

To perform a transition well you will need good posture and balance combined with the ability to stop and start quickly.

In the midcourt an effective method you can use to change direction (perform a transition) is a split jump (*see* page 52). In this way you can halt your movement in one direction, transfer your body weight during the jump and on landing rebound in a new direction. You can also slow down your movement ready to push off into a new direction by using a checking step as described in the section on Stopping.

Awareness Exercises

1ST METHOD

Use a bounce start to travel from the midcourt centre to the forecourt, rearcourt and sides of the midcourt. *See* Fig 19. Perform a transition and recover to the centre using a split jump to stop.

Practise this at different speeds and to different parts of the court.

2ND METHOD

Approach the centre from different parts of the court. *See* Fig 20. Perform a split jump and on landing rebound away into a new direction.

3RD METHOD

Practise transitions in different directions at different speeds.

LUNGE AND RECOVERY

A lunge is simply a large extending step on to your flexing racket leg which is performed in various directions in the court. The ability to lunge and recover is an essential part of badminton.

Most players appear to learn and use the full lunge in which they stretch out as far as possible to hit the shuttle. This is usually an indication that they are late getting to it, which, in addition, will usually make them late recovering into position to cover the opponent's next shot.

As well as mastering the full lunge and your recovery from it you should also learn and master the half lunge, a partially extended step. This will be less demanding and allow you to maintain your

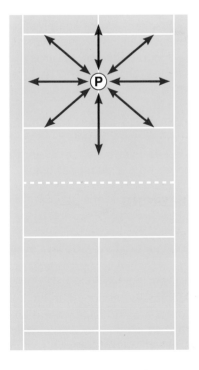

Fig 19 *left*
Transitions away from the centre

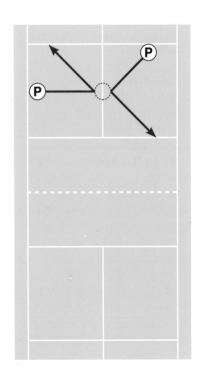

Fig 20 *right*
Transitions at the centre

Plate 13 – Full Lunge

Plate 14 – Half Lunge

posture and balance while hitting the shuttle. It will also enable you to make a quicker recovery.

The Lunge

When travelling at speed it is important that you make a preparatory slowing down movement (a checking step) immediately prior to the lunge. This is done by turning the non-racket foot out-wards at a 45-degree angle and bending your knee to lower your centre of gravity and to pre-pare for the thrust forwards on to the racket foot. The non-racket foot can be turned outwards at the side, directly behind or crossed behind the racket foot. The action is similar to that of a fencer lunging forwards to attack an opponent. See plates 13 and 14.

The Recovery

From the outstretched lunge position there are two types of recovery to a more comfortable 'feet shoulder width apart' stance. First, you can trans-fer your body weight backwards towards your non-racket foot, flexing the non-racket leg while

you do so. Second, you can bring your extended non-racket leg towards your racket foot in one continuous movement as the lunge is performed, flexing it while you do so to get into a comfortable stance from which you can start quickly to travel into position to cover your opponent's replies. Watch that fencer in action and you can learn this movement quite quickly.

Awareness Exercises

Take up a forward attacking stance and practise half and full lunges and both types of recovery.

Start from the midcourt and travel towards the forecourt to practise the 'checking step' and the lunges and ways of recovering. Repeat this in the midcourt and rearcourt.

Practise approaching the lunges at different speeds and recovering quickly. Select several action phrases using the lunge and recovery to approach and recover from a hitting position.

JUMPING AND LANDING

JUMPING

Jumping is an athletic/gymnastic type of activity. If you enjoy jumping then you will enjoy practising the variety of jumps you can use to smash, clear, drop from the rearcourt and midcourt and to kill the shuttle in the forecourt. Fortunately there are only five basic jumps which you have to learn in order to perform the variety of jumps used in

Plate 15 - Diagonal Jump

Plate 16 – Spin Jump

Plate 17 – Scissor Jump

badminton.

The five basic jumps are:

● take off one foot to land on the same foot
● take off one foot to land on the other foot
● take off one foot to land on two feet
● take off two feet to land on one foot
● take off two feet to land on two feet.

If you can imagine yourself or other players jumping to hit the shuttle you will 'see' that you and they will only use one or other of the five basic jumps.

Consider, for example, the following badminton jumps (Plates 15,16,17):

● diagonal jump to the forehand rearcourt (one foot to two feet)
● spin jump in the forehand rearcourt (one foot to two feet)
● scissor jump to the backhand rearcourt (one foot to the other foot)
● vertical jump smash (two feet to two feet)
● side jump smash in midcourt (one foot to two feet)
● forward jump to forecourt (one foot to the same or to the other foot), as when attacking the low serve in doubles.

As jumping is an athletic/gymnastic-type activity there is often a sequence of actions performed. There is the approach run (travel phase), the take-off (from one or two feet), the flight and the landing. During the flight you will hit the shuttle and then, on landing, perform a transition to start the recovery travel phase to get into position to cover the probable replies.

LANDING

There are three types of landing depending on how high or far you jump.

Deep Landing

After a high jump, e.g. vertical jump or diagonal jump you will approach the ground on a vertical flightpath and usually land by bending your knees to absorb the force of the landing.

Running Landing

After a distance jump in which you 'fly' on a horizontal pathway you will usually land and take several steps to slow down before recovering, e.g. a scissor jump smash after receiving the flick serve.

Rebound Landing

When your flight path is a mixture of distance and height it is effective to perform a rebound jump on landing to prevent travelling any further after landing, e.g. a forward jump into the forecourt to attempt a kill at the net.

In all landings it will be important to keep a good posture, balance and to land lightly. After landing you will often perform a transition to recover your position to cover the opponent's probable replies.

Awareness Exercises

● Experiment with different badminton jumps using the five basic jumps.
● Run and jump for height and/or distance and try out the different sorts of landings. Make sure that you land lightly.
● Practise rebound jumping on the spot from two feet to two feet.
● Try out the various badminton jumps with emphasis on the approach run, take-off, flight, stroke cycle and landing.

SPECIFIC PRACTICES FOR BODY SKILL

When practising any body skill it is helpful to 'walk through' (do them at walking pace) the exercise to get the feel of the movement and to work out how the actions are performed. Then you can add the travel phases and increase your speed to an appropriate game speed.

The following practices should help you to improve your body skill in actual play. Do each exercise at medium pace for 30-60 seconds.

Shadow Badminton Exercises

PRACTICE 1: POSTURE AND BALANCE

Play a game of shadow badminton with the emphasis on posture and balance. Keep your back straight, your head up and eyes focused forwards as you play.

PRACTICE 2: STARTING AND STOPPING

Play a game of shadow badminton with the emphasis on starting and stopping. Show clearly a controlled stop and the speed of acceleration in the start. Use the split jump to stop in the centre midcourt and the bounce start to travel away from the midcourt.

PRACTICE 3: TRAVELLING

Play a game of shadow badminton with the emphasis on using different step patterns and moving quietly, with *soft feet*.

PRACTICE 4: TRANSITIONS

Play a game of shadow badminton with the em-

phasis on performing quick smooth changes of direction. Use the split jump in the midcourt to make the transition from one direction to another.

PRACTICE 5: LUNGE AND RECOVERY

Play a game of shadow badminton with the emphasis on the full and half lunges and the different types of recovery. Focus on the different approaches to the lunge, good balance and posture and the appropriate recovery.

PRACTICE 6: JUMPING AND LANDING

Play a game of shadow badminton with the emphasis on the different jumps and landings. Focus on the height and distance in the flight and the quietness of the landing.

Comment: If you practise these body skill components regularly you should improve your skill in moving when you play in formal competition.

PRACTICE 7

Use all the body skill components while playing shadow badminton for periods of 30-60 seconds. Play at medium pace and take your time as you focus on the quality of your movement. You will find that if you try to use *soft feet* throughout you should improve the quality of your movement.

ACTION PHRASES

All action phrases will include posture and balance, stopping and starting, travelling and transitions. You can select action phrases for different situations in the game. In the forecourt and midcourt many action phrases will involve the half lunge and recovery, especially when you are hitting the shuttle from below net height and near the ground. In the midcourt and rearcourt many action phrases will involve jumping and landing, especially in doubles.

In these practices the purpose is to repeat specific action phrases which contain various body skill components. To do this requires a reasonable level of fitness. I would advise you therefore to rest between each set of repetitions as in interval training. (*See* chapter 13, page 131).

I will give you two examples of action phrases and then you can devise your own for developing your body skill when hitting the shuttle from different parts of the court.

Examples

Here are two action phrases. One focuses on the lunge and recovery and one on jumping and landing. *See* Figs 21 and 22.

Comment: Do ten repetitions and then rest for about 30-45 seconds or until you feel ready to start another set of repetitions.

JUMPING AND LANDING

You can use any of the standard badminton jumps in this practice, e.g. vertical jump, scissor jump. I have chosen the diagonal jump for this exercise.

Comment: Do five repetitions and then rest for about thirty seconds, or until you feel ready to start another set of repetitions or another action phrase.

DEVELOPMENT: Practise the other jumps and increase the height and/or distance that you jump. This will also help you to practise your landings. If you jump for height then you will use a deeper landing to land quietly. If you jump for distance you will use a rebound jump or take extra steps on landing to control your landing before you recover to the midcourt.

You can practise these jumps with or without a shuttle. Obviously if you use a shuttle you will require a good feeder who can feed skilfully enough to make you have to jump for a height and/or distance. If you want to hit shuttles as you jump then be prepared for some practice with your feeder before he gets his timing and accuracy right.

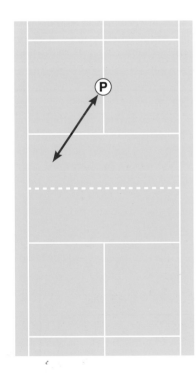

Fig 21
Lunge and Recovery

(left)
Begin from the centre MC as shown in a sides attacking stance.
Start with a jump/bounce start. Travel to the FC and lunge into the hitting position.
Perform your stroke and then recover to travel backwards to the centre MC.
As you arrive perform a split jump to change direction (transition) and repeat the action phrase.

(right)
Begin from the centre MC as shown in a sides attacking stance.
Start with a jump/bounce start. Travel to the forehand RC and jump (diagonal jump) into a hitting position.
Perform a smash in flight and land softly with a deep landing or a rebound jump and change direction (transition) to recover and travel to the MC.
As you arrive perform a split jump to change direction and repeat the action phrase.

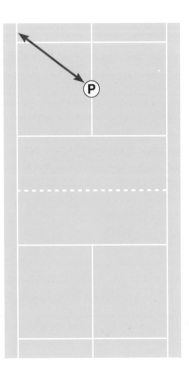

Fig 22
Jumping and Landing

CHAPTER 9

Know Your Strokes, Correct Your Faults and Practise to Improve

Your strokes should always be used as tactical moves. Through playing building shots or attempted winning shots your opponent will be forced to respond in some way, either to your advantage if you play a good shot, or to his advantage if it is a poor shot.

Because strokes are used as tactical moves I usually refer to them as stroke-moves. Well-played stroke-moves will depend on your technical skill. If you cannot perform a particular stroke or do so badly then your tactical skill will be limited. It is important therefore that you can perform all the stroke-moves effectively. For this reason you will need to make sure that your strokes are technically correct. You should, therefore, know your strokes, the common faults that may occur, their causes, how to correct them and then how to practise to improve your technical and tactical skill in performing them. In addition you need to learn how your opponent might reply so that you can decide which position to travel into to cover them. The purpose of this chapter is to provide you with this information.

Please remember that all stroke-moves take place within an **action phrase** (*see* Fig 23) which requires body skill. This is something you should consider when analysing your strokes and trying to correct any faults that arise.

How you start and approach the shuttle (approach travel phase) and when you start to recover can affect how you hit the shuttle. A particular fault in performing the stroke may be due to some weakness in the approach travel phase. The cause might be your slowness to start or the step pattern you have used to travel. Alternatively it could be that you try to recover before you have completed the stroke; you **snatch** at the shuttle because you travel away from the hitting position too soon.

Fig 23

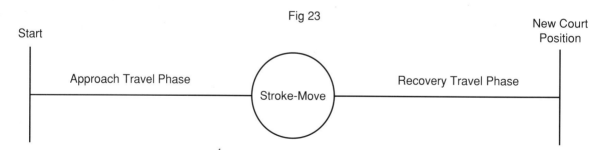

BODY SKILL FAULTS AND CORRECTIONS

Here are some general body skill faults which often occur during the action phrases. Refer to these if you have any difficulties in getting into the hitting position, during the hit and in leaving the hitting position.

COMMON FAULTS	POSSIBLE CAUSES	CORRECTIONS
Late getting into the hitting position.	Slow start from your court position.	Use bounce start. Use split jump.
	Poor stance.	Adjust your stance.
	Poor posture and balance.	Adjust your posture and balance.
Not in balance during the hitting phase.	Not stopping or slowing down to hit the shuttle.	Practise stopping. Practise the lunge. Practise your landing after a jump.
	Poor posture and balance.	Adjust your posture and balance.
Weight falling backwards after you hit the shuttle.	Poor balance and posture.	Adjust balance.
	Not stopping.	Practise stopping.
	Incorrect hitting position.	Adjust hitting position.
	Poor landing after a jump.	Practise jumping and landing in balance.
Slow getting back into a new court position.	Slow start.	Use effective starting technique.
	Slow in changing direction.	Practise transitions.
	Incorrect step pattern.	Adjust step patterns.
	Poor recovery after the lunge.	Adjust recovery and practise it.
	Poor landing and transition after your jump.	Use appropriate type of landing and practise landing lightly and making a quick transition.

YOUR STROKES, COMMON FAULTS, CAUSES, CORRECTION AND PRACTICES

The *stroke-moves* have been grouped into rearcourt, midcourt and forecourt stroke-moves. I have *analysed* them under a number of *headings* which will be easy to follow once you have examined the stroke that you want to improve.

All the *parts of the action phrase* will be included in the analysis although, most times, I will be unable to comment on your court starting position as I will not always know where that is.

The *common faults* and their *possible causes* will also be included as will some advice on how to *correct* them.

A technical and tactical practice for a stroke will be included where I think it might be helpful. If you would rather design your own practices then read chapter 11.

DESCRIPTION OF THE STROKE-MOVE ANALYSIS HEADINGS

Tactical Use

The stroke-move may be used as either a building shot or an attempted winning shot to obtain a certain response from your opponent in accordance with the principle of attack. Some stroke-moves may serve both functions. When this is so the primary use will be stated first.

Opponent's Probable Replies

The tactical move that you play will not only cause your opponent to respond by having to travel to some place on the court but will also allow him to make certain replies which you must get into position to cover. If you hit a clear as a building shot, for example, your opponent could reply with a smash, clear or dropshot. Your task should be to get into position to cover the strongest threat to you. In this case it will probably be the smash; so you would travel to the midcourt and take up a sides defensive stance.

Court Starting Position

The position you have taken up to cover the opponent's replies to your previous shot.

Approach Travel Phase

The method you will use to start and to travel to the hitting position.

Court Situation

You will be situated in the centre or your forehand or backhand sides of the rearcourt, midcourt or forecourt when you perform the stroke-move.

Hitting Position

This is the position you have arrived in to hit the shuttle. It is here that you actually hit the shuttle. You will only do so effectively if you have got into the correct hitting position, in balance and where you cannot fail to perform the stroke-cycle fluently.

Stroke-Cycle

When using any stroke you should perform a cycle of movement which begins from the racket starting position and returns in front of you ready for the next stroke. This cycle can be described as: the racket starting position, the preparation (which you may begin while you are still travelling to the hitting position), the hitting phase and recovery to a starting position somewhere in front of you.

Racket Starting Position

This varies according to your court position and your opponent's probable replies. Your racket should be held ready to hit the shuttle wherever it may be. You will hold it in front of you 'as a weapon'. Your hand should be partially cocked at the wrist and your arm flexed at the elbow. You should now be ready to *prepare* your racket to hit the shuttle from anywhere in the space around you. This is known as the 'attack position' (*see* plate 18, page 65).

Preparation

From a starting position you take the racket head back and prepare to hit the shuttle. How far you take it back depends on how hard you want to hit the shuttle. When the shuttle is in front of you at the net you need only move your hand to prepare your racket head. Simply cock the hand. *See* plate 18. If the shuttle is above your head or high to one side you must take the racket head back much

further, ready to hit the shuttle very hard. In this case you would adopt the smash position (a throwing position) (*see* plate 19, page 65).

Hitting Phase

You may use a throwing action as in most forehand overhead shots, the drive and some underarm shots, e.g. the high serve, but on impact the racket head will be used in a tap, push or whip action with either a flat or glancing hit of the racket face.

Racket Recovery

After hitting the shuttle you should return your racket to a starting position with or without a follow through, depending on the stroke you have played. When you play a clear or a smash you will follow through before you recover. When you perform a backhand clear, which uses the tap action to hit the shuttle, there will be no follow through.

Recovery Travel Phase

The method that you will use to travel into position to cover your opponent's probable replies.

New Court Position

The position that you take up in the rearcourt, midcourt or forecourt to cover your opponent's probable replies.

PRACTICES FOR THE STROKE

I have included a technical and tactical practice for each stroke. As I explained in chapter 5 there is a progression of stages that you should follow when practising your strokes and a different aim at each stage. Ideally you should practise the complete action phrase which includes your travel phases and your stroke. If you are not ready for this then you could just practise the stroke from the hitting position until you feel ready to add the travel phases. In fact with some strokes this will be the best method to use, e.g. the smash and dropshot.

I have described each practice as if you are ready to practise your *consistency* level when doing the complete action phrase. If you are not ready then go back to the stage you feel is right for you. If you are not sure what that is then refer to chapter 5.

Let me remind you that in a technical practice the focus is on your SELF and how you perform the actions; whereas in a tactical practice the focus is on the OTHER player and what you can make him do.

OVERHEAD REARCOURT STROKE-MOVES

SMASH
POWER SMASH AND SLICED SMASH. *See Fig 24.*

Tactical Use	as a building shot it is used to hit the shuttle quickly downwards at the opponent to force a specific reply or to move the opponent out of position to the sides of the court. As an attempted winning shot it is used to hit a winner or to force a weak reply.
Opponent's Probable Replies	lob to the rearcourt, block to the forecourt and drive or push to the midcourt.
Court Starting Position	variable
Approach Travel Phase	walk, run, side-step or jump into the hitting position.
Hitting Position	your shoulders, if not your feet and body, behind the shuttle which is high and in front of you. *See* plates 19 and 20, page 65.
Stroke-Cycle (a throwing action)	
RACKET STARTING POSITION	in front of you with partially cocked hand.
PREPARATION	take up a sideways throwing stance, the **smash position**. Twist your shoulders as you prepare your racket and get into a throwing position.
	NOTE: Some players prepare with their racket hand fully uncocked and then fully cock it during the throwing action just prior to hitting the shuttle. This creates a whiplash effect and increases the racket head speed so giving a stronger smash. *See* plate 21, page 65.
HITTING PHASE	
grip	forehand or multipurpose.
racket head control	whip action.
racket face use	flat (for power smash), glancing (for sliced smash), and pointing downwards on impact with shuttle.
racket recovery	**flat hits**: follow through forwards along the line of flight of the shuttle before allowing your racket arm to go across your body to recover to a starting position in front of you. **glancing hits**: your follow through will be across the line of flight of the shuttle.
Recovery Travel Phase	walk or run towards the centre midcourt.
New Court Position	approaching or already arrived at the centre midcourt.

Fig 24
Shuttle trajectories

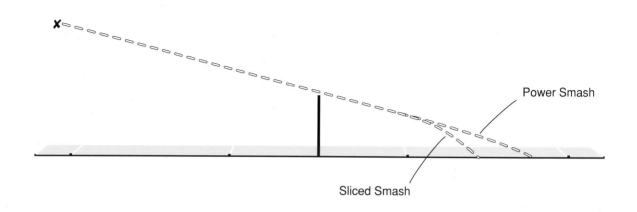

Power Smash

Sliced Smash

COMMON FAULTS	POSSIBLE CAUSES	CORRECTION
The shuttle goes horizontal instead of down. **The shuttle goes into the net.**	Incorrect hitting position. Wrong racket face angle.	Adjust your hitting position. Adjust racket face angle.
The shuttle doesn't go in the intended direction.	Incorrect hitting position. Wrong racket face angle. Follow through in different direction.	Adjust hitting position. Adjust racket face angle. Check throwing action and direction of your follow through.
Too much or too little slice.	Wrong racket face angle. Wrong grip. Follow through in wrong direction.	Adjust racket face angle. Adjust grip. Adjust throwing action and direction of follow through.
Loss of power.	Incorrect hitting position. Inadequate preparation.	Adjust your hitting position. Adjust your preparation in the stroke-cycle.
	Not enough racket head speed on impact.	Adjust hitting position. Grip racket gently. Faster arm throw in hitting phase.
	Wrong racket face angle on impact.	Adjust racket face for flat hit.
	Poor throwing action.	Practise stroke-cycle.

Plate 18 – Attack Position

Plate19 – In the smash position, preparing to throw the racket head at the shuttle. Note the racket hand is uncocked.

Plate 20 – In the smash position but prepares with the racket hand partially cocked.

Plate 21 – *(left)*
Hand cocked
prepared for smash

Fig 25

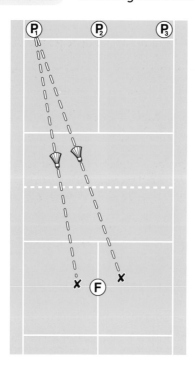

Fig 26

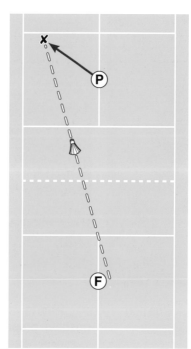

PRACTICES FOR THE SMASH

These will apply for power and sliced smashes and for straight and cross-court smashes.

TECHNICAL

Aim of practice: consistency in fluency and accuracy.

REPETITIONS: Ten, five to your feeder's forehand side and five to his backhand side.

Advice: Do this in two phases.

PHASE 1: Stand in a hitting position in the rearcourt, either P1, P2, or P3 as shown in Fig 25, and hit smashes to your feeder's forehand and then to his backhand while he lobs to you in a continuous rally. If he cannot control your smash then ask him to serve single shuttles for you to smash

PHASE 2: Stand in the midcourt in a sides attacking stance. Ask your feeder to serve high to the rearcourt while you do a bounce start and travel to the rearcourt to get into your hitting position. Smash the shuttle and recover to the midcourt. As you arrive your feeder should serve high again for you

to perform a split jump transition and travel back to the rearcourt.

DEVELOPMENT: There are several ways to develop this practice.

First, by smashing from the sides and centre of the rearcourt. *See* Fig 25.

Second, by adding the travel phases and jumping backwards to smash caused by your feeder serving a faster, lower feed. *See* Fig 26.

Third, by adding stage 5, *uncertainty*, to your practice. Ask your feeder to lob the shuttle to the sides or centre of your rearcourt as he chooses so that you cannot anticipate where his lob will go.

TACTICAL

Aim of practice: consistency in making your feeder play a backhand lob or a forehand lob reply, or making him travel to the sides of the court or forwards and sideways to hit the shuttle from near the ground. The purpose of such a practice is not 'I am going to hit a smash practice' but rather 'This is what I am going to make you practise.' The smash is simply your means of making the other player respond in a particular way. You should practise in order to do this consistently.

FOREHAND CLEAR

The three types of clear are described below, i.e. the standard clear, the attack clear and the defensive clear. *See* Fig 27.

Standard Clear **Tactical Use**	building shot, used to move the opponent out of position into the rearcourt.
Attack Clear **Tactical Use**	building shot/attempted winning shot, to move the opponent out of position into the rearcourt and to catch him out with a faster lower shuttle trajectory and so make him late getting to the shuttle.
Defensive Clear **Tactical Use**	building shot, to move the opponent into the rearcourt and to make time for you to recover into position to cover the probable replies.
Opponent's Probable Replies	Smash, clear or drop
Court Starting Position	variable
Approach Travel Phase	walk, run, side-step or jump into the hitting position.
Hitting Position	your shoulders, if not your feet and body, behind the shuttle which is high and in front of you. *See* plates 19, 20, of the smash position.
Stroke-Cycle (a throwing action)	
RACKET STARTING POSITION	in front of you with partially cocked hand.
PREPARATION	take up a sideways throwing stance, the **smash position**. Twist your shoulders as you prepare your racket and get into a throwing position.
HITTING PHASE	
grip	forehand or multipurpose.
racket head control	whip action.
racket face use	flat and pointing upwards on impact relative to the height that you want to hit the shuttle.
racket recovery	follow through forwards along the line of flight of the shuttle before allowing your racket arm to go across your body to recover to a starting position in front of you.
Recovery Travel Phase	for standard and high defensive clears walk or run to centre midcourt to defend against a possible smash. For attack clears travel towards centre midcourt to cover a possible smash or a weak reply. Yet also be ready to attack a high defensive clear.
New Court Position	centre midcourt.

COMMON FAULTS	POSSIBLE CAUSES	CORRECTIONS
The shuttle doesn't go on the desired trajectory.	Wrong racket face angle on impact Incorrect hitting position.	Adjust angle of racket face. Adjust your hitting position.
The shuttle doesn't go in the Intended direction.	Incorrect hitting position. Wrong racket face angle.	Alter hitting position. Adjust angle of racket face.
Lack of force, the shuttle doesn't reach the rearcourt.	Incorrect hitting position. Slow racket head speed. Wrong racket face angle.	Adjust hitting position. Adjust throwing action. Increase racket head speed. Use flat face.
Late getting into the hitting position.	Slow start. Poor step pattern.	Use appropriate start. Adjust your step pattern in your approach travel phase.
Slow recovering after the hit and late getting back to the new court position.	Poor balance during the stroke-cycle. Staying too long in the hitting position. Slow start to the recovery travel phase.	Adjust posture and balance. Start recovery travel phase immediately after hitting the shuttle. Adjust your start or your transition in the hitting position.
Slow in travelling	Incorrect step pattern, e.g. steps too large.	Adjust your step pattern in the recovery travel phase.

Fig 27
The Clears

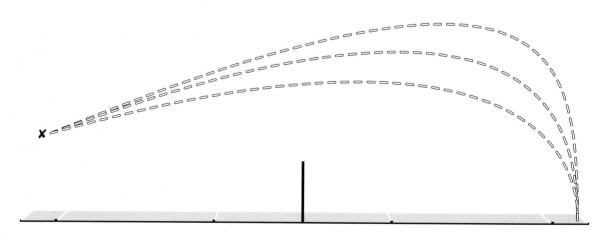

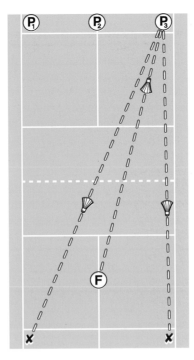

Fig 28

PRACTICES FOR THE CLEARS

Use the procedure below to practise your standard clear, attack clear and defensive clear in turn. This will apply for both straight and cross-court clears.

TECHNICAL

Aim of practice: consistency in fluency and accuracy.

REPETITIONS: sets of ten.

Advice: Do this in two phases.

PHASE 1: Stand in a hitting position. P1, P2 or P3 in the rearcourt and hit clears to your feeder positioned in F1, F2 or F3 in his rearcourt as your target. Play a continuous rally. If your feeder cannot do so then ask him to stand in the midcourt and feed single high serves continuously for you to clear to a target area in the rearcourt. *See* Fig 28.

PHASE 2: Add the travel phases to make up a complete action phrase. Start in the midcourt, travel to the rearcourt and return to the midcourt to take up a sides defensive stance or perform a transition. Use your split jump to stop or to perform your transition.

Position your feeder in the rearcourt or midcourt as for phase 1.

DEVELOPMENT: Add the element of **uncertainty**. Ask your feeder to lob the shuttle as he chooses to positions P1, P2 or P3 so that it is more difficult to anticipate where the shuttle will go.

TACTICAL

Aim of practice: consistency in moving your feeder out of position and making him play a clear from a selected area in his rearcourt.

The practice will use the same action phrases as the technical practice but you will simply change your focus and emphasis to what you can cause the OTHER player (your feeder) to do.

Start in the midcourt and ask your feeder to hit a high singles serve from the midcourt.

Travel to the hitting position in the rearcourt and hit a clear (standard, attack or defensive) and recover to your midcourt while you *look* to make sure that the feeder's feet are in the rearcourt when he hits the shuttle. You should arrive in your midcourt before he does hit the shuttle.

DROPSHOT
There are three dropshots used as moves in the game: the slow, fast and long drop. See Fig 29.

Tactical Use	all are used as building shots except for the fast drop which can also be used as an attempted winning shot.
Slow dropshot	also known as the *check-smash* because the smash action is used and the racket head speed suddenly checked just before impact to allow the racket head to hit the shuttle upwards and over the net. The purpose is to move the opponent out of position in the centre midcourt, near to the net in the forecourt and to force a weak reply.
Fast Dropshot	flat or glancing hit (slice), usually hit downwards towards the sides of the forecourt to move the opponent out of position sideways and forwards and make him return the shuttle from near the ground.
Long Dropshot	flat or glancing hit, to send the shuttle downwards towards the opponent's centre midcourt and allow you to travel to your midcourt centre to divide the angle of return and to cover his replies from low in the centre of his midcourt more easily.
Opponent's Probable Replies	net reply or lob to slow or fast drop shot. Reply to forecourt or push to midcourt or lob to rearcourt.
Court Starting Position	variable
Approach Travel Phase	walk, run, side-step or jump into the hitting position.
Hitting Position	your shoulders, if not your feet and body, behind the shuttle which is high and in front of you. *See* plate 19 of the smash position.
Stroke-Cycle (a throwing action)	
RACKET STARTING POSITION	in front of you with partially cocked hand.
PREPARATION	take up a sideways throwing stance, the *smash position*. Twist your shoulders as you prepare your racket and get into a throwing position.
HITTING PHASE	
grip	forehand, multipurpose, backhand.
racket head control	fast push action.
racket face use	flat or sliced hit relative to the stroke.
racket recovery	follow through after the shuttle *along* the line of flight for flat hits and *across* the line of flight for glancing hits before your racket arm recovers in front of your body.
Recovery Travel Phase	walk or run towards the central midcourt.
New Court Position	moving towards the central midcourt.

COMMON FAULTS	POSSIBLE CAUSES	CORRECTIONS
Fast dropshot goes into the net.	Not in correct hitting position. Wrong racket face angle. Incorrect hitting action.	Adjust hitting position. Adjust racket face. Use a push action.
Fast dropshot carries too far into opponent's court.	Wrong racket face angle. Racket head speed too fast. Hitting too hard.	Adjust racket face. Slow down racket head speed. Hit the shuttle gently.
Fast dropshot hit out of the side lines.	Wrong direction of throwing action. Racket face direction incorrect. Incorrect follow through.	Redirect throwing action Adjust racket face direction. Adjust your follow through.
Slow dropshot goes too high.	Incorrect hitting position. Racket face angle wrong.	Adjust hitting position. Adjust racket face angle.
Slow dropshot falls into the net.	Incorrect hitting position. Incorrect racket face angle. Incorrect racket head speed. Wrong hitting action.	Adjust hitting position. Adjust angle of racket face. Increase racket head speed. Use push action.
Your opponent anticipates the shot and meets the shuttle early each time.	Incorrect hitting position. No deception.	Adopt the smash position. Use the check-smash action.
Long dropshot travels horizontally and not down.	Incorrect racket face angle. Incorrect racket head speed.	Adjust racket face angle. Slow down racket head speed.
Long drop falls short or into the net.	Incorrect racket face angle. Incorrect racket head speed. Wrong hitting action. Incomplete throwing action.	Alter racket face angle. Increase racket head speed. Use a fast push action. Complete your follow through.

Fig 29 Shuttle Trajectories

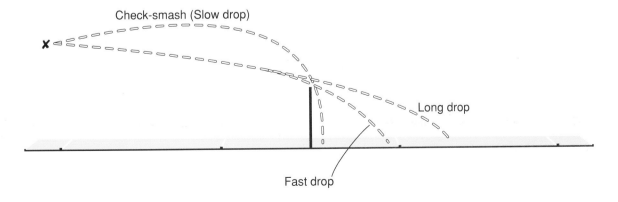

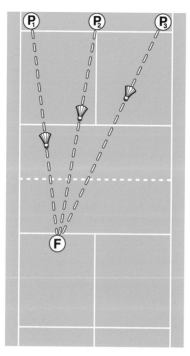

Fig 30

Play a continuous rally. If your feeder cannot do so ask him to start each repetition with a high singles serve from the midcourt.

PRACTICES FOR THE DROPSHOTS

These will apply for all the dropshots.

TECHNICAL

Aim of practice: consistency in fluency and accuracy.

REPETITIONS: sets of ten.

Advice: Do this in two phases.

PHASE 1: Stand in the hitting position in the rearcourt (P1, P2, or P3) and hit dropshots to your feeder, positioned behind the service line as you decide, while he lobs to you in a continuous rally. *See* Fig 30.

PHASE 2: Add the travel phases so that you can perform the complete action phrase. Ask your feeder to allow the shuttle to drop nearer the floor before he lobs it **high** to allow you time to recover

after your stroke. Start in the midcourt and recover *towards* there after each dropshot.

DEVELOPMENT: Add **uncertainty** to the practice. Ask your feeder to lob the shuttle to P1, P2 or P3 as he chooses to make it difficult for you to anticipate the shuttle and hence more demanding.

TACTICAL

Aim of practice: consistency in making your feeder play a lob from different positions in his court, i.e. near the ground and close to the net, near the ground and at the sides of the forecourt, from low in his centre midcourt. This will, of course, depend on what sort of dropshot you are practising to manipulate the other player.

You can remain in your hitting position or perform an action phrase each time you hit the shuttle, i.e. recover towards your centre midcourt.

Your feeder should stand in his centre midcourt in a sides defensive stance and travel into position to lob the shuttle to your rearcourt before recovering to his midcourt to take up a sides defensive stance. If he lobs the shuttle high enough he should have time to do this.

BACKHAND CLEAR

Tactical Use	building shot, to move the opponent out of position into the rearcourt.
Opponent's Probable Replies	Clear, drop or smash.
Court Starting Position	variable
Approach Travel Phase	walk, run, side-step or jump into the hitting position.
Hitting Position	shuttle is high and between you and the back line.
Stroke-Cycle	
RACKET STARTING POSITION	hold your racket in front of you in partially cocked hand.
PREPARATION	twist your shoulders and your trunk to the backhand side and cock your hand fully ready to hit the shuttle.
HITTING PHASE	
grip	backhand, multipurpose or forehand depending on how far the shuttle is away from you.
racket head control	tap action.
racket face use	flat.
racket recovery	no follow through – immediate recovery of racket in front of you.
Recovery Travel Phase	take a backward step on to your non-racket foot prior to turning to walk or run to the midcourt.
New Court Position	centre midcourt.

COMMON FAULTS	POSSIBLE CAUSES	CORRECTIONS
Lack of power – shuttle doesn't reach the rearcourt.	Incorrect hitting action. There is a follow through.	Use a strong tap action. Do not follow through. Rebound racket head on impact.
	Incorrect hitting position. Insufficient racket head speed. Wrong grip.	Alter hitting position. Increase racket head speed. Use backhand or multipurpose grip.
	Incorrect preparation.	Fully cock the hand in the preparation.
Does not go in the intended direction. Goes to high or low.	Incorrect racket face angle.	Adjust racket face angle.

Plate 22 – *(left)*
Backhand Clear

Fig 31 *(right)*

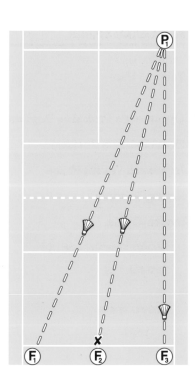

PRACTICES FOR THE BACKHAND CLEAR

TECHNICAL
Aim of practice: consistency in fluency and accuracy.

REPETITIONS: sets of ten.

Advice: Do this in two phases.

PHASE 1: Stand in a hitting position, P in the rearcourt and hit backhand clears to your feeder positioned in F1, F2 or F3 in his rearcourt as your target. Play a continuous rally *See* Fig 31. If your feeder cannot do so then ask him to stand in the midcourt and feed single high serves continuously for you to clear to a target area in the rearcourt.

PHASE 2: Add the travel phases to make up a complete action phrase.
Start in the midcourt, travel to the rearcourt and return to the midcourt to take up a sides defensive stance or perform a transition. Use your split jump to stop or to perform your transition.
Position your feeder in the rearcourt or midcourt as for Phase 1.

DEVELOPMENT: Add the element of **uncertainty** by asking your feeder to hit a clear to your forehand corner which will make it more difficult for you to anticipate the shuttle and help you to improve your speed off the mark.

TACTICAL
Aim of practice: consistency in moving your feeder out of position and making him play a clear from a selected area in his rearcourt.

The practice will use the same action phrase as the technical practice but you will simply change your focus and emphasis to what you can cause the OTHER player (your feeder) to do.

Start in the midcourt and ask your feeder to hit a high singles serve from the midcourt.

Travel to the hitting position in the rearcourt and hit a clear and recover to your midcourt while you watch to make sure that the feeder's feet are in the rearcourt when he hits the shuttle.

You should recover to your midcourt before he does hit the shuttle.

Play a continuous rally. If your feeder cannot do so ask him to start each repetition with a high singles serve from the midcourt.

BACKHAND SMASH

Tactical Use	attempted winning shot/building shot, to force a weak reply, to move the opponent out of position to the sides of the midcourt, to make the opponent hit the shuttle up from near the floor.
Opponent's Probable Replies	block to the forecourt, push to midcourt, lob to the rearcourt.
Court Starting Position	variable
Approach Travel Phase	walk, run, side-step or jump into the hitting position.
Hitting Position	shuttle is high and between you and the rearcourt.
Stroke-Cycle	
RACKET STARTING POSITION	hold your racket in front of you in partially cocked hand.
PREPARATION	twist your shoulders and your trunk to the backhand side and cock your hand fully ready to hit the shuttle.
HITTING PHASE	
grip	backhand, multipurpose or forehand.
racket head control	whip action.
racket face use	flat/glancing.
racket recovery	no follow through of arm – hold the hit position for a moment and then recover your racket in front of you. See plate 23, page 76.
Recovery Travel Phase	take a backward step prior to turning to walk or run towards the midcourt.
New Court Position	approaching or already at the centre midcourt.

COMMON FAULTS	POSSIBLE CAUSES	CORRECTIONS
Shuttle goes into the net.	Wrong hitting position. Wrong racket face angle. Arm following through.	Adjust hitting position. Adjust racket face angle. Stop arm movement on impact.
Shuttle goes horizontal.	Wrong hitting position. Wrong racket face angle.	Adjust hitting position. Adjust racket face angle.
Loss of power.	Arm following through. Lack of racket head speed. Too much slice.	Stop arm movement on impact. Use whip action. Adjust racket face angle.
Shuttle does not go in the intended direction.	Wrong racket face angle. Wrong hitting position.	Adjust racket face angle. Adjust hitting position.

Plate 23 –
Backhand Smash

Fig 32

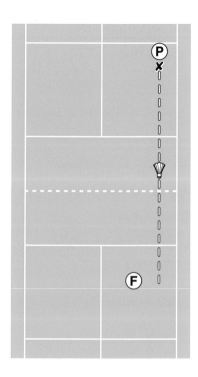

PRACTICES FOR THE BACKHAND SMASH

TECHNICAL
Aim of practice: consistency in fluency and accuracy.

REPETITIONS: sets of ten.

Advice: Do this in two phases.

PHASE 1: Stand in a hitting position, P on the edge of the rearcourt (long service line) and hit backhand smashes to your feeder positioned in the midcourt. Play a continuous rally. If your feeder cannot do so then ask him to stand in the midcourt and feed single high serves continuously for you to smash to a target area in the midcourt. *See* Fig 32.

PHASE 2: Add the travel phases to make up a complete action phrase.
Start in the midcourt, travel to the edge of the rearcourt and return to the midcourt to take up an attacking stance or perform a transition. Use your split jump to stop or to perform your transition. Position your feeder in the midcourt as for Phase 1.

DEVELOPMENT: Add the element of *uncertainty* by asking your feeder to hit a lob to your forehand corner which will make it more difficult for you to anticipate the shuttle and help you to improve your speed off the mark or in changing direction.

TACTICAL
Aim of practice: consistency in moving your feeder out of position and making him play a lob from a selected area in his midcourt.

The practice will use the same action phrase as the technical practice but you will simply change your focus and emphasis to what you can cause the OTHER player (your feeder) to do.

Start in the midcourt and ask your feeder to hit a lob from the centre midcourt. Travel to the hitting position in the rearcourt and hit a smash and recover towards your midcourt while you watch to make sure that the feeder has to travel to hit the shuttle from low in his midcourt. You should recover towards your midcourt before he does hit the shuttle.

Play a continuous rally. If your feeder cannot do so ask him to start each repetition with a lob from the midcourt.

BACKHAND DROPSHOT

There are three types of dropshot used in the game: the slow, fast and long drop. Refer to pages 70–72 for a description of these.

Tactical Use	all used as building shots except for the fast drop which can be used as an attempted winning shot.
Opponent's Probable Replies	net replies and lobs to fast and slow dropshot net reply, push to midcourt and lob to long dropshot.
Court Starting Position	variable
Approach Travel Phase	walk, run, side-step or jump into the hitting position.
Hitting Position	shuttle is high, level with you or between you and the rearcourt.
Stroke-Cycle	
RACKET STARTING POSITION	hold your racket in front of you in partially cocked hand.
PREPARATION	twist your shoulders and your trunk to the backhand side and cock your hand fully ready to hit the shuttle.
HITTING PHASE	
grip	backhand, multipurpose or forehand.
racket head control	push action (racket arm slightly flexed).
racket face use	glancing/flat.
racket recovery	follow through with your racket and shoulders (they untwist) to recover your racket in front of you.
Recovery Travel Phase	take a backward step prior to turning to walk or run to the midcourt.
New Court Position	centre midcourt.

PRACTICES FOR THE BACKHAND DROPSHOT

TECHNICAL

Aim of practice: consistency in fluency and accuracy.

REPETITIONS: sets of ten.

Advice: Do this in two phases.

PHASE 1: Stand in a hitting position in the rearcourt and hit backhand dropshots to your feeder positioned in his midcourt or close to the forecourt as your target. Play a continuous rally. If your feeder cannot do so then ask him to stand near the forecourt or in the midcourt and feed single high serves continuously for you to dropshot to a target area in the forecourt.

PHASE 2: Add the travel phases to make up a complete action phrase.

Start in the midcourt, travel to the rearcourt and return to the midcourt to take up an attacking stance or perform a transition. Use your split jump to stop or to perform your transition.

Position your feeder in the midcourt as for Phase 1.

DEVELOPMENT: Add the element of **uncertainty** by asking your feeder to hit a net reply occasionally which will make it more difficult for you to anticipate the lob and also improve your speed off the mark.

COMMON FAULTS	POSSIBLE CAUSES	CORRECTIONS
Fast dropshot goes into the net.	Incorrect hitting position. Wrong racket face angle. Wrong hitting action.	Adjust hitting position. Adjust racket face angle. Use a fast push action.
Fast dropshot carries too far into opponent's court.	Wrong racket face angle. Racket head speed too fast. Too much force.	Adjust racket face angle. Slow down racket head speed. Hit the shuttle gently.
Fast dropshot hit out of the sidelines.	Wrong direction of follow through. Incorrect racket face direction. Starting recovery travel phase too soon.	Adjust follow through. Adjust racket face. Stay in the hitting position until after impact.
Slow dropshot goes too high.	Racket face angle wrong. Incorrect hitting position.	Adjust racket face angle. Adjust hitting position.
Slow dropshot falls into the net.	Incorrect hitting position. Incorrect racket face angle. Insufficient racket head speed. Wrong hitting action.	Adjust hitting position. Adjust racket face angle. Increase racket head speed. Use a push action.
Long dropshot falls short or into the net.	Incorrect racket face angle. Incorrect racket head speed. Wrong hitting action. Insufficient follow through.	Adjust racket face angle. Increase racket head speed. Use a fast push action. Complete the follow through.
Long dropshot travels horizontally or too far into the court.	Incorrect racket face angle. Incorrect racket head speed. Wrong hitting action.	Adjust racket face angle. Slow down racket head speed. Use a fast push action.

TACTICAL

Aim of practice: consistency in moving your feeder out of position and making him play a lob from a selected area in his rearcourt.

The practice will use the same action phrase as the technical practice but you will simply change your focus and emphasis to what you can cause the OTHER player (your feeder) to do.

Start in the midcourt and ask your feeder to hit a lob from the midcourt.

Travel to the hitting position in the rearcourt, hit a dropshot and recover to your midcourt as you watch to see from where the feeder has to make his reply.

Play a continuous rally. If your feeder cannot do so ask him to start each repetition with a serve from the midcourt.

LOW REARCOURT STROKE-MOVES

Clear, drive, and **dropshot** from below net height in your forehand rearcourt corner. *See* Fig 35.

Tactical Use	building shot, to move the opponent out of position to the rearcourt, to the sides of the midcourt, and to the forecourt.
Court Starting Position	usually midcourt.
Approach Travel Phase	walk, run and side-step into hitting position.
Hitting Position	half lunge position with racket foot pointing towards the shuttle which is to your rear between you and the rearcourt. *See* plate 24.

Stroke-Cycle

use a sidearm throwing action.

RACKET STARTING POSITION	in front with hand partially cocked.
PREPARATION	prepare for a throwing action.
HITTING PHASE	
grip	multipurpose or backhand.
racket head control	push action for dropshot; whip action for drive and clear.
racket face use	flat for lob, flat or glancing for drive and dropshot.
racket recovery	allow your shoulders to rotate forwards as you follow through to recover in front of you while you keep your weight on your hitting foot.
Recovery Travel Phase	walk, run or side-step towards the midcourt.
New Court Position	midcourt area.

Plate 24 –
In position to play
a drive

COMMON FAULTS	POSSIBLE CAUSES	CORRECTIONS
Shuttle does not go in intended direction.	Incorrect hitting position. You begin the recovery travel phase before completing the stroke-cycle (you pull away from the front foot). Your racket foot doesn't point towards the shuttle. Incorrect grip.	Adjust hitting position. Stay on the hitting foot until you complete the stroke-cycle. Point racket foot towards the shuttle Alter grip.
Shuttle goes into the net.	Incorrect racket face angle. Incorrect racket head speed. Wrong grip.	Adjust racket face angle. Increase racket head speed. Alter grip.
Shuttle doesn't travel full distance in the clear.	Incorrect racket face angle. Insufficient racket head speed. Pulling away from the hitting position. Insufficient follow through.	Adjust racket face angle. Use a faster arm action in the hitting phase. Stay on the racket foot until you have completed the stroke-cycle.

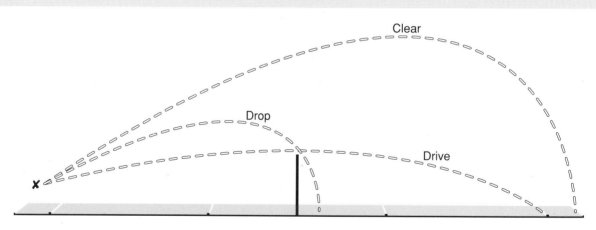

Fig 33
Shuttle Trajectories

PRACTICES FOR THE LOW REARCOURT STROKES

TECHNICAL

Aim of practice: consistency in fluency and accuracy.

REPETITIONS: sets of ten.

Advice: Do this in two phases.

PHASE 1: Stand in a hitting position in the rearcourt with your racket foot pointing towards the corner of the rearcourt. Ask your feeder to stand at the side of his midcourt and hit shuttles on a shallow arc towards the corner of the rearcourt. *See* Fig 34. Stay on your racket foot (*see* plate 24) during the hitting phase including your racket follow through and keep your eye on the point of impact even after you have hit the shuttle. Practise hitting drives, clears and dropshots from this position.

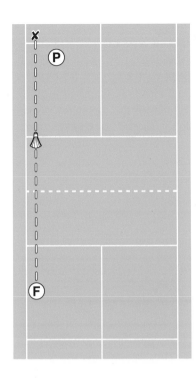

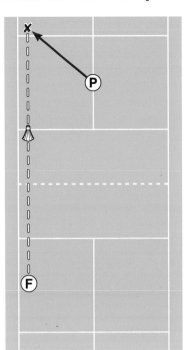

Fig 34 *(left)*
Fh RC

Fig 35 *(right)*
Travel phase to the Fh RC

PHASE 2: Add a travel phase to make up a complete action phrase. *See* Fig 35. Start in the midcourt, travel to the rearcourt and recover towards the midcourt ready to cover the probable replies from your shot.

DEVELOPMENT: Add an element of uncertainty by asking your feeder to hit the shuttle to the forecourt occasionally so that you cannot anticipate his shot.

TACTICAL
Aim of practice: consistency in manoeuvring your feeder out of position to the forecourt, rearcourt or midcourt.

Advice: Do this in two phases.

PHASE 1: Repeat phase 2 above and make your feeder travel to his forecourt, rearcourt or midcourt to play a reply to your shot.

PHASE 2: Develop this and allow your feeder to hit the shuttle to your forecourt occasionally so that you cannot anticipate his shot. When he feeds to your rearcourt then manoeuvre him to his forecourt, rearcourt or midcourt.

MIDCOURT STROKE-MOVES

When the shuttle is high in the midcourt the strokes are the same as those played from the rearcourt, i.e. the smash, clear and drop, though you would usually expect to use the smash from the midcourt as an attempted winning shot. Refer to the section on rearcourt strokes on pages 63–81. The strokes described below, therefore, are the drive, played when the shuttle is at net height, and the block, tap, push and lob, played when the shuttle is below net height. These are all used tactically as building shots. The explanations for the forehand strokes which follow will apply also for backhand strokes.

DRIVE

The shuttle is usually hit fast to skim the net horizontally. There are several ways of performing the drive. First, a sidearm smash from the sides of your midcourt; second, a fast hit from just in front of you or close to the sides of your trunk and usually played with a tap or whip action of the racket head. *See* Fig 36.

Tactical Use	building shot, to move the opponent out of position to the sides of the court and to catch him with the wrong grip or slow reacting to the speed of the shuttle and so cause him to play a late or weak reply, or an error.
Opponent's Probable Replies	counter drive, drop to forecourt or lob to rearcourt.
Court Starting Position	usually in the midcourt.
Approach Travel Phase	stay in position or side-step or lunge to the shuttle as necessary.
Hitting Position	the shuttle will be in front of you or at the sides.
Stroke-Cycle	
RACKET STARTING POSITION	in front of you.
PREPARATION	twist your shoulders to the right or left and cock your hand to prepare your racket.
HITTING PHASE	
grip	forehand, backhand or multipurpose.
racket head control	whip action for side arm smash. tap action for shuttles hit from in front of you.
racket face use	flat or glancing hit.
racket recovery	follow through as you recover from the side arm smash. rebound on impact in tap action, to prevent any follow through as you recover.
Recovery Travel Phase	recover to midcourt position.
New Court Position	midcourt.

COMMON FAULTS	POSSIBLE CAUSES	CORRECTIONS
Shuttle travels upwards.	Wrong racket face angle. Wrong grip.	Adjust racket face angle. Adjust grip.
Shuttle goes into the net.	Wrong grip. Wrong racket face angle.	Adjust grip. Adjust racket face angle.
Loss of power.	Poor hitting position. Too much slice.	Alter hitting position. Adjust racket face angle.
Lack of racket head speed.	Prepare earlier.	Throw racket head at shuttle. Use whip action.
Shuttle doesn't travel in intended direction	Follow through across your body. Wrong racket face angle. Wrong grip.	Follow through along intended line of flight of the shuttle. Adjust racket face angle. Adjust your grip.

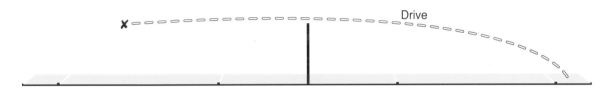

Fig 36 Shuttle trajectory

PRACTICES FOR THE DRIVE

TECHNICAL
Aim of practice: consistency in fluency and accuracy.

REPETITIONS: sets of ten.

Advice: Do this in two phases.

PHASE 1: Stand in the midcourt (see Fig 37) and rally with your feeder at medium pace. Ask your feeder to hit the shuttle at you or to one side. Practise sets of forehand drives, backhand drives and a mixture of forehand and backhand drives. Gradually increase the pace.

PHASE 2: Add the travel phase to make a complete action phrase.
Position your feeder as shown in Fig 38 at the side of the court.
You start in your centre midcourt and travel to the side of the court to hit the shuttle and recover to your midcourt to play the next drive.
Your feeder should drive the shuttle to the side of the court and to the centre of your court alternately.

DEVELOPMENT: Add the element of uncertainty by asking your feeder to drive to the side or centre of the court in any order. This will keep you alert and cause you to concentrate and respond quickly.

TACTICAL

Aim of practice: consistency in making your feeder return the shuttle from different places around his midcourt and use different grips.

Stand facing your feeder in your centre midcourt. Ask your feeder to return the shuttle to you in the centre midcourt.

Rally and make the feeder return the shuttle from the sides or centre of his midcourt and from different levels relative to the net, e.g. net height or lower. Make your feeder use the forehand and backhand grips; cause him to mistime the shuttle by changing the pace of the shuttle as you rally.

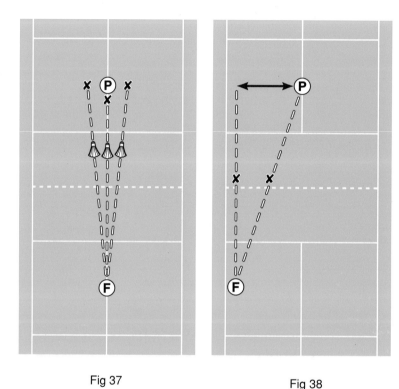

Fig 37   Fig 38

BLOCK AND PUSH

The strokes are very similar. The difference is in their use as building shots which results in a different trajectory of the shuttle.

Tactical Use	**The Block**. Building shot, used as a reply to the smash to hit the shuttle to fall steeply close to the net and to move the opponent out of position into the forecourt. **The Push**. Building shot, used as a reply to the smash to keep the opponent away from the net by hitting the shuttle to skim the net and travel downwards to land on or just beyond the short service line. **Note** The name of the stroke 'Push' is the same as the hitting action used to make it.
Opponent's Probable Replies	net reply or lob to the Block. net reply, push to midcourt or lob to the Push.
Court Starting Position	midcourt.
Approach Travel Phase	sides defensive stance in midcourt or side-step and/or half or full lunge towards side of court.
Hitting Position	shuttle hit at impact point in front of you or at the sides of your body. *See* plate 25.
Stroke-Cycle	
RACKET STARTING POSITION	racket held in front of you.
PREPARATION	twist your shoulder sideways on to the shuttle, bend arm and cock your hand.
HITTING PHASE	
grip	forehand, backhand or multipurpose.
racket head control	push action.
racket face use	flat or glancing.
racket recovery	follow through along line of flight of shuttle and then recover racket in front of you.
Recovery Travel Phase	**the Block**. Step forwards to edge of forecourt to threaten a net reply if opponent has to hit the shuttle from below the net. Step back to midcourt to sides defensive stance if your opponent can hit the shuttle from above the net. **the Push**. Adopt a sides attacking stance in the midcourt ready to attack the opponent's replies.
New Court Position	towards forecourt or in midcourt.

COMMON FAULTS	POSSIBLE CAUSES	CORRECTIONS
Shuttle goes into the net. Shuttle goes too high.	Wrong grip. Incorrect racket face angle. Alteration in hitting position during the hitting phase.	Adjust grip. Adjust racket face angle. Remain still during the hitting phase.
Shuttle travels too far into opponent's court.	Using too much force. Wrong grip. Incorrect use of racket head and racket face. Alteration in hitting position during the hitting phases.	Control racket head speed. Adjust grip. Use push action. Try glancing hit. Remain still during the hitting phase.
Shuttle does not go in intended direction.	Wrong grip. Not 'cocking' your hand.	Adjust grip. Cock your hand fully by pointing the end of your racket handle towards the shuttle prior to impact.
	Incorrect racket face angle. Not following through in the intended direction. Alteration in hitting position during the hitting phase.	Adjust racket face angle. Adjust your follow through. Stay in hitting position during the hitting phase.

Fig 39
Shuttle trajectory

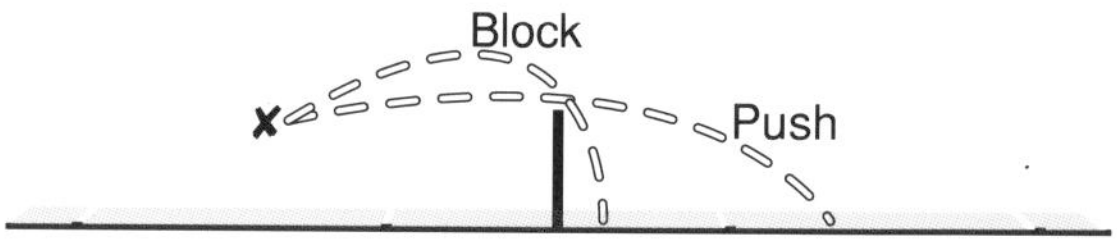

Block
x
Push

Plate 25 –
The block/push action

PRACTICES FOR THE BLOCK AND THE PUSH

TECHNICAL

In these practices you must be ready to move quickly sideways or backwards to get into a balanced hitting position.

Aim of practice: consistency in fluency and accuracy.

REPETITIONS: sets of ten.

Advice: Do this in two phases.

PHASE 1: Stand in the midcourt as shown in Fig 40 (a).
Serve the shuttle high to your feeder and ask him to smash to your forehand.
Block the shuttle to the side or centre of the forecourt and allow it to hit the ground.
Push the shuttle to skim the net and fall on to or just beyond the service line. Do this for ten repetitions on the forehand and backhand sides.

PHASE 2: Ask your feeder to smash the shuttle to the side of the court. This time travel to the side with a chassé and lunge to block or push the shuttle. *See Fig 40 (b).*
Do repetitions as for Phase 1.

DEVELOPMENT: Add the element of uncertainty. Ask your feeder to hit to either side of you or the sides of the court in any order.

TACTICAL

Aim of practice: consistency in moving the feeder out of position and making him play his reply to your block from below the net in the forecourt and your push from low in the forecourt/midcourt area.

Serve high. Your feeder should smash to your forehand and then approach the net at speed. Your task is to get the shuttle over the net, close to it and below net level before he can hit it. If you succeed then you can step forwards into an attacking stance and threaten his reply.

Complete sets of repetitions of this practice for forehand and backhand blocks.

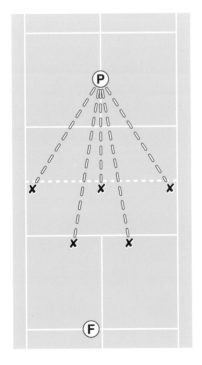

Fig 40 (a)

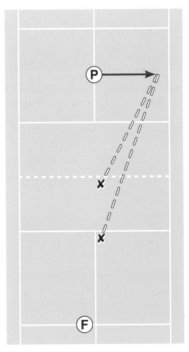

Fig 40 (b)

TAP

This is an example of when the name of the stroke-move is the same as the name of the hitting action used to make it.

Tactical Use	building shot and possible attempted winning shot, used as reply to the smash to hit the shuttle quickly into the forecourt away from an opponent who is rushing forwards after his smash. It should wrongfoot the opponent and possibly catch him out; hence it may result in a winning shot. *See* Fig 41.
Opponent's Probable Replies	net reply or lob.
Court Starting Position	midcourt.
Approach Travel Phase	stay in your midcourt position, sides defensive stance, or step forwards, or side-step and perform a half or full lunge towards the side of the court.
Hitting Position	shuttle is hit at impact point in front of or at the sides of your body. *See* plate 25, page 86.

Stroke-Cycle

RACKET STARTING POSITION	racket held in front of you.
PREPARATION	twist your shoulders sideways on to the shuttle, bend your arm and cock your hand.
HITTING PHASE	
grip	forehand, backhand or multipurpose.
racket head control	tap action.
racket face use	flat.
racket recovery	racket head rebounds on impact for immediate recovery in front of you.
Recovery Travel Phase	adopt a forward or backward attacking stance in the midcourt ready to attack the reply.
New Court Position	midcourt.

COMMON FAULTS	POSSIBLE CAUSES	CORRECTIONS
Shuttle goes into the net. Shuttle goes too high.	Wrong grip. Incorrect racket face angle. Altering your hitting position during the hitting phase.	Adjust your grip. Adjust racket face angle. Keep body weight going into the shot.
Shuttle travels too far into your opponent's court.	Too much force. Wrong hitting action.	Use a light tap action. Use a tap action.
Shuttle doesn't go in the intended direction.	Wrong grip. Incorrect racket face angle.	Adjust your grip. Adjust racket face angle.

PRACTICES FOR THE TAP

These will apply for forehand and backhand taps.

TECHNICAL

Aim of practice: consistency in fluency and accuracy.

REPETITIONS: sets of ten.

Adopt a sides defensive stance in the midcourt. Serve high to your feeder positioned in centre rearcourt.

Ask your feeder to smash to the sides of the midcourt each time you serve high, i.e. ten smashes to your forehand and ten smashes to your backhand. Side-step and lunge to the shuttle and reply to each smash with a tap cross-court to the side of the forecourt. *See* Fig 41.

DEVELOPMENT: Add the element of uncertainty and ask your feeder to smash the shuttle to either your forehand or backhand side as he chooses. This will cause you to concentrate more and to respond more quickly.

TACTICAL

Aim of practice: consistency in making your feeder have to change direction at speed and to hit the shuttle from near the ground (if you have not wrongfooted him and he can get to it in time).

Advice: In this practice you should include another shot so that the feeder cannot anticipate your cross-court tap. For that reason I have included the straight push reply hit straight down the line, though

you could also include the straight block or a lob.

Begin the practice as for the technical practice. This time, however, your feeder should try to hit a winning smash from your serve and then travel quickly forwards to attack your reply. If he charges forwards play the cross-court tap. If he changes direction early in anticipation of the cross-court tap then use your push down the line which should catch him out.

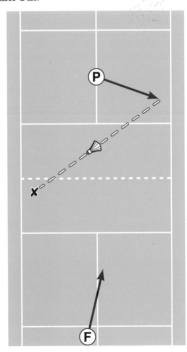

Fig 41
F smashes and travels forwards.
P steps forwards and taps shuttle
cross-court to the FC.

LOB

Tactical Use	building shot, used as a reply to the smash to send the opponent to the rearcourt. Usually hit high but can be played as an attempted winning shot when hit as a fast lob, on a lower trajectory, to catch out an opponent who rushes forwards after his smash.
Opponent's Probable Replies	smash, lob, drop.
Court Starting Position	midcourt.
Approach Travel Phase	stay in your midcourt position, sides defensive stance, or side-step and half or full lunge towards the side of the court.
Hitting Position	shuttle hit at impact point in front of or at your sides. *See* plate 25, page 86.
Stroke-Cycle	
RACKET STARTING POSITION	in front of you.
PREPARATION	twist your shoulders side on to the shuttle, bend your racket arm and cock your hand fully.
HITTING PHASE	
grip	forehand or multipurpose.
racket head control	whip action or strong tap action.
racket face use	flat.
racket recovery	follow through to recover if you use a whip action; rebound the racket head and recover directly after a tap action.
Recovery Travel Phase	adopt a sides attacking stance in the midcourt.
New Court Position	midcourt.

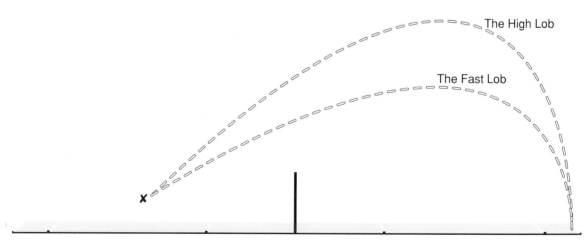

Fig 42
The High Lob and Fast Lob

COMMON FAULTS	POSSIBLE CAUSES	CORRECTIONS
Shuttle doesn't reach the rearcourt.	Wrong grip. Incorrect racket face angle. Not enough force.	Adjust your grip. Adjust racket face angle. Use a stronger tap or whip the racket head through quickly.
Shuttle doesn't go high enough.	Incorrect racket face angle. Not enough force.	Adjust racket face angle. Increase racket head speed with a stronger tap or a faster whip action.
	Racket face not below the shuttle.	Make sure that you hit the shuttle from below.
Shuttle doesn't go in the intended direction.	Racket arm does not follow through in direction of shuttle's flightpath. Incorrect racket face angle.	Adjust follow through. Adjust racket face.

PRACTICES FOR THE LOB

The practices should be used for forehand and backhand lobs.

TECHNICAL

Aim of practice: consistency in fluency and accuracy.

REPETITIONS: sets of ten on forehand and backhand lobs.

Advice: Do this in two phases.

PHASE 1: Stand in the hitting position in centre midcourt and ask your feeder to hit sets of ten smashes to your backhand side and then to your forehand side.
Play a continuous rally and keep the smasher in the rearcourt with deep lobs.

PHASE 2: Repeat the practice but now do the full action phrase: from midcourt to the side of the court and recover to the midcourt. Ask your feeder to hit sets of ten smashes to each side of the midcourt in turn.
You should lob high enough to allow you time to recover to a defensive stance in the midcourt before the next smash.

DEVELOPMENT: Add the element of **uncertainty**. Ask your feeder to hit sets of ten smashes at you, or close to your sides, or wide of you near the side lines. Practise returning all smashes with a high lob.

Advice: If you find this too difficult at first then ask your feeder to use medium-paced smashes so that you really do practise your technical skill in lobbing in a complete action phrase.

TACTICAL

Aim of practice: consistency in making your feeder hit smashes from the rearcourt.

The purpose of this practice is not simply to lob but to make the feeder play smashes from various parts of the rearcourt. For that reason ask your feeder to smash at you. Lob to the centre and sides of the rearcourt to keep your feeder pinned down in the rearcourt. If you lob short then your feeder will be allowed to try to hit through your defence for a winner. If the practice breaks down then serve high again and continue.

You can make this a **competitive practice** and conclude the practice when the feeder has hit three winning smashes.

SERVES

LOW SERVE

The description which follows applies to both forehand and backhand serves. *See* plates 26 and 27, page 93.

Tactical Use	building shot, used to force the opponent to hit upwards.
Opponent's Probable Replies	kill, net reply, push to midcourt/rearcourt, lob to rearcourt.
Court Starting Position	midcourt/forecourt area and usually close to the centre line though you may decide to serve from a wide position in doubles.
Approach Travel Phase	none.
Hitting Position	in balance with feet shoulder width apart, one foot behind the other slightly offset and pointing sideways to give an open stance. Shuttle held in front and on the racket side.
Stroke-Cycle	
RACKET STARTING POSITION	racket held in preparation position, bent arm and cocked hand.
PREPARATION	racket head taken backwards with bent arm and cocked hand.
HITTING PHASE	
grip	forehand, backhand or multipurpose.
racket head control	push action.
racket face use	flat or glancing hit.
racket recovery	follows through along the line of flight of the shuttle before recovering racket ready to threaten any net replies.
Recovery Travel Phase	step forwards to cover any net replies.
New Court Position	edge of forecourt.

COMMON FAULTS	POSSIBLE CAUSES	CORRECTIONS
Shuttle hit too high or into the net.	Wrong grip. Incorrect racket face angle. Wrong hitting action.	Adjust your grip. Adjust angle of racket face. Keep hand cocked and use a push action.
Shuttle hit in wrong direction.	Incorrect racket face angle. Not following through along line of flight of shuttle.	Adjust angle of racket face. Adjust your follow through.
Shuttle hit too far into your opponent's court.	Using too much force. Too much racket head speed.	Use a gentle push action. Slow down racket head.

Plate 26 –
Forehand Serve Stance

Plate 27 –
Backhand Low Serve Stance

PRACTICES FOR THE LOW SERVE

You might not think that you need to practise your low serve as you use it always in a game. If so you would be wrong. I am reminded here of the time when I was in Malmö in 1977 for the first World Championships. I was giving some practice to England's Jane Webster (later World Ladies Doubles Champion) on the next court to Tjun Tjun of Indonesia, then considered the world's best men's doubles player. He was practising his backhand serve which most players considered almost perfect. He did so for the two hours we were there and tried out different variations in using it. The practice paid off for he went on to win the Men's Doubles final.

Aim of practice: consistency in accuracy.

REPETITIONS: sets of ten.

Advice: Do this in two phases.

PHASE 1: Go on court with a box of shuttles and simply practise serving from different positions as you would in a game. For example you can serve from a wide position or stand further back in the court as in mixed doubles when the man serves. Keep a record of your score out of each set of ten repetitions. When you can serve ten out of ten accurately then you will have achieved your aim. Practise until you do so.

PHASE 2: Ask your feeder to attack your serve in order to increase the pressure on you. Keep practising until you can serve so accurately that the feeder cannot hit the shuttle downwards.

This practice will improve your concentration and should also increase your confidence in your ability to serve accurately under pressure. Of course, the real test will come in competition for which you will now be prepared.

FLICK SERVE

Tactical Use	attempted winning shot/building shot, used to catch your opponent out as you flick the shuttle over his head to the rearcourt as his weight moves forward for your low serve. This is useful for singles as well as doubles.
Opponent's Probable Replies	smash, drop, clear.
Court Starting Position	midcourt/forecourt area and usually close to the centre line though you may decide to serve from a wide position.
Approach Travel Phase	none.
Hitting Position	in balance with feet shoulder width apart, one foot behind the other slightly offset and pointing sideways to give an open stance. Shuttle held in front and on the racket side.
Stroke-Cycle	
RACKET STARTING POSITION	racket held in preparation position, bent arm and cocked hand.
PREPARATION	racket head taken backwards with bent arm and cocked hand.
HITTING PHASE	begin the forward movement of the racket head as if to serve low and then just before impact use a tap action.
grip	forehand, backhand, multipurpose.
racket head control	tap.
racket face use	flat.
racket recovery	racket head rebounds on impact as your racket arm follows through in the direction of the line of flight of the shuttle before recovering in front of your body.
Recovery Travel Phase	be ready to step forwards to threaten any weak replies if you hit an effective flick serve. If not, travel into a sides defence position in the midcourt.
New Court Position	forecourt or midcourt.

COMMON FAULTS	POSSIBLE CAUSES	CORRECTIONS
Opponent anticipates the flick serve.	The arm action is too fast into the impact point.	Use a push action in the hitting phase before you tap the shuttle upwards on impact.
Shuttle travels too high or too far.	Incorrect hitting action. Incorrect racket face angle.	Use a tap action. Adjust racket face angle.

PRACTICES FOR THE FLICK SERVE

Aim of practice: to be consistent in getting the shuttle past the receiver so that he either cannot hit it at all or cannot hit downwards.

When you perform a flick serve you should give your opponent the impression that you are about to perform a low serve. Thus you swing the racket head gently and slowly forwards as if you are about to push the shuttle over the net. The idea is to cause your opponent to sway forwards in anticipation of the low serve. If he does so then you have caught him out. Just prior to impact you accelerate the racket head forwards and tap the shuttle upwards over your opponent's outstretched reach.

You can practise the action without a feeder, but I would recommend that you set up a tactical competitive practice with your feeder.

Stand in the serving and receiving positions as for level doubles. You should hit low or flick serves. Your feeder should try to attack your serve. If he can hit down at the net or smash your flick serve then you have failed. If he cannot do so and you can catch him out with your flick serve then you have achieved your aims.

HIGH SERVE

Tactical Use	building shot, used to move the receiver to the rearcourt in singles. Used in mixed doubles to move the lady out of position in the rearcourt and so reverse the positions of the man and woman. Used in ladies' doubles and men's doubles against a weak attacker or to move the doubles team's front player to the rearcourt.
Opponent's Probable Replies	smash, drop, clear.
Court Starting Position	midcourt/forecourt area and usually close to the centre line though you may decide to serve from a wide position.
Approach Travel Phase	none.
Hitting Position	in balance with feet about shoulder width apart, one foot behind the other slightly offset and pointing sideways to give an open stance. Shuttle held in front and on the racket side.
Stroke-Cycle underarm throwing action.	
RACKET STARTING POSITION	racket held in preparation position, bent arm and cocked hand.
PREPARATION	racket head taken backwards with bent arm and cocked hand.
HITTING PHASE	swing your racket arm forwards and whip the racket head under the shuttle to hit it upwards.
grip	forehand, multipurpose.
racket head control	whip.
racket face use	flat.
racket recovery	racket head follows through in the direction of the line of flight of the shuttle before recovering in front of your body.
Recovery Travel Phase	travel to midcourt ready to defend against a possible smash.
New Court Position	midcourt.

COMMON FAULTS	POSSIBLE CAUSES	CORRECTIONS
Shuttle not hit high enough.	Incorrect hitting position. Wrong hitting action. Incorrect racket face angle. Insufficient follow through. Insufficient racket head speed.	Adjust hitting position. Use whip action. Adjust racket face angle. Follow through fully. Faster underarm throw and whip action.
Shuttle not hit far enough.	Not enough force. Wrong hitting action. Incorrect racket face angle. Insufficient preparation.	Increase racket head speed. Use whip action. Adjust angle of racket face. Cock your hand fully before the hitting phase.
Shuttle hit too far.	Too much force. Incorrect racket face angle.	Decrease racket head speed. Adjust racket face angle.

PRACTICES FOR THE HIGH SERVE

TECHNICAL AND TACTICAL

Aim of practice: to serve high with accuracy and consistently move your feeder to play his reply from the rearcourt.

REPETITIONS: sets of ten.

Advice: Do this in two phases.

PHASE 1: Practise serving high from the right and left courts and aim the shuttle to land near the centre line or the sideline, or between them in the rearcourt. Do this until you can achieve ten out of ten to a given place in the rearcourt.

PHASE 2: Position your feeder to receive the serve and practise high serves as in phase 1 until you can make your feeder play his replies from different places in the rearcourt.

DRIVE SERVE

Tactical Use	building shot/attempted winning shot in doubles, used to catch the receiver late in responding to the speed of the shuttle. Usually aimed to the backhand side.
Opponent's Probable Replies	block to forecourt, lob, counter drive.
Court Starting Position	about 1.2 metres from the front service line in the midcourt and usually close to the centre line, though you may decide to serve from a wide position.
Approach Travel Phase	none.
Hitting Position	in balance with feet shoulder width apart, one foot behind the other slightly offset and pointing sideways to give an open stance. Shuttle held in front and on the racket side.
Stroke-Cycle	
RACKET STARTING POSITION	racket held in preparation position, bent arm and cocked hand. *See* plate 26.

Drive Serve *continued*

PREPARATION	racket head taken backwards with bent arm and cocked hand.
HITTING PHASE	
grip	forehand or multipurpose.
racket head control	tap.
racket face use	flat.
racket recovery	your arm follows through after the tap action along the line of flight of the shuttle.
Recovery Travel Phase	step forwards ready to attack a weak reply.
New Court Position	on edge of forecourt.

COMMON FAULTS	POSSIBLE CAUSES	CORRECTIONS
Shuttle goes into the net.	Incorrect hitting position. Wrong racket face angle.	Adjust hitting position. Adjust angle of racket face.
Shuttle goes too high.	Incorrect hitting action.	Use a tap action as you swing your racket head forwards at speed.
	Racket hand uncocks.	Keep hand cocked throughout the hitting phase.
Shuttle travels too slowly.	Insufficient racket head speed.	Swing your racket head forwards very quickly and hit through the shuttle using a tap action during the swing.
Foul serve as racket head is too high.	Lifting racket head sideways as you hit the shuttle.	Keep your racket head below your hand.

PRACTICES FOR THE DRIVE SERVE

TECHNICAL
Aim of practice: to develop accuracy and consistency in driving the shuttle to skim the net as horizontally as you can achieve.

REPETITIONS: sets of ten.

Advice: Take care that you keep your racket head below the level of your hand when you drive serve. Some players drive from the side and lift their racket heads higher than their hand. If you do so you will be penalised for doing a fault serve.

Practise driving the shuttle to skim the net at speed towards the backhand side of your feeder. As your feeder will be expecting this ask him to block them back to you. However, notice at what point he actually hits the shuttle and use that to adjust your aim, if necessary.

TACTICAL
Use the drive serve as a surprise serve in informal competition. This is really the best place to practise it. If you are successful in doing this you will add a useful serve to your repertoire which you can use effectively and to your advantage in formal competition.

FORECOURT STROKE-MOVES

In the forecourt the shuttle will be hit from above net height, just below net height and near the ground. You will usually attempt a winning shot from above the net and a building shot from below the net. When the shuttle is high in the forecourt the smash can be used as an attempted winning shot. The smash will not be included below as it has been described in the section of rearcourt stroke-moves.

KILL

Tactical Use	attempted winning shot, used when the chance arises to hit an outright winner at the floor or at the opponent.
Opponent's Probable Replies	lob, drive, block.
Court Starting Position	forward or backward attacking stance on the edge of the forecourt.
Approach Travel Phase	step, run or jump forwards and upwards to hit the shuttle down from close to and above the net.
Hitting Position	shuttle in front of you at arm's reach distance, *'reach with your arm and hit with your hand'*. *See* plate 28.
Stroke-Cycle	
RACKET STARTING POSITION	in front of you.
PREPARATION	cock your hand.
HITTING PHASE	
grip	forehand or backhand.
racket head control	strong tap action.
racket face use	flat.
racket recovery	rebound on impact and immediate recovery.
Recovery Travel Phase	withdraw from the net with side chassé ready to attack any reply.
New Court Position	on edge of the forecourt.

COMMON FAULTS	POSSIBLE CAUSES	CORRECTIONS
Shuttle goes into the net.	Incorrect racket face angle. Wrong hitting action. Wrong hitting position. Wrong grip.	Adjust racket face angle. Use a tap action. Adjust hitting position. Adjust your grip.
Shuttle does not go downwards.	Incorrect racket face angle. Wrong grip. Wrong hitting position.	Adjust angle of racket face. Adjust the grip. Adjust hitting position.

Fig 43 *(above)*
Shuttle Trajectory: The Kill

PRACTICES FOR THE KILL

TECHNICAL

Aim of practice: consistency in fluency and accuracy.

REPETITIONS: sets of ten.

Advice: Do this in two phases.

Comment: The hitting action used here is the tap action. The practices are no different from those which you should do regularly in developing your racket skill. *See* chapter 7, page 44.

PHASE 1: Stand in the hitting position in the forecourt with your feeder positioned deep in his midcourt. Rally at speed with your feeder using forehand taps, then backhand taps and then a mixture of forehand and backhand taps.

PHASE 2: Add the travel phases so that you do the complete action phrase.
Stand on the edge of the forecourt astride the short service line in a forward attacking stance. Rally, each time stepping forwards to hit the shuttle before you chassé back to recover to the service line. *See* Fig 44.
NOTE Your racket foot remains in front as you approach the hitting position and recover from it.

DEVELOPMENT: Play 'three-shot' rallies. In these you hit two shots at speed to your feeder and on the third shot you kill the shuttle to the floor and recover. Your feeder serves again for you to repeat the three-shot rally. It is important that when you practise going for the kill you do actually see the shuttle hit the ground. It helps you to develop your adventurous attitude and your confidence.

FURTHER DEVELOPMENT: Add the element of

Plate 28

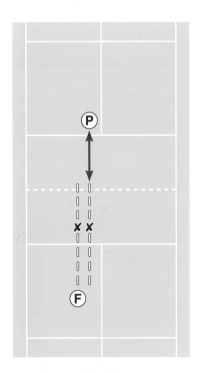

Fig 44

uncertainty by asking your feeder to return the shuttle to your backhand or forehand as he chooses. Now see what you can do at speed.

Comment: Never be bothered by errors when you are going for the kill from the net. At first you will make many but if you keep practising then eventually you will become more consistent and develop the good habit of hitting winners when chances arise in the forecourt.

BRUSH STROKE

Tactical Use	attempted winning shot/building shot, used when you cannot hit forwards to kill the shuttle for fear of hitting the net with your racket. So you *brush* the shuttle off the top of the net with a glancing hit from right to left or left to right.
Opponent's Probable Replies	drive, net reply, lob.
Court Starting Position	forward or backward attacking stance on the edge of the forecourt.
Approach Travel Phase	step, run or jump forwards and upwards to hit the shuttle down from close to and above the net.
Hitting Position	shuttle in front of you at arm's reach distance, *'reach with your arm and hit with your hand'. See* plate 28, page 99.
Stroke-Cycle	
RACKET STARTING POSITION	in front of you.
PREPARATION	cock your hand.
HITTING PHASE	
grip	forehand or backhand.
racket head control	fast push action.
racket face use	glancing.
racket recovery	follow through across the line of flight of the shuttle to hold the racket in front of you.
Recovery Travel Phase	withdraw from the net to the edge of the forecourt ready to attack any reply.
New Court Position	edge of forecourt.

COMMON FAULTS	POSSIBLE CAUSES	CORRECTIONS
Shuttle goes into the net.	Incorrect racket face angle. Wrong grip. Wrong hitting position. Wrong hitting action. Wrong use of racket face.	Adjust angle of racket face. Adjust grip. Adjust your hitting position. Use fast push action. Use glancing hit.
Shuttle does not go down.	Incorrect racket face angle. Wrong grip.	Adjust angle of racket face. Adjust grip.

PRACTICES FOR THE BRUSH SHOT

Refer to the practices for the Kill, pages 99–100.

PUSH

Tactical Use	building shot, used when the shuttle is net height or just below the top of the net, to hit the shuttle gently over the net into the forecourt or midcourt.
Opponent's Probable Replies	net reply, counter push, lob.
Court Starting Position	forward or backward attacking stance on the edge of the forecourt.
Approach Travel Phase	step forwards to push the shuttle over the net so that it falls into the forecourt or midcourt.
Hitting Position	shuttle in front of you at bent arm distance.
Stroke-Cycle	
RACKET STARTING POSITION	in front of you.
PREPARATION	cock your hand.
HITTING PHASE	
grip	forehand, backhand or multipurpose.
racket head control	gentle push action.
racket face use	flat or glancing.
racket recovery	part follow through along the line of flight of the shuttle before recovering the racket in front of you.
Recovery Travel Phase	withdraw from the net to the edge of the forecourt ready to attack any reply.
New Court Position	edge of the forecourt.

COMMON FAULTS	POSSIBLE CAUSES	CORRECTIONS
Shuttle hit into the net.	Incorrect hitting position. Wrong grip. Wrong racket face angle. Wrong hitting action.	Adjust your hitting position. Adjust your grip. Adjust racket face angle. Use push action and keep hand cocked.
Shuttle hit too hard.	Too much force. Incorrect hitting action.	Slow down racket head speed. Use a gentle push action.
Shuttle goes too high.	Incorrect racket face angle.	Adjust angle of racket face.

Fig 45 *(right)*
Shuttle Trajectory – The push

PRACTICES FOR THE PUSH

Refer to the practices for the Kill. *See* pages 99–100.

TUMBLER

In this stroke the shuttle rotates around its two axes. *See* Figs 46 (a), (b).

Tactical Use	building shot, used to make it more difficult for the opponent to play a controlled and effective reply from close to the net.
Opponent's Probable Replies	net reply, lob.
Court Starting Position	forward or backward attacking stance on the edge of the forecourt.
Approach Travel Phase	step forwards to hit the shuttle from close to the net.
Hitting Position	shuttle in front of you at arm's reach. *See* plate 29.
Stroke-Cycle	
RACKET STARTING POSITION	in front of you.
PREPARATION	cock your hand.
HITTING PHASE	
grip	forehand, backhand or multipurpose.
racket head control	upward push action.
racket face use	glancing.
racket recovery	part follow through along the line of flight of the shuttle before recovering the racket in front of you.
Recovery Travel Phase	withdraw from the net to the edge of the forecourt ready to attack any reply.
New Court Position	edge of the forecourt.

COMMON FAULTS	POSSIBLE CAUSES	CORRECTIONS
Shuttle goes into the net.	Wrong grip.	Adjust grip.
	Wrong racket face angle.	Adjust angle of racket face.
	Wrong use of racket face.	Use glancing hit.
	Wrong hitting action.	Use a push action.
	Wrong hitting position.	Adjust your hitting position.
Shuttle goes too high.	Too much force.	Use a gentle push action.
	Gripping racket too tightly.	Hold racket handle gently in your fingers.
	Wrong hitting action.	Use push action.
		Use a glancing hit.
	Incorrect racket face angle.	Adjust racket face angle.

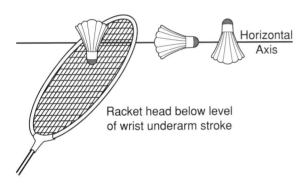

Racket head below level of wrist underarm stroke

Horizontal Axis

Fig 46a *(above)* and Fig 46b *(below)*

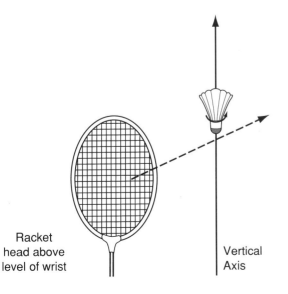

Racket head above level of wrist

Vertical Axis

Plate 29

PRACTICES FOR THE TUMBLER

There is a knack in playing tumblers and other sliced shots in the forecourt. The principle is obvious as you must make the shuttle rotate. However, there is no one way of achieving this and in my experience each player will develop his own individual way of hitting tumblers as he acquires the knack of doing so. The knack comes from practice. It is like learning to ride a bicycle. Suddenly you can do it – you get the knack.

TACTICAL

Aim of practice: consistency in fluency and accuracy.

REPETITIONS: sets of ten. These may be continuous sets without a pause. You should make a mental note of your consistency percentage as you practise.

Advice: Do this in two phases.

PHASE 1: Stand in the hitting position in the forecourt. See Plate 25. Ask your feeder to underarm throw the shuttle over the net for you to play a tumbler. Practise both forehand and backhand tumblers.

PHASE 2: Start in the midcourt. Ask your feeder to throw or hit the shuttle upwards as if he is blocking your smash from the midcourt. Travel forwards and play a tumbler and recover to the edge of the midcourt ready to threaten a net reply.

DEVELOPMENT: Play a continuous rally with your feeder. Both of you start from the short service line, step forwards to play your tumbler and recover to the service line ready to travel forwards again. Keep practising as you gain more control and skill in performing tumblers.

HAIRPIN NET REPLY

In this stroke the shuttle 'climbs' up and passes close to the top of the net before falling down into the opposite court.

Tactical Use	building shot, used to make it more difficult for the opponent to play a controlled and effective reply from close to the net, and to force a weak lob to the midcourt.
Opponent's Probable Replies	kill, net reply, lob.
Court Starting Position	forward or backward attacking stance on the edge of the forecourt.
Approach Travel Phase	a deep lunge to hit the shuttle from near the ground and close to the net.
Hitting Position	shuttle in front of you near the floor.
Stroke-Cycle	
RACKET STARTING POSITION	in front of you.
PREPARATION	cock your hand.
HITTING PHASE	
grip	forehand, backhand or multipurpose.
racket head control	upward push action.
racket face use	glancing or flat.
racket recovery	follow through along the line of flight of the shuttle before recovering the racket in front of you.
Recovery Travel Phase	withdraw from the net to the edge of the forecourt ready to attack any reply.
New Court Position	edge of the forecourt.

COMMON FAULTS	POSSIBLE CAUSES	CORRECTIONS
Shuttle goes into the net.	Incorrect hitting position. Wrong racket face angle. Incorrect hitting technique.	Adjust hitting position. Adjust angle of racket face. Use a push action.
Shuttle goes too high.	Too much force.	Use a gentle push action and reduce racket head speed. Stay in the hitting position during the hitting phase. Use a glancing hit.
Shuttle goes high enough but does not go over the net.	Wrong racket face angle.	Adjust racket face angle and follow through along the line of flight.

PRACTICES FOR THE HAIRPIN NET REPLY

TECHNICAL
Aim of practice: consistency in fluency and accuracy.

Practise the 'hairpin' as for the tumbler except that you should allow the shuttle to drop nearer the floor and your feeder should throw it so that it travels down close to the net. You will require good body skill in order to perform a deep lunge to get down to the shuttle.

LOB

Tactical Use	building shot, used as a reply to the dropshot or net reply to send the opponent to the rearcourt. Usually hit high but can be played as an attempted winning shot when hit as a fast lob, on a lower trajectory, to catch out an opponent who travels forwards to attack a net reply. *See* Fig 47.
Opponent's Probable Replies	smash, drop, clear.
Court Starting Position	midcourt.
Approach Travel Phase	bounce start and travel forwards to lunge into the hitting position.
Hitting Position	shuttle hit at impact point in front of you and near the ground. *See* plate 30, page 107.
Stroke-Cycle	
RACKET STARTING POSITION	in front of you.
PREPARATION	arm slightly flexed and hand cocked.
HITTING PHASE	
grip	forehand or multipurpose.
racket head control	whip action or strong tap action.
racket face use	flat.
racket recovery	follow through to recover if you use a whip action; rebound the racket head and recover directly after a tap action.
Recovery Travel Phase	recover to the midcourt and adopt a side defensive stance.
New Court Position	midcourt.

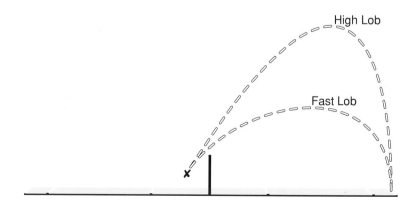

Fig 47
The High Lob and Fast Lob

COMMON FAULTS	POSSIBLE CAUSES	CORRECTIONS
Shuttle doesn't reach the rearcourt.	Wrong grip. Incorrect racket face angle. Not enough force.	Adjust your grip. Adjust racket face angle. Use a stronger tap or whip the racket head through quickly.
Shuttle doesn't go high enough.	Incorrect racket face angle. Not enough force.	Adjust racket face angle. Increase racket head speed with a stronger tap or a faster whip action.
	Racket face not below the shuttle.	Make sure that you hit the shuttle from below.
Shuttle goes too far and out of court.	Too much force. Incorrect racket face angle.	Use less force. Adjust racket face angle.
Shuttle doesn't go in the intended direction.	Racket arm does not follow through in intended direction. Incorrect racket face angle.	Adjust follow through. Adjust racket face.

Plate 30 – *(left)*
Lunge for the Lob

PRACTICES FOR THE LOB
The practices should be used for forehand and backhand lobs.

TECHNICAL
Aim of practice: consistency in fluency and accuracy in lobbing high to the rearcourt.

REPETITIONS: sets of ten on forehand and backhand lobs.

Advice: Do this in two phases.

PHASE 1: Stand in the hitting position near the forecourt and ask you feeder to hit sets of ten drops to your backhand side and then to your forehand side.
Play a continuous rally and keep the dropper in the rearcourt with deep lobs.

PHASE 2: Repeat the practice but now do the full action phrase: from midcourt to the forecourt and recover to the midcourt.

Ask your feeder to hit sets of ten drops to each side of the forecourt in turn. You should lob high enough to allow you time to recover to a defensive stance in the midcourt before the next dropshot.

DEVELOPMENT: Add the element of uncertainty. Ask your feeder to hit sets of ten drops to either side of the forecourt as he chooses to try to catch you out. Practise returning all drops with a high lob.

TACTICAL
Aim of practice: consistency in making your feeder hit his drops from the rearcourt.

The purpose of this practice is not simply to lob but to make the feeder play his drops from various parts of the rearcourt. For that reason ask your feeder to drop to you using fast sliced drops and slow drops (check smashes). Lob to the centre and sides of the rearcourt to keep your feeder pinned down in the rearcourt. If you lob short then your feeder will be allowed to try for an attempted winner with a smash.

If the practice breaks down then serve high again and continue. You can make this a *competitive practice* and conclude the practice when the feeder has hit three winning shots.

CHAPTER 10

Analysing and Correcting Your Technical Faults

Your first task is to *identify the problem* you are having in hitting the shuttle. The first indication you will have if something is wrong is that your movement doesn't feel right – it may be too slow, awkward or lacking in control; or in what happens to the shuttle – it doesn't go where you want it to go.

You will need to know your strokes quite thoroughly to analyse them and correct your faults. If you are not quite sure about a particular stroke then refer to chapter 9 and read up on the stroke you are having problems with. Each stroke has been written out to show clearly its parts in order from the time you set off to travel into position to hit the shuttle to the time you return into position to cover your opponent's possible replies.

This is how I would try to solve a technical problem.

PROBLEM

The shuttle travels horizontally when I smash, I find it difficult to hit it down steeply.

DIAGNOSIS

The hitting position was correct before the hit which means that I was then behind the shuttle and was able to hit it downwards. I stepped forwards just before I hit the shuttle which would have altered my hitting position slightly. I would now be under the shuttle instead of behind it and this would mean that my racket face was pointing forwards and not downwards on impact with the shuttle. This would also account for my loss of power as, during the throwing action, the racket head would not have gained maximum speed before impact.

ANALYSIS

Stroke move:	forehand smash
Court Starting Position	OK.
Approach Travel Phase	OK.
Hitting Position	OK.
Stroke-Cycle *throwing action*	
RACKET STARTING POSITION	OK.
HITTING PHASE	OK.
grip	OK
racket head control	slightly less power than usual.
racket face use	hit the shuttle horizontal instead of downwards.
racket recovery	OK.
Recovery Travel Phase	seem to step forwards just before I hit the shuttle.
New Court Position	OK.

CORRECTION

Do not step forwards to begin the recovery travel phase before I have hit the shuttle. Maintain my hitting position and stay behind the shuttle until after impact.

PRACTICES

Ask my practice partner to 'feed' shuttles one at a time for me to practise maintaining my hitting position until after I have hit the shuttle. Ask him to feed them so that they fall in front of me to make sure I will be behind the shuttle. Once I have got the correct feel of the stroke he can feed the shuttle higher and deeper so that I have to travel backwards into the hitting position.

COMMENT

If this does not work repeat the complete analysis process and examine each part of the stroke to be sure that each one is satisfactory. If this is difficult, refer to the stroke in chapter 9 and examine it carefully to remind yourself of all the parts. Even then you may have to try out several different corrections before you find the right one. Do not be put off by this; it is quite usual for this to occur.

When I am coaching I always go through this procedure. I may find the faults and their corrections more quickly than you will but that comes from lots of experience. But even then I will expect to make the wrong diagnosis occasionally and have to repeat the procedure. All coaches experience this at some time or other and if they do then you should expect to also.

When analysing and making corrections try not to confuse yourself by making too many corrections at the same time. The general rule is: *Keep it simple by working on one correction at a time*.

Create Your Own Practice Programme

Ideally you should be the best judge of your own game and the parts you will need to practise to improve your play. This chapter will help you to devise your own practices using a combination of the individual strokes described in chapter 9.

DEVISING YOUR OWN PRACTICES

Practise Your Strokes and Action Phrases

In a game you perform your strokes as part of an action phrase (*see* Fig 6, page 18) in which your approach travel phase to the hitting position is linked to your recovery travel phase into position to cover your opponent's probable replies. As your rallies in singles and doubles are made up of action phrases you should aim to practise your strokes within an action phrase.

You can however, and it is usual to do so, first practise a stroke by extracting it from a particular action phrase and practise it on its own to develop your technical or tactical skill. To do this you would stand in the appropriate hitting position and then keep practising until you had **grooved** the stroke so that you can hit the shuttle accurately and with consistency. When you are satisfied with it then you should add the travel phases before and after the stroke and practise the whole action phrase. Alternatively you could practise the stroke within the whole action phrase from the outset. The choice is yours and will depend on what stage you are at in your practice.

From Single to Combination Stroke Practices

The practice routines in this chapter lead you to combine several strokes to make your practice more **complex**. You will find that your practices will range from **easy to difficult** and **simple to complex**, depending on the number of strokes

you decide to use within a practice. In a complex practice, for example, you may decide that you want to practise a clear followed by a net return followed by a scissor jump cross-court smash from your backhand rearcourt. *See* Figs 48 (a), (b) and (c).

If you use the recommended procedure and know how to practise individual strokes you should find it easy to devise your own practice routines. You should learn how to do this so that after taking part in formal competition you can create specific practices for different aspects of your game. I have already explained the procedures in chapter 5 (pages 29–38) for technical and tactical skill practices but I will remind you of them again. They consist of a number of progressive stages.

TECHNICAL SKILL

The focus here is on your SELF and how you do what you do.

Stage 1: Practise to develop the 'feel' of the stroke.

Stage 2: Practise to develop your accuracy.

Stage 3: Practise to develop your consistency.

Stage 4: Add the travel phases to practise the stroke as part of an action phrase.

Stage 5: Add the element of **uncertainty**.

TACTICAL SKILL

The focus here is on the OTHER player and what you can make them do.

Stage 1: Decide on the game situation and the action phrase.

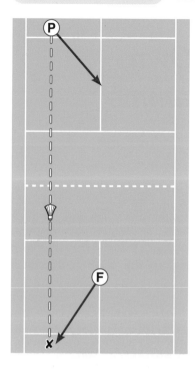

Fig 48 (a)
P clears.

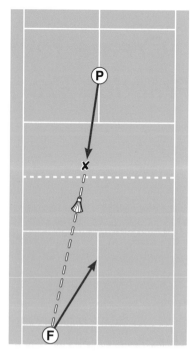

Fig 48 (b)
P travel to Fc.

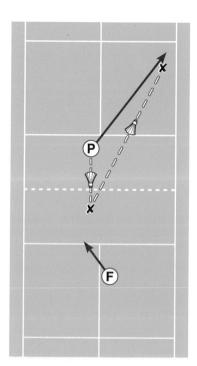

Fig 48 (c)
Plays net reply and travels to
RC to smash lob from F.

STAGE 2: Decide how you will start the practice and end it.

STAGE 3: Develop the practice by adding more action phrases.

STAGE 4: Increase the degree of difficulty.

STAGE 5: Add the elements of *uncertainty and competition*.

Make Use of the Practice Procedure

In a tactical practice it will be necessary to follow the procedure as written whereas in technical practice you do not have to go through the procedure from stage 1 to stage 5 each time you practise a stroke. It depends on the stroke and what you want to improve.

You could begin at stage 1 and practise the 'feel' of the stroke if that is what is needed, or begin at stage 5 and add some uncertainty into the practice. You may even begin at stage 1 and, from there jump straight to stage 4, or begin at stage 4 and go back to stage 1 to make some minor correction. It is entirely up to you how you move around in these stages.

Decide on your Practice Aims and Standards

In a technical practice there are three main aims which are synonymous with the standards you should achieve. These are:

- fluency and ease of performance of your actions
- accuracy
- consistency.

These aims apply even when you add the *travel phases* and *uncertainty* at stages 4 and 5. The addition of these two stages should not affect your aims. If you cannot achieve these standards in the later stages then you should go back to stage 1 perhaps and make whatever corrections are necessary.

In a tactical practice your aims will be related to achieving the standards of *effectiveness* and *consistency* in using your strokes as building shots or attempted winning shots.

Set Practice Targets and Measure your Success in Practice

It is pointless to practise without knowing whether or not you are improving as a result of your practice. You should have some way of measuring your improvement. This is quite easy to do.

Let's continue with your forehand clear as an example and assume that in practice your accuracy only has a success rate of 50 per cent, five out of ten. Obviously this is not good enough so you decide to improve it. You decide on the *realistic* target of 70 per cent success rate, seven out of ten.

As you usually repeat things to get them right in practice, you can now organise your practice into a set number of repetitions. Sets of ten repetitions will measure your improvement. Complete one set of ten repetitions and record how many times you were accurate. If you only get six out of ten accurate, 60 per cent success, then do another set of ten repetitions and count your score again. Keep doing this until you achieve your target of seven out of ten, 70 per cent success.

If you do this easily then it could be that you are better than you judged so do another set and try to achieve 80 per cent success.

If you can improve your success rate in stages 4 and 5 then you should show an improvement in competition. This will in turn increase your confidence and with it your chances of winning.

Develop Your Technical Practice and Extend Yourself

It is sensible to make your practices more demanding. This will force you to extend yourself and help you to improve your standard of play. There are several ways of doing this:

● *Increase the number of repetitions you do* (the amount of practice). If you have been doing ten repetitions of your forehand clear then keep increasing this until you can do fifty repetitions. This will place demands on your concentration, determination and fitness.

● *Increase the speed at which you practise.* If you have been practising the standard clear in an action phrase then ask your practice partner to hit attack clears to give you less time to get into position to hit your clear. This will also place extra demands on your concentration, determination, fitness and body skill.

● *Increase the distance and height that you jump.* If you are practising jump smashes then practise jumping higher or further to hit the shuttle. This will place extra demands on your fitness as well as your body skill.

● *Add the element of uncertainty.* Ask your practice partner to play dropshots as well as the attack clear so that you cannot anticipate the clear and cheat yourself by starting early.

Fitness

The harder you practise the fitter you must be. If you increase your work rate (*the intensity*) in the practice and increase the quantity (*volume*) of work then you will need to be fit. The work itself will help to make you fitter but this should be in addition to any fitness training you are doing.

Mental Attitude

Good-quality practices will also help to develop some aspects of your mental attitude. They will help to develop concentration in keeping your focus on the practice, determination to get a specific part of your game right, self-discipline which will help you to maintain regular practice, regardless of whether or not you want to do it, and self-confidence which will grow with the knowledge that you can do the work and achieve good standards of play. You can read more about mental attitude in chapter 15.

Devise Your Own Practices

You should now be able to make up your own practices. To help you further I have devised a practice form which you can photocopy and use to make up practices when you need them. *See* page 116.

The practice form has an explanation written beside each heading. I have provided an example of how I would use it to work out a practice for the forehand lob. Once you have grasped the idea make some copies of the blank practice form and devise some practices for yourself.

Once you get into the habit of practising in this organised way you will find that you won't need to use the practice form. In the meantime it should help you to practise successfully.

STROKE PRACTICE FORM

STROKE   whatever stroke you need to practise.

PRACTICE STAGE   from 1 to 5 in the practice procedure stages.

AIM(S) OF PRACTICE   the standard you want to achieve when using the stroke:
                                   fluency, accuracy, consistency.

TARGET SCORE   success rate you want to achieve: percentage score or your
                                   score out of ten, e.g. 70 per cent or seven out of ten.

HITTING POSITION   from where you hit the shuttle, e.g. forecourt, midcourt or
                                   rearcourt.

FEEDER'S POSITION   where your practice partner stands to 'feed' shuttles to you.

ACTION PHRASE   the approach and recovery travel phases before and after
                                   you play the stroke. This will be illustrated on the court
                                   diagram.

PRACTICE

NUMBER OF   how many times you will perform the practice,
REPETITIONS   ten repetitions, fifty repetitions.

NUMBER OF SETS   the number of times the agreed number of repetitions are
                                   performed, e.g. five sets of ten repetitions.

INSTRUCTIONS   inform the players how to do the practice.

DEVELOPMENT   in what ways you will develop the practice to extend yourself.
OF PRACTICE

STROKE PRACTICE FORM

STROKE — *forehand lob*

PRACTICE STAGE — *4*

AIM(S) OF PRACTICE — *to improve consistency in playing the forehand lob.*

TARGET SCORE — *80 per cent, eight out of ten.*

HITTING POSITION — *forehand forecourt.*

FEEDER'S POSITION — *forehand rearcourt.*

ACTION PHRASE — *midcourt to forecourt and recover to midcourt.*

PRACTICE

NUMBER OF REPETITIONS — *ten.*

NUMBER OF SETS — *five.*

INSTRUCTIONS — *P serves high, and takes up MC sides defence stance.*

f drops to P's forehand FC.

P travels and lunges into the hitting position, lobs and recovers to centre MC into sides defensive stance.

f plays another dropshot.

Practice continues.

DEVELOPMENT OF PRACTICE — *add uncertainty by asking your feeder to hit the occasional clear to try to catch you out.*

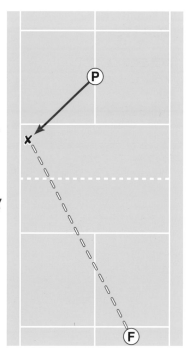

Fig 49

STROKE PRACTICE FORM

STROKE

PRACTICE STAGE

AIM(S) OF PRACTICE

TARGET SCORE

HITTING POSITION

FEEDER'S POSITION

ACTION PHRASE

PRACTICE

NUMBER OF REPETITIONS

NUMBER OF SETS

INSTRUCTIONS

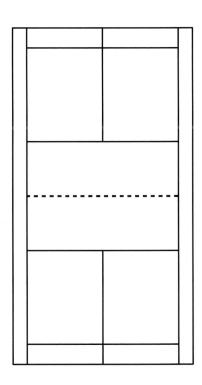

DEVELOPMENT
OF PRACTICE

CREATING YOUR PRACTICE PROGRAMME

This is quite easy to do if you know what you want to practise. Let me remind you that you will practise to learn a new skill, to raise your standards in performing the skill, and finally to maintain your standards of performance. You should now know what strokes, and what aspects of your racket and body skill you should practise, so all you need now do is decide how much time you can allow for practice and then plan a programme.

This is simply a matter of listing your strokes on a practice programme form. You can devise your own form or if you prefer make use of the one I have designed below. I will use the following shorthand to make it easier to write the programme.

Rearcourt = RC
Forecourt = FC   Forehand = fh
Midcourt = MC   Backhand = bh

Now look at the practice programme form.

TECHNICAL PRACTICE PROGRAMME FORM

NAME: Tanya Groves

DATES: From: 5, 7, 93   To: 3, 8, 93   DURATION: 4 weeks

Stroke	Hitting Position	Feeder's Position	Practice Stage	Repetitions	Sets	Comments
fh clear	fh RC	bh RC	4	20	1	
fh clear	bh RC	fh RC	4	20	1	
bh clear	bh RC	fh RC	3	10	5	
fh smash	fh RC	Centre MC	3	10	5	
bh smash	bh RC	Centre MC	2	10	3	
fh fast drop	fh RC	fh MC/FC	3	10	3	
fh check smash						
bh block						
bh lob						

Add other strokes as you choose

I think you should have the idea by now and will be able to complete your own practice programme form. The **Comments** column is for you to write any notes about what you want to improve or how you want the feeder to feed or introduce **uncertainty** if you are doing a Stage 5 practice.

An important consideration in practising is not to waste time. If you plan your programme carefully you won't waste time and if you raise your standards in practice you should become a better player in competition.

CHAPTER
12

Learn How to Practise Your Technical Skills Under Pressure

If you want to be a good player you should learn to hit the shuttle from any part of your court to any part of your opponent's court.

The practices in this chapter will help you to gain overall control of your court, no matter how fast and how long the game. If you do them you should have reached a good standard of technical skill and a reasonably high level of fitness as they are quite demanding. They will also develop your mental toughness with respect to your determination, perseverance and concentration.

Many coaches use these types of practice and you may be familiar with them. However, in my opinion, too many coaches do not understand how

to use them effectively and often players do not improve as they should when practising them. If you do not have a coach and work with a practice partner then you should find the practices quite easy to do, providing you know what you are trying to achieve and that you do them properly.

WHAT ARE THE PURPOSES OF THE PRACTICES?

The purposes of these practices are to improve your technical skill, i.e. your racket skill, your

THE ZONES

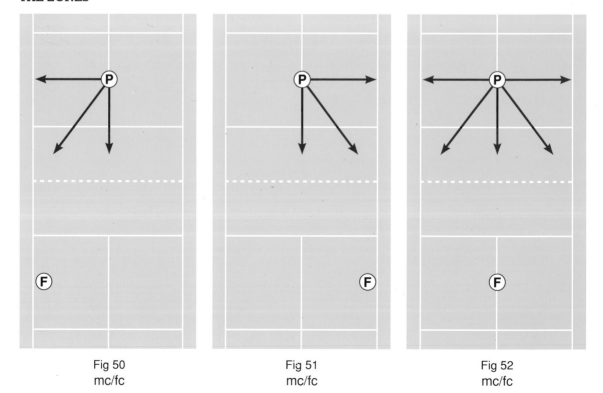

Fig 50
mc/fc

Fig 51
mc/fc

Fig 52
mc/fc

strokes and your body skill, and to develop your accuracy and consistency as you perform continuous action phrases in all parts of the court.

When you do them remember that any shot you play will be a building shot or an attempted winning shot. If, for example, you hit a clear then you should make sure that it is either a high defensive clear or a standard or an attack clear, and try to recover into position to cover the replies before you travel to play the next shot. In other words you should make sure that you maintain your tactical standards even though you will be doing a technical practice.

Now let's get started.

ZONE PRACTICES

The idea here is that you simply divide the court into zones and practise within a zone until you can travel to and return any shuttle that is hit into that zone. The practices start in single zones and then are made more demanding and beneficial by linking several zones.

Your practice partner (your feeder) plays an important part in feeding from several different court positions to make sure that you play a range of strokes in the zone. I have suggested several court positions where your feeder can stand to rally with you in your zone. You should experiment and place your feeder in different parts of the court according to what situations you want to experience. You decide.

Aims of Practice

To develop your skill in moving and to improve your accuracy and consistency of strokes from all parts of the court.

Practice Stage(s): 4 and 5

There will be a high degree of uncertainty which will increase the difficulty of the practices and make them more game-like. *See* chapter 5, pages 32–3 for a description of the practice stages.

How do I do the practice?

You start from the centre midcourt and then rally with your feeder. He hits the shuttle away from you to the sides or corners of your zone, or at you in the centre of the midcourt or as you are still travelling

THE ZONES *continued*

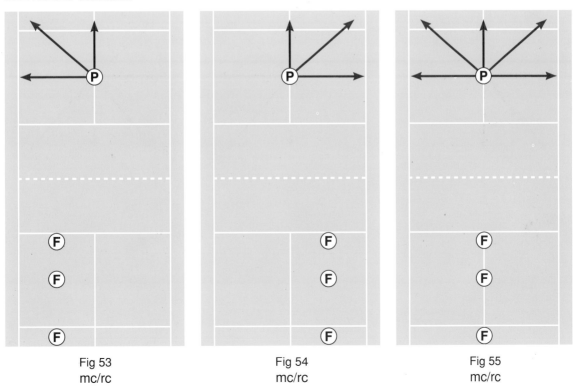

<table>
<tr><td>Fig 53
mc/rc</td><td>Fig 54
mc/rc</td><td>Fig 55
mc/rc</td></tr>
</table>

to recover your position.

Where should my feeder stand?
I have positioned your feeder in several places in the diagrams. You can place him elsewhere if you both decide that is better for you.

How hard must I practise?
You should work at a rate which allows you to stay on the oxygen energy system (*see* pages 130–134) as your main fuel supply. On that basis the speed of the practice must be at a rate which will allow you the time to get to the shuttle and time to recover to the midcourt. You will be expected to travel very quickly to get to the shuttle but you must take your time when performing the stroke to gain accuracy and not make an error. ***Don't rush your strokes!*** You should decide on the speed with your practice partner.

INTENSITY: If you are using your feelings as a guide (see chapter 13, page 131) then make the pace about somewhat hard.

How long shall I practise for?
Your fitness level will determine how long you practise within each zone and although the practice will help to develop your fitness you should make sure that the emphasis is on the development of your technical skill. As you will operate on your oxygen energy system and depend on your 'heart and lungs' endurance you can probably rally for 1-3 minutes.

DURATION: 1-3 minutes and then have a recovery period of half or of the same duration.

RALLIES: the amount of time will allow you to rally for about 30-100 shots.

Which zones shall I practise in?
Ideally you should practise in each zone until you feel confident that you are in complete control of that area of the court. If you do not have time for this in one session then select one or two zones only for each practice session.

THE ZONES *continued*

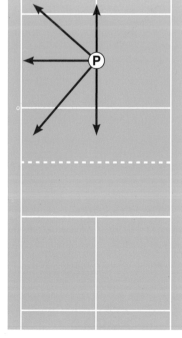

Fig 56
fc/mc/rc

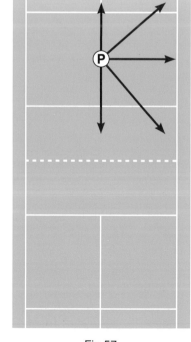

Fig 57
fc/mc/rc

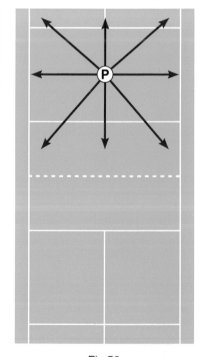

Fig 58
rc/mc/fc

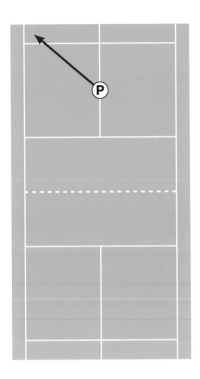

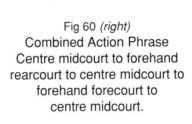

Fig 59 *(left)*
Single Action Phrase
Centre midcourt to
forehand rearcourt.

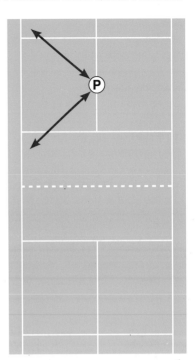

Fig 60 *(right)*
Combined Action Phrase
Centre midcourt to forehand
rearcourt to centre midcourt to
forehand forecourt to
centre midcourt.

ACTION PHRASE PRACTICES

The emphasis here is on developing your technical skill in doing action phrases at various speeds within the oxygen energy system. The rallies can be speeded up or slowed down as you agree with your feeder.

Your feeder will be positioned in the rearcourt so you will practise lobs and clears only as building shots within each action phrase. These are reasonably easy to perform and should help you to become very skilful in performing all aspects of an action phrase. They include single action phrases and combined action phrases. *See* Figs 59 and 60.

Rather than draw the court each time to show an action phrase I usually draw one as an arrow with a '●' to show the court starting position. *See* Fig 61.

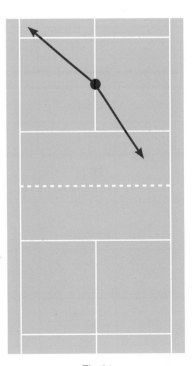

 shows the court starting position

 shows the direction and distance travelled

Fig 61

Aims of Practice
To develop your skill in moving, your accuracy and your consistency.

Practice Stage: 4
There will not be any uncertainty in this practice.

How do I do the practice?
You simply travel from your midcourt starting position to the shuttle, hit it back to your feeder and recover to your starting position before your feeder hits the shuttle back again. Make sure that you hit good building shots each time.

Where should my feeder stand?
He can stand in the left, centre or right rearcourt as you decide. This will allow you to hit straight and cross-court clears and lobs with accuracy and consistency.

How hard must I practise?
Work at a rate which allows you to stay within the oxygen energy system. A somewhat hard steady rate of work.

How long shall I practise for?
As you are doing repetitions to develop accuracy and consistency I have started you off at 10 repetitions for each action phrase. You can increase this up to anything between 10 and 50 repetitions.

Use this Action Phrase Practice Programme
Now look at the chart below which provides you with an action phrase programme.

ACTION PHRASE	STROKE	FEEDER'S POSITION	REPETITIONS	COMMENTS
	fh clear			
	fh clear			
	bh clear			
	fh/bh clear			
	fh lob			
	bh lob			
	fh/bh lob			
	fh clear fh lob			
	bh clear bh lob			
	fh clear bh lob			
	bh clear fh lob			
	fh/bh clear bh/fh lob			

CONTINUOUS RALLY PRACTICE

The idea here is that you learn to control the whole court and play the complete range of possible strokes. This will involve numerous action phrases, a high degree of uncertainty and a feeder with high-level racket and stroke skill. Your feeder will adopt various court positions during each long rally to enable him to play all the stroke-moves from his rearcourt, midcourt and forecourt. Your task will be to return the shuttle to him throughout the rally.

This practice is excellent for developing your technical skill. It also helps to improve your fitness and mental attitude. A high level of concentration, determination, perseverance and patience is required to do the practice properly and without error. It is an excellent confidence-building practice.

Aims of Practice

To develop your skill in moving and your racket and stroke skills.

Practice Stage: 5

You will experience a high level of uncertainty.

How do I do the practice?

Stand positioned in your centre midcourt as shown in Fig 62, with your feeder in his first court starting position ready to begin the rally. Your feeder should call out what he wants when he changes his court position after he has worked you from one position. He should call:

'Shots to the rearcourt forehand, centre, backhand.'
'Shots to the midcourt forehand, centre, backhand.'
'Shots to the forecourt forehand, centre, backhand.'

Your task will be to return the shuttle to the feeder with whatever building or attempted winning shot seems best.

Where should my feeder stand?

In the various positions indicated in Fig 62 in the rearcourt, midcourt and forecourt.

How hard must I practise?

You should work at a rate which allows you to operate on your oxygen energy system. The pace therefore should be fairly light to somewhat hard

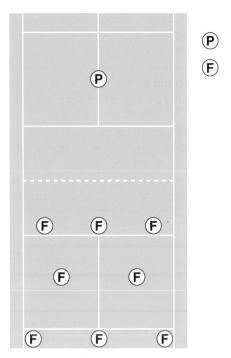

Fig 62

in the early days and then increase this to somewhat hard to hard. You can build up to making it very hard providing that you stay within the oxygen energy system.

How long shall I practise for?

I usually begin with players doing about 1½-2 minutes' work and the same amount of rest for about 3 repetitions. Gradually I would increase this depending on the fitness level to 5 repetitions of 3 minutes (15 minutes total time) until they can do 6 repetitions of 5 minutes or 3 repetitions of 10 minutes (30 minutes total time). The rest interval is usually the same amount or half the amount of time. As I have mentioned previously, high-level technical practices must conform to the fitness training methods of interval training.

MULTIFEED PRACTICE

The purpose of this practice is not so much to develop your technical skill but to quicken your reactions. You can develop your reaction speed in several ways. These are:

● Your speed in anticipating where the shuttle will be hit, which comes from 'reading' your opponent's body language correctly. This is something that you already do when you play against opponents whose game you know well.

● Your speed in transmitting the appropriate message from your brain to your muscles – the message that says 'Respond now!'

● Your speed of movement to the shuttle which will depend on how efficient your 'fast twitch muscle' fibres are and whether you have sufficient energy. I expect you have experienced times when you know what you want to do and your body just doesn't want to know.

● Your speed of movement from the shuttle into position to cover the opponent's next shot.

Aims of Practice
To improve your reaction and movement speed.

Practice Stage: 5
There will be constant uncertainty to the extent that there may be a lowering of your standard of technical skill.

How do I do the practice?
You start from the centre midcourt and then simply try to reach and hit any shuttle with whatever type of shot seems appropriate. As soon as you have hit or missed one shuttle you must recover very quickly to get to the next one which your feeder will hit.

Where should my feeder stand – and what does he try to do?
The position of your feeder may vary. See Fig 63.

In the rearcourt he will be more effective standing on a table or a chair so he can hit overhead clears, smashes and drops from a high position.

In the midcourt and forecourt he can remain on the floor to hit shuttles mainly upwards or drive them at you from shoulder height.

The feeder will require a large supply of shuttles, carried in a box or a multishuttle holder. He should be able to hit shuttles to various parts of your court in a regular rhythm.

The success of this practice is dependent on the skill of your feeder. His task is to stretch you, to make you change direction quickly, sprint, jump,

twist and turn all at a very fast pace. It will, however, be ineffective if he makes the practice too difficult for you. He should hit shuttles so that you can just get to them with an effort.

How hard must I practise?
Obviously you have got to work very hard to move very quickly. You will be using your anaerobic energy system (*see* page 134) rather than your oxygen system as your main fuel supply. You can practise using your oxygen system but you would move at a slower pace and you might not gain the same benefits. The fitness demands of this practice are very intensive. You need a good range of flexibility, strength and power and endurance to complete the exercise without risking injury. *If you have not developed these fitness components you would be advised not to do this practice*.

Generally you should work at an intensity of 85 –100 per cent effort. This means that you will be working anaerobically using your lactic energy system and your phosphagen energy system (*see* page 134).

How long shall I practise for?
As the intensity and duration of this practice is determined by your fitness you must practise within the time-scales allowed for anaerobic training. The practice must take the form of interval practice in which you work and then rest for the recommended period of time. For example if you are working at 100 per cent intensity then you will work for 10–20 seconds and then rest for 5 times that period, 50–100 seconds, the work/rest ratio being 1:5.

THE PRACTICE ROUTINES
I have devised three variations of this practice, each one describing how to do intensive practice using the anaerobic energy system or the oxygen system. If you do not follow this procedure and do not allow the recommended time to recover you will find that you will not be able to keep up such a high work rate and you will lose the benefits of the practice.

1ST PRACTICE (phosphagen energy system)
Duration of Practice: 10–20 seconds.
Intensity: 100 per cent – very very hard.

| Sets: | 10 (each one of 10–20 seconds). |
| Work/Rest Ratio: | 1:5. A rest period of 50–100 seconds of active recovery, i.e. walk around as you recover. |

2ND PRACTICE (lactic energy system)

Duration of Practice:	30-60 seconds.
Intensity:	90 per cent for 30 seconds to 80 per cent for 60 seconds – very hard.
Sets:	5.
Work/Rest Ratio:	1:3.

3RD PRACTICE (oxygen system)

Duration of Practice:	1½–2 minutes.
Intensity:	70–80 per cent – hard (close to your anaerobic threshold).
Sets:	5.
Work/Rest Ratio:	1:1 or 1:1½ depending on how fit you are.

Do not forget

The emphasis is on your developing the various aspects that make up your reaction speed. It is not to develop your fitness although this will be developed in the practice. If you focus on reaction speed then you can adapt the practice as you do it. You may for example ask your feeder to concentrate on developing your reaction speed in going backwards or changing direction to your non-racket side. This is not simply an exercise in 'retrieve the shuttle' but rather an attempt to improve your skill and speed in reacting and moving in different ways in different parts of the court.

Final Comment

There are many variations on these sorts of pressure practices. I am sure that you will have experienced others. What I hope you will understand is that the intensity and duration of a pressure practice should be related to your current fitness levels. You should only practise as hard as you are capable of and for the recommended fitness work/rest period for a practice of that intensity.

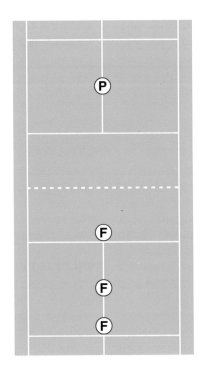

Fig 63

chapter 13

Get Yourself Fit for Badminton

You only have one body: make certain that you know how to take care of it.

This chapter outlines how you can get fit by creating your own fitness training programme. Getting fit is a gradual process which can be enjoyable so long as you know what you are doing. With a planned approach to fitness training you can forget about the 'pain barrier' or other such labels. There are good reasons why fitness training must be hard work but there is no reason why you must suffer in order to get fit. If at any time you are suffering and in pain then you are doing the wrong training or you are medically ill, e.g. a fever, injury. In either case you must stop to adjust your training schedule or visit a doctor.

It is not only in fitness training that you might be suffering unnecessarily. It can also happen when you are supposedly practising. I say supposedly because I have seen coaches pushing their players hard for 5–15 minutes and longer with totally inadequate rest periods in multifeed sessions of continuous 'chase and get back the shuttle'-type rallies. I have often wondered whether the coaches knew what they were actually trying to develop in their players and certainly the players did not, otherwise they would have changed their coaches. The result of such work is usually excessive fatigue, a lowering in the standard of technical skill, little opportunity for decision-making and so no development of tactical awareness and tactical skill improvement, an increased risk of injury and extra days to recover. When you have read this chapter you should be able to understand what such a coach is actually doing to your body and whether it is what it needs. Get to know your body and how far it can be pushed. If at any time you feel that a coach or feeder is forcing you to work too hard then stop and discuss the matter with your coach and find out what he is trying to achieve.

WHAT YOU NEED TO KNOW

There are several important questions you should consider in creating your own fitness programme. These are:

- Am I in good health and able to train for fitness?
- What is fitness?
- What do I need to do to get fit?
- How fit do I need to be?
- How do I maintain my fitness?

CREATE YOUR OWN FITNESS PROGRAMME

AM I IN GOOD HEALTH AND ABLE TO TRAIN FOR FITNESS?

If you are playing regularly at a good standard of play and suffer no ailments then you could say that you are in good health. If, however, you have any medical problems, e.g. get out of breath easily, suffer from asthma, get headaches or blurred vision when you play and tend to be injury-prone with backache, sore joints and muscle strains then you should ask your doctor to give you a medical check-up and some advice about what activities you can and cannot do. *If you have any doubts whatsoever please check with your doctor before you start any fitness programme*.

WHAT IS FITNESS?

Fitness refers to your physical and mental states. I am sure that you have gone on court feeling fit and yet proved to be quite unfit after a few minutes' hard play. Alternatively you could go on court knowing that you are superbly fit and yet not feel fit. To be fit for play you should be in a good physical and mental state.

The main purpose of fitness training is to make sure that you can last the pace in a hard game and recover quickly from fatigue. If you are not fit you will start to make errors, opt out of the work by going for quick winners, lose your confidence and become frustrated and angry with yourself. In short, you will play below standard and usually lose. Your mind may be willing but your body is not.

WHAT DO I NEED TO DO TO GET FIT?

Fitness Components To get fit you should develop certain fitness components which include: endurance (stamina), flexibility, strength, speed and power. You should also know how to maintain the correct body weight.

Exercise You will develop these fitness components by exercising in different ways, i.e. fitness training.

Diet You will need *fuel* for energy to do the work and this you will get from eating the correct foods. You will also need sufficient fluid (water) to keep you hydrated. Insufficient fluid may cause early fatigue and damage to your health.

Rest You will need *time* to *rest* and *recover* from the exercise so you can refuel and allow your body to change towards its improved physical state.

Fitness Standards You should set some fitness goals which are to some extent built into the fitness components. Imagine the ultra-fit player who is tireless, strong, fast, powerful, agile, flexible, lean, athletic and muscular. Whether you intend to train to reach this level of fitness depends on the level at which you play. If you are striving to become fitter to get on to the club team such a degree of fitness, though useful, might well be more than you need. If, however, you want to become a world-class player then you will have little choice but to train to reach this standard of fitness.

General Rules You should follow these general rules, usually known as the *Principles of Training* which will act as guidelines when planning your fitness programme. They will help you to decide how much training you should do and when you should to it.

1 Build up a general level of fitness.
2 Train *specifically* for badminton.
3 Design a programme for your *specific* fitness needs. General training may be all right for a group of players but eventually the programme must be designed to cater for your particular needs.
4 *Overload* your training. Increase the amount of exercising that you do in training.
5 Allow time for your body to *adapt* to the work overload in training.
6 Make your training *progressive*. Overload your training in a gradual progression.
7 Vary your training to make it more interesting and enjoyable.
8 *Measure* and *keep a record* of your progress.
9 *Diet* properly. Eat the right amount and type of food for your needs and do so at the right time; drink sufficient water even if you do not feel thirsty.
10 Allow for a fall in your fitness level if you cannot train for any reason, e.g. because of injury.
11 Make sure that you **rest** properly.
12 **Balance** your training, practice and competition with your social life. But make sure that you place these in the appropriate order of priority according to what you want to achieve.

HOW FIT DO I NEED TO BE?
Performance Level

This depends on your present *performance* level, e.g. club or local district league team player, which is usually decided by how skilful you are. You should be able to play at your present performance level without risk of injuring yourself due to a lack of fitness. This is the minimum level of fitness you should have. If you are a club player you might find that you can get fit enough to play at the required performance level by regular play rather than by specific fitness training.

At the higher levels of play you must be prepared to compete against players of a higher skill performance level which may require you to become fitter to cope with their level of play. Likewise, if you aspire to world-class play you should become as fit as you can possibly be even if such a level of fitness is, at first, more than you need to cope with the demands of your current level of play. In this case even if your fitness level does exceed your skill performance level you are going to need that fitness in order to do the work in practice and competition to raise your skill performance to a higher level.

Choice

You have two choices. You can get fit enough to play at your present performance level only, or you can get fit enough to play at higher performance levels, which may mean that you become fitter than you presently need to be.

HOW DO I MAINTAIN MY FITNESS?

Once you have reached a certain fitness level then you can reduce the amount of overload and just do sufficient exercise on each of the fitness components to maintain your current level of fitness. If you have achieved a high level of fitness you will not be able to maintain your fitness by just playing games. You will have to continue your training even though you may reduce the amount of training that you do. The reason for this is that fitness training exercises are carefully designed and your programme is organised to develop the fitness components; they ensure that all aspects of your fitness are developed and that you can meet the varying physical demands of practice and competition.

How will I know whether my fitness level is not being maintained?

You can get yourself scientifically tested by an exercise physiologist at a sports clinic. Alternatively you can judge yourself. You may be slower and weaker, you may not be able to match or last the pace of the game, you tire too quickly and you are taking two days to recover instead of recovering after a good night's sleep. Ask any good athlete about fitness and he will confirm that once you have reached a high level of fitness you will certainly know if you are losing it and need to do more training.

Advice

Don't try to learn and remember the technical words or descriptions in this chapter. Just read on and at the end you should gain a good working knowledge of how to improve your fitness. If any part interests you then read that again later.

HOW DO I GET FIT?

The main components of getting fit are training (exercise), rest and diet. Training includes everything to do with practical exercise and so I will explain that first. Rest (recovery) time will be included as part of the training programmes and will be apparent to you as you read through this section. Diet is discussed further on in this chapter.

Training

The purpose of training is to make your body function more efficiently. To do this you must improve the level of efficiency of your fitness components.

Different types of exercise are used for this purpose, e.g. running, skipping, stretching and weight training. Exercise is *work*. When you exercise you move. All movement is dependent on muscular contractions of varying degrees of intensity and rate over a period of time. When you smash, for example, your muscles will contract more intensely than when you do the low serve.

To improve the efficiency of your muscles you should consider:
a) the quality of their contraction which affects your muscle strength
b) the supply of energy to your muscles.

Muscular Contraction

Your muscles comprise two types of muscle fibre. These are *slow*- and *fast-contracting* fibres – usually known as *slow-twitch* and *fast-twitch* fibres. You will use your slow-twitch fibres to a greater extent in endurance-type activities, whereas you will use your fast-twitch fibres more in speed activities. As badminton is a game that entails both, though in doubles there is a greater emphasis on speed than endurance, any training must include exercises which develop both types of muscle fibre. You should do, therefore, endurance, strength, speed and power exercises.

Energy Supply

Your muscles require a constant supply of energy. This energy comes from two main sources: the oxygen from the atmosphere and the chemical energy that comes from food. Both undergo a complex series of changes before being converted into the energy used for muscular activity. There are two types of energy system. These are the aerobic energy system, which is dependent on oxygen; and the anaerobic energy system which is dependent on chemicals obtained from food and which are stored in the muscles. (*See* pages 131 and 134) Right now let's begin with how you would prepare for and recover from training, practice and play.

How should I prepare for and recover from hard exercise?

You should always prepare properly for hard work and allow enough time to recover properly afterwards. I know many players who don't warm up before a game; they do it during the first game. They are the slow starters who usually take the first eight points to warm up by which time they are often losing the game. 'I always lose the first game,' they say, as if that were quite acceptable. If you are one of these then try warming up before you play and you might be surprised at the difference. If you are playing against one of these players then, if you win the first game, make sure that you keep the pressure on in the second game. Be prepared for them to start playing better now that they have warmed up, so fight hard to maintain your lead and win.

PREPARATION – WARM-UP

The purpose of warming up is:

● to raise your body temperature
● to warm and stretch your muscles and so increase your flexibility for play
● to increase your heart rate (HR)
● to increase the volume of oxygenated blood to the working muscles.

The reasons for warming up are to make sure that you are physically and mentally ready for intense activity, i.e. you can make a flying start, and it reduces the risk of muscle injury.

I recommend four stages for a complete badminton warm-up, although this can vary according to whether you are warming up for formal competition or informal competition, practice or training.

STAGE 1: Five minutes' continuous exercise to raise your heart rate and increase your oxygen uptake, e.g. jogging, running, skipping. Then walk about for a minute or two and begin:

STAGE 2: Stretching exercises to 'loosen' you up for play. Make sure that you stretch all the main muscle groups in the body. *See* pages 132 – 133.

STAGE 3: Do fast reaction movements. *See* pages 140–1 for speed exercises.

STAGE 4: Simulate the game movements, e.g. shadow badminton.

Recovery – Cool-Down

The purpose of cool-down is to help you to recover quickly from the hard activity. It will:

● lower your heart rate and body temperature
● help to remove waste deposits from your body
● help to prevent stiffness and soreness in your muscles after hard exercise
● help to save energy.

The cool-down should include jogging, walking and some stretching. You should change into dry clothes to speed up the cool-down.

FLEXIBILITY
What is flexibility?

When you are flexible, also referred to as supple or mobile, you will be able to increase the range of movement at your joints. You will, for example, be able to touch your toes easily, lean backwards, twist your shoulders to prepare for the smash, perform full lunges and perhaps even do the splits.

Why do I need flexibility?

With greater flexibility you should be able to move more easily, reduce the risk of possible injury and improve your skill in moving.

Slow Stretching – how to become flexible?

You simply stretch your muscles by a process known as **slow stretching** which is the form most recommended by physiotherapists. It is also known as active stretching because you will use your own muscle strength to stretch other muscles.

How does a muscle stretch?

A muscle is made up of many fibres, once described to me as similar to a packet of spaghetti. *See* Fig 64. Each fibre is crimped. Stretching straightens out the crimp so that the muscle extends and allows you to move your limbs further. There is of course a limit to how far you can stretch a muscle fibre. This is because your muscle has a built-in safety device called the **stretch reflex**. As you stretch your muscle a reflexive contraction occurs to prevent it stretching any further and causing damage to the muscle.

Muscle

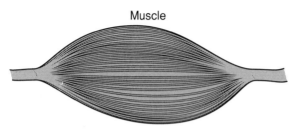

Fig 64

If you stretch **quickly** there is a **strong** reflex contraction. You cannot stretch any further, or you may tear the muscle fibres. If you stretch **slowly** there is a **weak** reflex contraction. You could stretch further more easily without doing damage.

How do I overcome the stretch reflex?
You must overcome the stretch reflex if you want to improve your flexibility. An effective way to do this is by **active stretching** done **slowly** (slow stretching). Active stretching also helps to strengthen some muscles as well as stretch others.

How long must I stretch for?
Six seconds is considered to be the minimum time required to overcome the stretch reflex, although some exercise physiologists recommend holding the stretched position for up to thirty seconds. I find that doing four repetitions of 10–12 seconds for each muscle group works well in increasing my flexibility. However, to achieve the maximum benefit your stretching must start from the **end position**. For example if you place your arms vertically above your head now and press backwards that will be your **end position**. It is as far as you can stretch at this moment. Now if you press back further for 10–12 seconds you will find that you can stretch beyond that end position. This is what you

want to achieve in all the stretching exercises included below.

How often must I stretch?
I would recommend a minimum of three times each week on alternate days and a maximum of six days each week. You will find that this will be beneficial particularly if you also include the stretching exercises as part of your warm-up.

EXERCISES TO IMPROVE YOUR FLEXIBILITY
There are many books containing stretching exercises and even though I am sure that you will know many exercises I have included here a few of those which I find useful for badminton players.

SLOW STRETCHING EXERCISES
The purpose of each exercise is to stretch the muscles at a particular joint or part of the body, e.g. knee joint. The stretching helps you to increase your range of movement at that joint, i.e. your *flexibility*. This helps general movement in play and improves the capacity to play harder, lessens the risk of injury and helps you to recover quickly after hard exercise. After each exercise, 'shake out' loosely to release any muscle tension built up doing the exercise. Breathe normally.

DEVELOPING YOUR ENDURANCE
You need to have good endurance (sometimes called stamina) to train or play for long periods of time. There are two main types of endurance:*

Long-Term Endurance – the capacity of your heart and lungs to work efficiently in supplying large supplies of oxygen to your working muscles for long periods of time. It is also described as **aerobic (oxygen)** endurance or **heart and lungs** endurance. Oxygen is required at your working muscles as energy. Your lungs, blood and heart are all involved in this transfer and must be highly efficient to ensure that oxygen reaches your muscles with the minimum of delay.

Short-Term Endurance – also known as **anaerobic endurance** involves the supply of energy for short intense bursts of work, e.g. when you perform a quick jump smash or sprint from the rearcourt to the forecourt. Anaerobic means without oxygen

---

* Dr Craig Sharp, *Developing Endurance*, National Coaching Foundation Resource Pack, page 4.

and in your *anaerobic energy system* the energy is obtained from chemicals stored in your muscles.

You may also be familiar with the phrase *local muscular endurance* which is the capacity to repeat movements continuously without getting too tired, e.g. doing press-ups or hitting fifty clears. This type of endurance usually depends mainly on the oxygen energy system for its supply of energy and should therefore be included as part of your training for long-term endurance.

To improve your endurance you will need to develop the *system* in your body which provides you with the *fuel* to do the work and then removes the *waste deposits* that are left as you use up the fuel. The fuel provides you with the energy for the type of endurance work you are doing. When a car gets its energy from petrol and air fuel it uses up and removes the waste deposits through the exhaust system. Your body operates in a similar way.

When you develop your endurance you must develop your energy systems; the aerobic energy system and the anaerobic energy system.

DEVELOP YOUR AEROBIC (OXYGEN) ENERGY SYSTEM

This is used as the main energy supply for your long-term endurance. Your heart and lungs must become very efficient in taking oxygen from the air and sending it via your blood to your working muscles. In this system oxygen is the fuel used to provide the energy for your muscles.

The *amount* of oxygen that you are able to take from the air and send to your working muscles is know as VO2 Max – the maximum volume of oxygen. You can increase this amount with training and so increase the amount of fuel you can obtain for energy.

Training will increase the size of the chambers of your heart and also strengthen the muscles of your heart. As your heart is like a pump, that means you will pump out more oxygenated blood with each beat. A trained heart will beat slower than an untrained heart when doing the same amount of work. It will be more efficient.

How do I develop my aerobic (oxygen) system?

You can do this in two ways:

- By doing *continuous exercise* at the same rate. We call this *steady state* exercise.

- By doing *interval training* in which you exercise, rest, exercise, rest etc.

What volume (quantity) of work is required?

Steady State Training If you do steady state training for a minimum of twenty minutes three times each week you will improve your aerobic endurance. Such training should usually be done in the off-season. This will be sufficient as a start but if you want to play at higher levels of play then you would expect to increase this to doing 30–40 minutes five times each week. It is also beneficial to do your training on the same days as you do your flexibility exercises.

Interval training If you do interval training for five repetitions of three minutes' exercise with a three-minute rest interval between each repetition you will also improve your fitness. This type of training is a good progression from continuous steady state training as you can begin to train at higher speeds as the badminton season gets nearer.

How intensely (hard) must I exercise?

Usually intensity of exercise is related to the effect it has on your heart rate. Obviously the harder the exercise the higher your heart rate. When you are just starting steady state training then it is wise to exercise at what is called *conversation rate*. That is, you can talk as you exercise. As you get fitter you can increase the intensity so that it is difficult to talk without getting out of breath. This would also apply when you are doing interval training. Do not, however, train too hard to develop your aerobic energy system as you will risk going into your anaerobic energy system and then you will not improve your long-term endurance.

Rely on your Feelings!

My advice here is rely on your feelings to guide you. You can train at a fairly light intensity or one that is somewhat hard. The harder it is the more intense it will be. If you possess one of the heart monitor watches then you can still use your feelings but also check your actual heart rate on the monitor. This will give you a more accurate indication of how intensely you are training and how fit you are becoming.

JOINT	STARTING POSITION	EXERCISE	HOW TO PERFORM IT	REPETITIONS	MUSCLES STRETCHED	BENEFITS
Knee & Ankle	Legs tensed	Foot Extension	Press feet and toes forwards to full extension to a slow count of **12** and then release	4		Greater thrust in lunge and jumps. Helps to slow down and change direction quickly and landing and balance
Knee & Ankle	Legs tensed	Foot Contraction	Pull feet and toes towards you. Hold for slow count of **12** and release	4		Cushions landing after jumps and helps thrust away from the floor. Important for agility and balance
Knee Joint & Hip Joint	Legs tensed throughout exercise	Alternate Leg Raising	Stretch foot and raise right leg to slow count of **6**. Repeat with other leg	4		Stretches hamstrings and allows maximum thrust when you lunge and jump
Knee & Hip Joint	Both legs tensed	Knee to Chest contraction	Lift knee to chest and keep resting leg tensed. Press knee down for count of **12** and release. Do **4** reps. and repeat with other leg	4 each leg		Helps jumps and lunges and general agility
Hip Joint	Sitting on floor	Knee Presses	Press knees towards floor. Hold for count of **12** and release	4	Inner side of thigh	Greater flexibility in lunge. Aids recovery
Lower Back, Hips, Knees & Shoulders	Legs flexed	Back Extension	Slide hands down shins, drop head towards knees and reach towards toes. Keep legs tensed. Hold for count of **12** and release	4		Greater flexibility for stretching out for shuttles in play
Lower Back, Hips, Knees & Shoulders	Legs tensed	Back & Leg Extension	Slide hands forwards on floor between legs. Legs as far apart as possible and held tensed. Hold for count of **12** and release	4		Greater stretch in side and forward lunges and backward scissor jump to **RC**
Side Trunk, Lower Back, Hips, Knees & Shoulders			Reach forward over one leg. Other leg is flexed. Count of **12**	4		Helps lunge and stretching movements in forecourt and jump smashes. Helps twisting movements

JOINT	STARTING POSITION	EXERCISE	HOW TO PERFORM IT	REPETITIONS	MUSCLES STRETCHED	BENEFITS
Hip, Chest		Back Arches	Arch back and lift chest and head by pushing with hands. Hold for **12** seconds and release. Keep hips on floor	4		Helps arching back for smash and good posture (upright) when lunging and recovering
Knee & Ankle	(a) Feet together Legs tensed (b)	Plié	Keep feet flat on floor. Lower trunk by bending knees and pressing knee directly over the feet. Count **12** slowly. Straighten legs slowly Count of **12**. (a) Right leg (b) Left leg	4 4		Helps jumps and landings, lunge and recovery. General agility and speed. Helps balance and posture
Hip, Knees & Lower Back	Legs tensed. Arms held in balance. Face front foot	Lunges	Rear foot turned outwards. Front foot forward. Lower body in lunge. Press for **12** seconds. Return to starting position	Right leg × **4** Left leg × **4**		Greater strength and control in lunge. Improves balance
Hip, Lower Back, Knee	As above	Forward Splits	Support weight on two chairs. Stretch front foot forward into splits. Count **12** and release	Right leg × **4** Left leg × **4**		Greater strength and control. Helps lunge and recovery
Shoulders	(a)	Shoulder Press	Press shoulder back to count of **12**. Release	4		More preparation in overhead strokes. Greater power
	(b) Arms straight	Shoulder Stretch	Stretch shoulder and arms upwards to count of **12**. Release	4		More stretch in reaching for shuttle
	(c)	Backward Stretch	Bend arms and reach down back. Press to Count of **12**. Release	4		More stretch in backward movements
Shoulders & Trunk		Trunk Twists	Twist trunk to right to look behind you. Press for count of **12**. Release. Do **4** reps and repeat on left side	4 right 4 left	Muscles of trunk	Greater range of movement in twisting for **fh** and **bh** shots
Trunk		Side Leans	Lean over on side and press down for count of **12**. Release	4 right 4 left	Side muscles	Helps reaching for shuttle and leaning to intercept overhead shots

What endurance training methods shall I use?

There are several methods you can use: running, cycling, skipping, shadow badminton, continuous rallying.

What happens if I go too fast?

If you do this you will also use your **anaerobic energy system** (without oxygen). There is only sufficient fuel in this system for a short period of maximal work, i.e. 40–60 seconds. When that is used up you will slow right down or stop – take deep breaths, refuel with oxygen and try to remove some of the waste products that you have built up.

DEVELOP YOUR ANAEROBIC ENERGY SYSTEM

First, I will explain how this functions.

The **fuel** used is the chemicals in your muscles. The main one is **glycogen** which comes from **carbohydrates** provided in the food you eat. There are two energy systems which operate in this system. These are the **lactic** energy system and the **phosphagen** energy system.

The Lactic Energy System

Glucose from your blood or **glycogen** from your muscle cells are used to produce energy. The by-product is **pyruvate** which converts to **lactic acid**. This system provides you with about 30–40 seconds of fuel if you are exercising intensely. You must work at over 80 per cent intensity effort to produce lactic acid.

What happens when the fuel is used up?

Lactic acid is a waste product which will cause you to seize up and have to slow down and revert to the **oxygen energy system** until you have diffused the lactic acid (the waste deposits) from your muscles to the blood and cleared it away in the blood.

Example: You may have experienced this at school in athletics. If you have ever had to run a 400-metre race and seized up on the last bend after about 40 seconds' running you will have slowed down and changed to your oxygen system and taken deep breaths to recover.

How long does it take to clear the lactic acid away from the blood?

When you are training it is usually recommended that you should allow twice the time to recover as your work takes, i.e. 1:2 is the ratio of work to rest (active recovery). In actual fact there may be a level of lactic acid in your blood even after ten minutes of rest. Though a work: rest ratio of 1:2 is appropriate for training purposes, particularly when you are also developing your capacity to tolerate lactic acid in your blood, it is insufficient to remove all the lactic acid. You will find that as you continue to do your work intervals the lactic acid level will rise. It is mainly for that reason that only two sets of ten repetitions are advised and that you take a rest (active recovery) of ten minutes between sets.

The Phosphagen Energy System

This uses a chemical called phosphocreatine as its fuel. It provides fuel for 5–10 seconds' work depending on how intensely you work. You must work at 100 per cent intensity to use this energy system. When you have done so you will require 5–6 times as long to recover, e.g. if you run at 100 per cent effort for ten seconds you will require 50–60 seconds' rest to recover.

How shall I train my Energy Systems?

When you exercise, therefore, you can use all three energy systems to obtain fuel for your needs. Oxygen is the main fuel supply and the others provide a different fuel to give you a short supply of energy for intense work. When you have used these up you must slow down and use the oxygen system for a time until you have cleared away the waste deposits and refuelled.

When you train you must train to develop all these energy systems so that in a tournament you can either play fast and stay on the oxygen system where there is a constant supply of fuel; or you can play fast using an anaerobic energy system and recover more quickly after intense rallies.

Each energy system must be trained separately. It is possible to train all the systems separately in the same training session or day. If you do so you must start with the more intense anaerobic training and progress to the less intense aerobic training. Hence you will train your phosphagen energy system, then your lactic acid system and finally your oxygen system.

Opposite is an example of how a well-trained fit

player will have the advantage over an unfit player of equal ability.

Imagine that as the game continues the pace of the rallies increases. At the point when the players are playing at ten miles per hour the very fit player's heart rate is still quite low and he is still using his oxygen system alone. But the less fit player finds that his heart rate increases so much that he cannot obtain sufficient oxygen and he has to use his anaerobic energy system also.

What are the implications?

Let us assume that the rally at ten miles per hour has lasted forty seconds and the less fit player has been using his lactic energy system. You know now that there will be an increase in the level of lactic acid in his blood. He will normally require eighty seconds to recover to some extent as the work: rest ratio in training is recommended as 1:2, and even then there would still be a level of lactic acid in the blood. Unfortunately for this player the interval between rallies usually ranges from eight to twenty seconds. Consequently the less fit player cannot recover fully before the next rally. The next rally starts and the fit player decides to play another long rally at a fast pace. The less fit player

soon goes anaerobic again and as he has not recovered fully he has to slow down to use his oxygen system. He cannot keep up with the pace and so loses the rally again.

The anaerobic threshold

With training the very fit player has raised the level at which he must resort to his anaerobic energy system. He can play at an intense pace for longer periods of time and maintain a lower heart rate and function on his oxygen system. The rate of play would have to become very intense to increase his heart rate and cause him to use his anaerobic energy system. The less fit player is unable to play at the same pace and soon reaches a threshold, the *anaerobic threshold*, at which point he must switch from using his oxygen system solely to using his anaerobic energy system also.

Raising your anaerobic threshold

Through regular long-term endurance training (steady state and interval) you will develop your aerobic energy system, thus allowing you to do more work aerobically. This will also allow you to increase your work rate up to your anaerobic threshold.

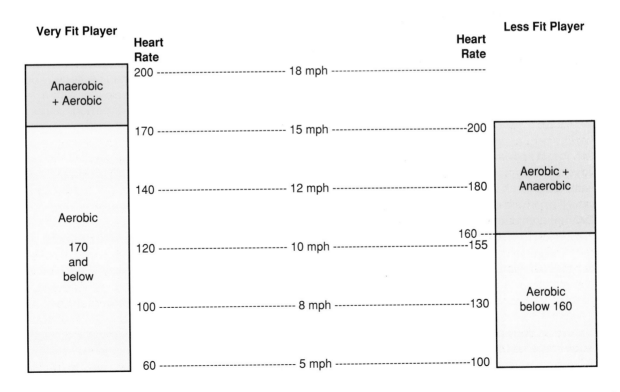

TRAIN TO DEVELOP YOUR OXYGEN ENERGY SYSTEM

This training will help to develop your heart and lungs endurance. Always start with a warm-up (stages 1 and 2) and cool down to recover.

1ST METHOD: Steady State Training (continuous exercise) – running or cycling

VOLUME: Minimum of 20 minutes 3 to 5 times each week.
You can build this up to 40 minutes' training.

INTENSITY: Start at fairly light, increase this to somewhat hard.

Advice: If you are not very fit when you begin you can combine running and walking until you are fit enough to run continuously. Remember that you should not suffer as you exercise. Gradually overload your training and enjoy the exercise.
Set yourself a target and try to increase the distance you run or cycle in the time.

2ND METHOD: Interval Training – running or cycling

VOLUME: 15 minutes minimum – 5 repetitions of 3 minutes – 3 to 5 days a week. You can increase this up to 30 minutes – 6 repetitions of 5 minutes.

INTENSITY: Hard but not too hard.

WORK: RECOVERY RATIO: 1:1 or 1:½ which would be more appropriate for an endurance effect as you get fitter.

Advice: Do not start intense interval training until you can run for a minimum of twenty minutes continuously at a somewhat hard pace. Then you can alternate steady state with interval training so that you complete three to five aerobic sessions each week in the off-season.

3RD METHOD: On-court interval training – shadow badminton

VOLUME: 15 minutes: 5 repetitions of 3 minutes, 3 times each week on alternative days. Increase this to 5 times a week and also increase the volume up to 6 repetitions of 5 minutes or 3 repetitions

of 10 minutes.

INTENSITY: Hard but not too hard.

WORK: RECOVERY RATIO: 1:1 or 1:½ as you get fitter.

4TH METHOD: On-court interval training – continuous rallies
This is similar to the third method except that you rally continuously with a feeder.
See Fig 65. The feeder stands in different hitting positions in the court during the work period of 3–10 minutes and hits the shuttle anywhere into your court. Your task is to hit the shuttle to the feeder who also functions as a target. Although the aim of the session is fitness training you should still concentrate on hitting good building shots with accuracy and consistency: and move skilfully as you perform the body skill components.

Comment: This is a very effective method which I often use when training players since any fitness improvements are directly related to badminton fitness. It also demands a very high skill level from any player or feeder (practice partner or coach). This is particularly so if the feeder is hitting smashes, attack clears, and using deception. In fact I remember one particular session with Paul Whetnall who was then the English National Singles Champion, a world-class player and seeded 7 in the All England Championships. I was the feeder and kept the rallies going at an intense pace. We completed 3 repetitions of 10 minutes with a 3-minutes rest between each work period. During the total time of 30 minutes Paul made only 2 errors. We reckoned that if he could keep that pace up for 30 minutes and only make 2 errors he could contend with most players in singles which was the case with one exception at the time, Rudi Hartono, the great Indonesian singles player.

TRAIN TO DEVELOP YOUR ANAEROBIC ENERGY SYSTEM

The training methods used here will take the form of interval training as you must allow time to recover after short periods of intense exercise.

First I will explain how to train the lactic energy system and then the phosphagen energy system in off- and on-court training.

LACTIC ENERGY SYSTEM

METHOD: Off-court: running/cycling.
On-court: shadow badminton action phrases.

VOLUME: 10 minutes minimum.
Do 2 sets of 10 repetitions of 30 seconds' work.
Set 1: 30 seconds x 10 repetitions.
Set 2: 30 seconds x 10 repetitions.

INTENSITY: 80–90 per cent effort.

WORK: RECOVERY RATIO: 1:2. 30 seconds' work and 60 seconds' rest.
Take 10 minutes' rest between sets.

Advice: You can do one set on one day and the second set on another day if you wish. In the recovery interval you should walk around and keep active. This will help to clear away the waste deposits and aid your recovery.

PHOSPHAGEN ENERGY SYSTEM

METHOD: Off-court: running/cycling.
On-court: shadow badminton action phrases.

VOLUME: 3 minutes 20 seconds minimum.
Do 2 sets of 10 repetitions of 10 seconds.
Set 1: 10 seconds x 10 repetitions.
Set 2: 10 seconds x 10 repetitions.

INTENSITY: 100 per cent.

WORK: RECOVERY RATIO: 1:6. 10 seconds' work and 60 seconds' recovery.
Take 10 minutes' rest (active recovery) between sets.

Advice: Warm up and cool down thoroughly.

Comment: If you ever combine anaerobic training with aerobic training make sure that you begin with the anaerobic interval training. Do the intense work when your muscles are properly rested and capable of hard work with less risk of injury.

DEVELOP YOUR STRENGTH, POWER AND SPEED

These three fitness components are interrelated. Strength is your capacity to exert a force; power is your capacity to exert that force very quickly and

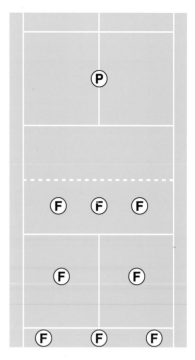

Fig 65
The feeder should keep about six shuttles to hand to keep feeding in case the rally breaks down.

speed is your capacity to move quickly over a distance. I don't have to tell you that you already do use these components in play.

Strength can be developed specifically by weight training using your own body weight, dumbbells, free weights or those of the multigym type now found in most sports centres. If you want to do weight training (with weights) obtain expert advice on what and how to do it before you start.

Power can be developed specifically by weight training and also by doing *plyometrics* which is a means of developing the *explosive power* you should possess.

Speed can be developed specifically by doing badminton-related exercises very quickly.

I will describe how to develop each fitness component in turn.

STRENGTH

The simplest method and the one I will describe here is **circuit training** in which you will use your own body weight to develop these components. I should also add that doing repetitions in a body circuit will also develop your local muscular endurance as will practising strokes to develop consistency.

METHOD: Body weight circuit training

There are numerous exercises that you can do. I like to keep them quite simple and add more to my circuit as I get fitter or to develop different muscle groups. As a badminton player you will need a good basic general body strength, e.g. shoulders and arms, trunk, upper and lower legs. The following circuit should help to develop this general strength. It is based on the principle of progressive overload.

VOLUME: 3 sets of repetitions of certain exercises. Do them 3 to 5 times each week.

INTENSITY: Perform them quickly but with good quality movement, i.e. complete each exercise properly.

Advice: Choose the A, B or C circuit. Go through the circuit 3 times (sets) in the order from 1 to 6. You can do repetitions from different circuits until you can do C circuit completely. When that becomes easy then increase the number of repetitions or add another set. Take adequate rest between exercises.

Exercise	Circuit and repetitions		
	A	B	C
1 Press-ups	10	15	20
2 Sit-ups (with bent knees)	10	15	20
3 Back Lifts	10	15	20
4 Squat Thrusts	5	10	15
5 Dips (using chair)	5	10	15
6 Tuck Jumps	5	10	15

DESCRIPTION

PRESS-UPS: On knees or fully prone position. (*See* Fig 66.)

SIT-UPS: Bent knees – hands on front of thighs – sit up and slide your hands to your knees and then lower your body to the floor.

BACK-LIFTS: As you arch your back make sure that you keep your feet and hips on the floor. (*See* Fig 67.)

BURPEES: Squat position. Thrust your legs backwards to extend them and then bring them forward to your knees again.(*see* Fig 68.)

DIPS: Hold chair as shown. Bend arms and straighten so pushing yourself up and down on the chair. (*See* Fig 69.)

TUCK JUMPS: Jump up and bring your knees to your chest. Rebound on landing. Repeat the tuck jump. (*See* Fig 70.)

POWER

In badminton it is explosive power that you will need most particularly in starting, changing direction, jumping and landing, and hitting. Once you have built up your basic strength and flexibility then you can focus on developing your explosive power. An effective method of doing this is plyometrics.

What is Plyometrics?

Plyometrics applies to movements in which you load your muscles very quickly and so activate the muscles' stretch reflexes to operate and cause an equally quick and additional powerful contraction of those muscles which you experience as the feeling of a rebound action in them. In effect the muscles are 'charged' with the result that they become stronger so that you can exert more force with them. The bounce start is a typical example of plyometric action. As you get ready to move, you bend your knees quickly which causes the stretch reflex in your thigh muscles to activate, your muscles contract and you feel the rebound in your muscles from which you can accelerate from the spot. Another example is in the throwing action. If you prepare to smash and take your shoulder back quickly then you will feel a bounce in your shoulder muscles which you can use to accelerate your arm forwards in a very fast powerful smash action. Try it again now that you know what to focus on.

It is limiting therefore, for coaches to teach you the throwing action by the old-fashioned method of starting with your racket head behind you in a 'scratching your back' position. The stretch reflex

Fig 66

Fig 66(a)

Fig 67

Fig 68

Fig 69

doesn't operate to help you to develop explosive power.

What Plyometric Exercises should I do?

There are exercises for all parts of your body but I would recommend that you work mainly on your legs which is where you will need explosive power for badminton. In normal play you will also be developing a certain amount of explosive power as you practise and play. If you want to learn more about plyometrics refer to the recommended book (*see* page 192).

Leg Exercises Light quick rebound jumping exercises. Do only one set of the following exercises and rest between each set. If you do too many you may overload your muscles and joints and risk injury. Emphasise the explosive reactive movements and make sure that you contact the ground for only a fraction of a second in these jumps. Work:rest ratio is 1:6 for each exercise.

BOUNCE START: Read pages 51–2.
Do 10 repetitions of the bounce start in different directions.
Forwards –10; backwards – 10; sideways – 10.

TUCK JUMPS: 10. (See Fig 70.)

ASTRIDE JUMPING: 10. (See Fig 71.)

SIDE TO SIDE JUMPS: 10. (See Fig 72.)

HOPPING FOR HEIGHT AND DISTANCE: 10 hops on your right leg; 10 hops on your left leg.

TWO-FEET JUMPS FROM SIDE TO SIDE: 10.

SCISSOR JUMPS: alternate legs 10. (See fig 73.)

VOLUME: Perform these exercises two to three times each week on alternate days.

Advice: Make sure that you are fully warmed up, i.e. fully stretched before you do these exercises and do more stretching when you have completed them.

SPEED
If you want to move fast you must be able to quickly contract your muscles. How quickly they contract will depend on how well you have developed your 'fast-twitch' muscle fibres and how effectively you can 'charge' your muscles by doing a 'get ready' movement (plyometrics). Your speed of movement will also depend on how flexible you are. To develop speed you must train or practise at speed. Here are some simple and effective badminton-related exercises for different parts of your body.

Feet and Legs
The following exercises are done on the spot.

● PATTER STEPS Stand upright with your weight on the balls of your feet. Prepare yourself and

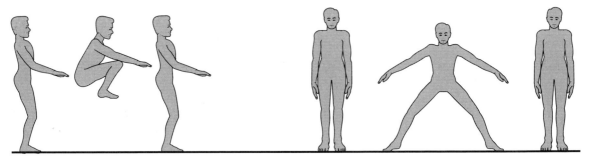

Fig 70

Fig 71

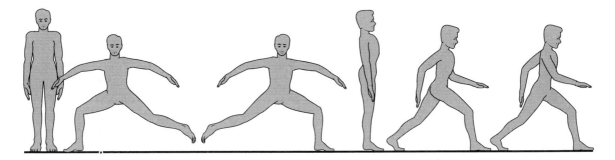

Fig 72

Fig 73

begin running on the spot with very fast small light steps, your feet hardly leaving the ground. Run for 5 seconds and rest for 5–10 seconds. Do about 5 repetitions.

● ASTRIDE JUMPS Get ready as in the previous exercise. Begin astride jumping very fast with your knees flexed throughout and your feet just skimming the floor. Work for 5 seconds and rest for 5-10 seconds. Do about 5 repetitions.

● SCISSOR JUMPS Get ready in balance with one foot in front of the other. Keep your knees flexed throughout and change your feet positions rapidly. Work for 5 seconds and rest for 5–10 seconds. Do about 5 repetitions.

● KNEE RAISING SPRINT Sprint on the spot with light steps raising your knees hip height as fast as possible. Work for 5 seconds and rest for 5–10 seconds. Do about 5 repetitions.

Hip Swings

These exercises are useful when performing a split jump or changing direction in the midcourt from forwards to backwards and vice versa, or from the right to the left, or left to right.

● Stand in a sides defence stance with your knees flexed and trunk and head upright. Lean forwards so that your shoulders are ahead of your feet. *See* Fig 74. This is your starting position. Get ready. Jump forwards, both feet skimming the ground to place them in front of you. Then repeat the action to place your feet behind you. Do this very quickly, swinging your hips forwards and backwards to place your feet in front of you or behind you. Do 10 repetitions.

● Repeat this exercise but this time swing your hips from side to side to place your feet on your right and left sides. *See* Fig 75. Do 10 repetitions.

Trunk and Shoulder Twists

You often have to twist your trunk to make a quick preparation for overhead forehand and backhand strokes. And for the smash this quick preparation

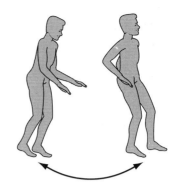

Fig 74

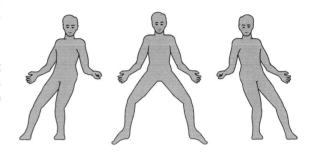

Fig 75

can have a plyometric effect and help to charge your muscles and give you extra power. It sometimes helps to do this exercise while holding a pair of dumbbells.

● Stand upright with your racket held ready in front of you. Keep your knees flexed and then twist your shoulders and trunk rapidly to your right and left. Do 3 sets of 10 repetitions with a rest between each set.

Fast Hands

You need fast hands to hit fast particularly in the midcourt and forecourt. The hand operates from your wrist joint which is constructed to allow a range of movements. The range of movement depends on how much your muscles will stretch and the speed of movement depends on the contractile strength of your fast-twitch muscle fibres. A good exercise to develop fast hands is *chopping*.

● CHOPPING: Hold your hands up in front of you with your palms facing. 'Chop' with your hands, up and down as fast as you can. Do this for 5 seconds and then rest for 5–10 seconds. Do 10 repetitions.

FIND OUT HOW FIT YOU ARE

It is usual to test your fitness in some way at the start of your fitness training programme. In this way you can measure your progress and set yourself some fitness goals.

There are several ways of testing your fitness depending on how accurate a test you want to make. A thorough scientific fitness test is advisable for top-class players. If you are not competing at this level, however, there are various 'field tests' which you can use: for example, the Loughborough VO2 Maximum Test ('Bleep Test'), the Harvard Step Test or the twelve-minute run which tests your endurance. Finally there is the 'Have a go and rely on your feelings' test. I tend to use all these methods when working with players.

I must admit however that, in general, it is the 'Have a go and rely on your feelings' test that I use most; and it is this one which I believe you will find the easiest to use.

THE 'HAVE A GO AND RELY ON YOUR FEELINGS' TEST

First you must plan a simple fitness programme and decide what exercises you will include to develop your fitness components. Let us assume that you will test your endurance, strength and flexibility.

TEST YOUR ENDURANCE

You want to build up to a twenty-minute run three times each week. Test yourself by having a go at running for twenty minutes. If you are out of breath after five minutes or your legs get too tired and it feels like hard work then you are not fit or are running too fast. If you ran for five minutes before you had to stop, build up to twenty minutes by running for 3–5 minutes at a gentle pace, then walk for 2–3 minutes and run for another 3–5 minutes and so on until you have completed twenty minutes.

Do this from 3 to 6 times a week until you can run for 20 minutes non stop. When you can do so increase your pace to make it somewhat hard work and try to increase the distance that you run.

In this way you test yourself by relying on your

feelings to measure your progress, and to decide how much training you can do.

TEST YOUR STRENGTH

Have a go at the circuit training and find out how many sets and repetitions you can do. Rely on your feelings to measure your fitness and adjust the circuit to suit you

TEST YOUR FLEXIBILITY

Have a go at the flexibility exercises. Here you simply want to know how far you can stretch. If you cannot stretch far you will experience a tight feeling in your muscles. That will be your starting point. Regular stretching exercises will help you to stretch further before you get the tight feeling

Comment: It should be obvious to you that by relying on your feelings and actually finding out what you can achieve each time you train that you will be using an ongoing test whenever you do train. This will only be of value to you if you are doing the right sort of exercises to develop your badminton fitness.

DIET

I do not intend to go into detail about diet but if you are interested in knowing more then I have recommended several books for reference and I am sure that if you visit any library you will find more. A preoccupation of most people these days seems to be with diet with regard to losing weight. You should be concerned with diet to ensure that you consume the right balance of foods and drink for your physical needs. It is surprising how many players do not eat properly or take insufficient water when working hard in training, practice or play. The food you eat should provide the fuel for the energy you need in work, for growth and to make your body function properly. The main foods are carbohydrates, fats and protein.

CARBOHYDRATES

There are two types of carbohydrates.
Simple: These are found in chocolate, sweets, sugar, cakes and energy drinks. As you might expect in this form they contain other foods including quite a lot of fat or sugar which make them less nutritious. The criticism of sugar is that it only provides calories, is low in nutritional value and,

therefore, not good for your health if eaten in sizeable quantities. In addition if you take in too much sugar in simple carbohydrates then your body actually compensates by reducing the sugar levels in your blood. The extra energy is then stored as fat and your reduced blood sugar level may actually cause fatigue. So do not eat sugary foods, or take sugary drinks before you play.

Complex: These are considered to be beneficial to your health. They have a more complex structure than simple carbohydrates and, with regard to your dietary and energy needs, are more nutritious. They are found in wholemeal bread, pasta, brown rice, peas, beans, potatoes, cereals, fruit and nuts, and root vegetables.

What should I eat?
You should eat plenty of complex carbohydrates.

How much should I eat?
It is recommended that carbohydrates should provide about 40–45 per cent of your diet each day. A man will eat about 250–350 grams daily and a woman about 150–300 grams. The harder you exercise the more carbohydrates you will need.

FATS
You will know that there is much discussion on fats with respect to the sorts of fats that we eat. There are the saturated fats found in meat, cheese and butter and the unsaturated fats found in vegetable oils and fish. It is believed that you ought to eat more unsaturated than saturated fats for health reasons although there are conflicting views about this. You should eat some fats because they play an important part in making your body function as well as being a source of energy.

How much should I eat?
It is recommended that fats should provide 35–40 per cent of your daily diet. A man should eat about 100–150 grams, a woman about 75–130 grams.

PROTEIN
Protein is a source of amino acids which are essential for your body's needs. The main foods for protein are meat, fish, dairy products and also vegetable proteins which come from cereals, peas, beans and nuts. So if you are a vegetarian you can easily obtain sufficient protein for your needs just as you can obtain sufficient fats.

How much should I eat?
It is recommended that protein should provide about 10–15 per cent of your diet each day, that is about 100 grams for a man and 75 for a woman.

FIBRE
It is important that your diet contains fibre as it helps your gut to function properly. Fibre is found in seeds, peas, beans and vegetables. Start the day right and have a look at your breakfast cereals and select those which are high in fibre. You need about 15–25 grams each day.

WATER
It is essential that you drink sufficient water to balance that which you lose when you sweat during training, practice and competition. If you do not then your body will overheat and you will inevitably suffer from heat exhaustion. When this happens your blood does not circulate around your body efficiently and the muscles do not receive the fuel they need for the work they are doing; hence it takes a greater effort to play and you tire more quickly.

Water is necessary to regulate your body temperature and to ensure that you can perform well when you train, practice and compete.

The advice given by nutritionists is that you should always be fully hydrated before you start intense exercise. During exercise (training, practice and competition) make sure that you often drink small amounts of fluid. If you are working hard and losing water constantly then you should be replacing it just as constantly. Keep yourself fully hydrated and you will not come to much harm through lack of water. The advice is that you should also not take carbonated drinks which are not good for you for various reasons.

What, when and how much should I eat before, during and after hard training, practice and competitive play?
When you exercise you get your energy from glycogen which is the form of the carbohydrate stored in your liver and muscles. As this is used up you need to restock the stores by eating more carbohydrates. If you are using a lot of energy the

current advice is that you should increase the amount of carbohydrates that you eat. Ideally you should eat more complex than simple carbohydrates. It might be necessary for you to increase your daily intake of carbohydrates up to 50 per cent of your diet.

When shall I eat?

You must eat carbohydrates after exercise simply to restock your glycogen reserves. Of course you can eat other foods as well but carbohydrates are essential. It is now recommended that you eat within the first hour of finishing exercise, if not sooner, even if you do not feel like eating. You will restock your reserves and recover more quickly if you do eat then. If you do not you may find that you tire more quickly when you exercise the following day.

How often and how much you eat will depend on how much you are exercising and using up glycogen in training, practice and play. If you are exercising throughout the day then you need to be refuelling continually with more smaller smacks rather than three large meals. This would be the policy you might adopt throughout a tournament. If you are in serious training and competition my advice is as follows:

- Have a good breakfast of complex carbohydrates.
- Make sure that you drink plenty of water so that you are fully hydrated at all times and do this during training, practice and competition.
- Check your diet to make sure that it contains the recommended amounts of carbohydrates, fats, protein and fibre. And if you need more food then add complex carbohydrates rather than protein or fat.
- Make sure that you eat carbohydrates within the first hour after hard exercise.
- Take a rest day so that you can stock up with carbohydrates and give your liver and muscles time to refill their glycogen stores.
- Have your main meal prior to strenuous exercise at least 3-4 hours before competition, rigorous training and practice to allow time for it to digest.
- During competition eat regular carbohydrate snacks, e.g. bananas, cereal bars, and drink water and fruit juices.

REST

Rest is an essential part of fitness training.

- You need rest to allow your body to adapt to the increasing amount of work you are doing. Hard exercise causes physiological changes in the body which need time to take place, e.g. your heart and lungs and your muscles.
- You need rest to refuel your glycogen reserves and to recover fully before you work again. If not you will find that instead of getting fitter you get progressively more tired and risk possible injury.
- You need rest to take a mental break. The saying 'all work and no play makes Jack a dull boy' will also apply to you.

Do you 'listen' to your body?

It is quite usual for players, once they become committed to training and getting fit, to feel guilty if they miss their training. So, no matter how they feel, they go out and train even when really they should take a complete day off to do something entirely different, eat well or to recover from a slight strain. In my experience this can do more harm than good.

So, 'listen to your body' and if it is telling you that it has had enough and needs a rest or wants more fuel, then do as it says and rest. And REST even if it is not your set rest day. You will be better for it and your performance will benefit.

PLAN YOUR OWN TRAINING PROGRAMME

You should now have sufficient information to achieve the following two aims.

1 Build up a good basic level of fitness for your needs throughout the playing season.
2 Maintain and, if possible, gradually increase that level during your main competition season.

Why do I need to increase my fitness level during the playing season?

During the season, if you are playing in good competition, your skill level will improve as will that of your opponents. The games can be longer and harder to win; hence you will need to improve your fitness level accordingly.

The higher you progress as a player the higher should be your fitness level. You will find that you must maintain a constant high fitness level throughout the season which is difficult to do. Unlike track athletes and swimmers, badminton players do not tend to try to peak physically for a big event. They are more like football players who must retain a constant high fitness level throughout their season. The way to do so is to take 'recovery periods' to rest and refuel; to recharge your batteries. I often think of these as troughs in your fitness plateau. *See* Fig 76.

How do I create my own Fitness Programme and what training exercises shall I include?

The most successful approach is that which meets the requirements of exercise physiologists, the sports scientists who design fitness programmes. Any programme must also be designed in accordance with the principles of training. *See* page 127.

I usually design a three-stage programme which start with the first stage before the season begins, continues during the first half of the season with the second stage and concludes with the third stage in the second part of the season.

STAGE 1

My advice is to develop four main fitness components:

- develop your 'heart and lungs' endurance (the oxygen energy system)
- develop your local muscular endurance
- develop your flexibility
- develop your strength.

I usually allow at least three months for off-court training to build up this basic fitness level and try to connect it with on-court practice and play. It is possible to increase your fitness levels in less time than this, e.g. two months but I usually take longer because I prefer my players to build up slowly. Until these components are sufficiently developed to a reasonable level of fitness you will find that you will be limited in how hard you can work in prac-

tice; the possibility of injury is also increased. Refer again to the description of these components and how to train them and get started.

STAGE 2

Now the season has started. My advice is to:

- gradually increase your endurance by improving your aerobic energy system and raising your anaerobic threshold
- maintain your flexibility
- increase your strength
- develop your anaerobic energy systems – lactic and phosphagen
- develop your power and speed.

You should allow three months' training on- and off-court to develop these components and to raise your fitness level. You should maintain some volume of work to retain your flexibility exercises and to increase your strength gradually. You may find that you can improve your oxygen system by interval training to raise your anaerobic threshold and thereby reduce the volume of work as you begin to develop your anaerobic energy system. You should train regularly to develop your power and speed.

Refer again to the description of these components and how to train them when you are ready to start.

STAGE 3

This is now in the second half of the season and I am assuming that the major important tournaments are now your target. You should train off-court sufficiently to maintain your flexibility exercises, strength, power and speed though they will also be developed in pressure practices and competition on court. Your on-court training should be designed to raise your anaerobic threshold, to maintain the efficiency of your anaerobic energy system and to maintain and if possible to continue to develop your speed and power.

Refer to the relevant sections to read how to do this when you are ready to start stage 3.

Fig 76 Fitness Levels

CHAPTER 14

Injuries and How You Can Try to Prevent Them

PHYSICAL INJURIES

The main purpose of fitness training is to strengthen and improve the efficiency of your body to ensure that you can cope with the physical demands of badminton. Exercise, recovery and rest time and the right sort of food and fluid are the main ingredients of a fitness training programme. In addition a proper warm-up and cool-down period (*see* page 129), good technical skill, proper equipment, clothing and footwear; and safe and suitable playing conditions are all necessary to safeguard you against possible injury.

If any of these things are ignored or neglected you may risk injury to your muscles, tendons, ligaments and bones. These can occur as bruises, pulled and strained muscles, torn tendons and ligaments, fractured and broken bones.

WHAT ARE MUSCLES, TENDONS AND LIGAMENTS?

Muscles are made up of lots of fibres. The function of muscle is to move your bones (as levers) at your joints, e.g. knees and ankles. To do this some muscles contract (shorten) while opposite groups stretch to allow your bones to move. Muscle tissue has a rich supply of blood which is one reason why you usually recover more quickly from muscle injuries than from tendon or ligament injuries.

Tendon is the name given to the tissue which connects your muscle to your bone. *See* Fig 77. Tendons do not receive such a rich supply of blood as muscles and so they usually take longer to heal.

Ligaments connect your bones together and ensure that your bones move within a certain range.

They can be narrow (cord-like) or wide (belt-like). Ligaments receive a very limited blood supply and, if injured, take longer to heal than tendons. Players with ligament injuries often have the joint strapped up to prevent any movement while the ligament heals.

Bones provide the supporting bony structure of your body.

WHAT FORMS OF INJURY ARE THERE?

There are three main forms. These are:

Overuse Injuries These usually appear with gradual increasing pain over a period of time, e.g. shin splints, backache, tennis elbow, badminton shoulder.

Traumatic Injuries These are sudden injuries which are caused by either an external force (a blow or a knock), or an *internal* **force** (your muscle strength or a joint twisting), e.g. an Achilles tendon tear, a knee cartilage tear, and a ligament tear as your foot twists over. In badminton the cause will more often be an internal force.

Overload Injuries These are often a combination of overuse and traumatic injuries. Your muscles, tendons, or ligaments may gradually weaken until suddenly they become damaged.

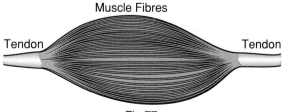

Fig 77

What can cause injuries in badminton and what can you do to try to prevent them?

Let's consider each form of injury and identify some causes.

OVERUSE INJURIES

Causes:

One-sided play which may result in an extended racket arm, an enlarged racket shoulder and trunk, a sideways tilt of your spine in the opposite direction to your racket arm.

Prevention: Exercise both sides of your body by doing regular stretching exercises for flexibility, body circuit training, weight training, or regular swimming. Make sure that you do a thorough warm-up and cool-down each time you train, practise or play.

Excessive Repetition which may result in shoulder and elbow injuries resulting from excessive clearing and smashing practices.

Prevention: Reduce the number of repetitions in practice and take frequent rests and/or changes of activity so that your body can adapt to the workload. Rely on your common sense and feelings and stop your game when you begin to feel any pain or it is becoming hard work.

TRAUMATIC INJURIES

Causes:

Lack of flexibility, inadequate warm-up, lack of strength, poor technical skill, poor footwear, a slippy floor, trying too hard.

Prevention: From reading why these happen, it should be obvious what steps you can take to reduce the risk of traumatic injuries.

Make sure that your body can cope with the physical demands of the game, always play in the right clothing and footwear for the conditions, check the floor surface, improve your technical skill and warm up properly.

OVERLOAD INJURIES

Causes:

- Excessive repetitive actions in practice and in training and ignoring the warning signals that you are becoming too tired.
- Poor technique.
- Not taking sufficient rest breaks. (See page 134 on anaerobic training.)
- Running on hard surfaces with inadequate footwear and/or poor technique which may cause compression injuries such as shin splints, tendon and ligament injuries particularly in the knees, hip joint and lower back.
- Weight training with too heavy a weight.
- Weight training with poor technique. Back injuries often result from this.
- Inappropriate fitness training exercises, e.g. deep knee bounces.
- Using shuttles which are too slow when performing smashes and clears.
- Inadequate diet causing fatigue.
- Inadequate liquid intake causing dehydration and muscle cramps (*see* page 143).
- Not warming up and cooling down properly.

Prevention It is also obvious here that you should be avoiding all the things that may cause overload injuries. Make sure you:

- Warm up and cool down properly.
- Improve your technical skill.
- Vary your practices and training.
- Get adequate rest (recovery) breaks and take in sufficient food and drink during training and practice.
- Make sure that your training programme, e.g. strength training, is suitable for you.

YOUR MENTAL ATTITUDE AS A POSSIBLE UNDERLYING CAUSE OF INJURY

Your mental attitude can cause you to tense up, lose concentration, try too hard, not try hard enough, give up easily, not prepare properly and use sloppy techniques.

Causes:

- Pressure from the expectations of others.

- Feeling cheated.
- Your ambitions.
- Personal, social and financial problems.
- Ignorance.

Prevention:

- Set realistic goals, be honest about your performance and learn to play for yourself and not others.
- Develop tactics for dealing with cheats and decisions that go against you.
- Adopt a sound personal philosophy about winning and losing in competitive sport.
- Learn and practise the actor's golden rule, 'The show must go on', and when it does learn to perform up to standard whatever your personal problems. If you cannot perform under pressure then you should seriously consider whether you ought to play until you have resolved your problems.
- Study the game and all aspects of your craft and become knowledgeable.

HOW SHALL I TREAT AN INJURY?

You should always refer to a qualified medical practitioner if you ever suffer from any type of sports injury.

Here is some general advice which you should follow if you do suffer an injury.

- Do not continue to train or play if you do have an injury.
- Visit your doctor or a physiotherapist as quickly as possible to find out what sort of injury you have and what treatment you need.
- Follow their advice. If you are not happy with it do not ignore it but obtain a second qualified medical opinion.
- Buy a book on sports injuries. There are several good ones available which I have listed on page 192.
- Do not try to short-cut the healing process by starting practice and training too soon.

Develop a Winning Attitude and Exploit Your Opponent's Attitude

CHAPTER
15

What we need is an enthusiastic but calm state of mind and intense but orderly work. *
Mao Tse-tung

For many players attitudes are usually the most complex aspect of their performance and inextricably bound up with their skill and fitness. With hard work and practice it is relatively easy for players to attain a high standard of fitness and technical skill and then, with lots of competition, to develop a good level of tactical skill in the game. Many players do this and yet do not achieve the sort of success they are capable of solely because their attitude lets them down.

You are far more likely to play well if you have the right sort of attitude. And if you can exploit your opponent's attitude in play then you could increase your chances of beating him. This chapter, therefore, examines mental attitudes, how you might develop winning attitudes and how you might exploit your opponent's attitudes. By understanding more about them you will understand how to develop the ones you need and get rid of those you don't want.

WHAT IS A MENTAL ATTITUDE?

Mental attitudes are connected with people's behaviour. I imagine that you may sometimes judge people's attitudes by the way they behave in certain situations. When I watch players I judge their attitude as *appropriate* if they seem to be behaving as they should in the game, and *inappropriate* if they don't. Typical examples of *inappropriate* attitudes are: dropping your head and shoulders after losing a rally (a sort of 'woe is me' attitude), racket throwing, not trying, a couldn't care less approach to the game, playing too safely, trying for impossible winners, blaming your racket, hit-

ting yourself with your racket, blaming yourself, getting frustrated, impatient, angry, getting rattled, giving up.

Some players may also experience other mental states such as feeling weak in the legs, or their side of the court will seem huge and their opponents' very small. Just think how useful it could be if you knew how to use such mental states to your advantage if your opponent is expressing them and, also how to 'help' your opponent to adopt some of them.

If part of your task in trying to win is to exploit your opponents' weaknesses then weaknesses in their attitude are just as fair game for exploitation as they are in their skill and fitness.

WHAT MENTAL ATTITUDES ARE APPROPRIATE AND HOW DO I DEVELOP THEM?

To answer this question you will have to take a closer look at the game, why you play it and how you should behave when you do so. When you have given some thought to these things we can go on to discuss how you might develop appropriate attitudes.

DO YOU HAVE A LOVE OF THE GAME FOR ITS OWN SAKE?

I will assume that you have taken up badminton *voluntarily*, because you consider it is a **worthwhile** game to play and that you continue to play for the enjoyment you get from the game. Your enjoyment may come from the exercise, from hitting the shuttle, the general movement about the court (sprints, changes of direction, jumps and landings, twists and turns), the challenge of the contest or because it is an **absorbing**, dynamic

---

*Quotations from *Chairman Mao Tse Tung,* Foreign Languages Press, Peking, 1972, p.229.

and *interesting* game to play. The more you play and want to get better the more you will *care about how you play* and so you will begin to take some *pride* in the way you play and any successes you may achieve. This being so I will assume that you are willing to *commit yourself* to working harder to achieve higher standards of excellence in your skill, fitness and your attitude and you want to try to become better if not the best player. At this stage it could be said that you have a *love of the game* and *value* it solely for the interest and enjoyment it provides.

A love of the game for its own sake is essential to your further development; it provides a strong foundation from which you can grow as a player. With it you will already have developed a number of important appropriate attitudes, e.g. care, interest, pride and commitment. If you can retain this love, and hopefully passion, for the game, then you should not have any difficulties in developing other appropriate attitudes. Neither should you develop any serious attitude problems.

WHAT HAPPENS IF I PLAY FOR OTHER REASONS?

You can play badminton for other reasons providing your prime reason is to play the game for its own sake. If, however, you lose your love of the game or let or other reasons take priority, e.g. to gain social prestige and status, money or to please others, then you could experience all sorts of attitude problems. This is because to achieve your goals you will need constant success; you will always be under pressure to win and if this is so then you will most probably experience the fear of losing which will inevitably lessen your chances of playing well.

The difference is in for whom you play the game. *Do you play it for yourself or do you play it for others?* If you are experiencing attitude problems which are affecting how you play then you should give this question some serious thought. If you really love the game for its own sake then you have no choice but to play it for yourself.

THE GAME AS A CONTEST AND THE ATTITUDES YOU NEED FOR COMPETITION

Your task in the contest is to compete with your opponent(s) to try to win. *Trying to win is the sole*

point of the game. It is because you are both trying to win that the game becomes interesting and challenging, for you are testing the performance of each other. The test takes time, because of the length of the game, and calls for a certain degree of skill from you to beat your opponent(s). The game should become more absorbing as the struggle to win becomes more difficult. You should be interested in and committed to the task of winning. To do this you will have to *persevere* in your efforts until the game is over. At the same time you will be expected to make a serious effort to win and show *determination* in doing so. Because of the nature of the game you will need to be *adventurous* in seizing any opportunity to attempt a winning shot. Such a commitment to trying to win will require complete *concentration* with all your attention being focused on defeating your opponent.

You will express attitudes of perseverance, determination, adventurousness and concentration if you are really committed to trying to win the contest. If you do not have these you should give some thought as to whether you are really trying to win. And if you are not then you should give some further thought as to what your actual purpose is on the court.

HOW DO I DEVELOP SUCH ATTITUDES?

You should play the game for its own sake which means playing it for yourself. You will then be free of the many pressures that can come from playing for status and prestige and for others. If the result matters only to you then there is no reason why you cannot give 100 per cent effort in trying to win.

I appreciate that it is difficult to give 100 per cent effort all the time and to keep your mind fully on the purpose of trying to win. Even if you play the game for yourself you will sometimes have doubts about whether you can succeed; you may lose your confidence if things are not going right or if you cannot do something; you may lose your concentration as you relax for a moment or think about what you will do when you have won.

When this happens during a game you will have to find your own way of overcoming the problem. This will involve some self-discipline. It takes self-discipline which develops in and through the work you do in practice and training. If you set yourself a programme of practice and training and stick to it rigorously, except of course when you are ill or for some other good reason, then you will develop self-discipline. To develop it you must practise it in daily life. Even if you do not feel like training or practice then get out and do it. Even if you don't feel like practising hard then work hard to make sure that you improve your standards. Even if you do not feel like training hard you should push yourself and train hard. If you are going to be easy on yourself then don't expect to develop an appropriate competitive attitude. And do not expect to win.

In informal and formal competition try to maintain high standards no matter who you play. Try to win as effectively as you can. If you are playing a lesser player then play your best and win love and love if you can, in as few rallies as possible.

To develop appropriate attitudes in the contest you have to practise them always. Never allow your standards to fall. And of course all this means HARD WORK which you can only do by adopting these attitudes. So as you practise to improve your skill and train to improve your fitness you will also be practising your attitudes. Don't be put off by this because if you really play the game for its own sake then the work should be a *labour of love*. You will enjoy it.

THE GAME AS A PART OF SPORT

Last, but of equal importance is another group of attitudes which arise from the fact that badminton is played as a social game. *The manner in which it is played* is therefore important. Humans have devised many sports throughout history, mainly for the purpose of enjoyment and to enhance the quality of their lives. There are many reasons why people play different sports as there are many reasons why people play badminton, but when it comes to competitive sports their main purpose should be to try to win.

This shouldn't alter the fact that the main reason why people take part in sport is for enjoyment. Consequently it would seem to negate the whole purpose of sport to try to win at the expense of enjoyment. Behaviour which lessens your own or others' enjoyment of sport should be avoided as undesirable. That is why 'fair play' is emphasised so much at the Olympic Games; without it sport would lose all meaning. It is for this reason that players who cheat or take drugs and do anything else to gain an unfair advantage should be con-

demned. They devalue the sport in general and themselves in particular.

In general because sport has so much to do with the quality of our lives moral values such as honesty, fairness, respect and consideration for others, including officials, spectators and other players, should also be reflected in your behaviour. These attitudes are as important as determination and concentration.

HOW DO I EXPLOIT MY OPPONENTS' ATTITUDES?

Just as you should try to find weaknesses in your opponents' skill and fitness then you should also try to find weaknesses in their attitudes. It is reasonable and fair to do so. This is however an area where gamesmanship can arise. There is a risk that you may go too far and act unfairly or not in the spirit of the game. Nevertheless within limits there is still plenty of scope to exploit any weaknesses in your opponents' attitudes. You can do this before a game, during a game and in between rallies. Here are a few examples.

Creating pressure on your opponent(s)

Imagine that you are favoured to win a contest against a keen rival who you know gets tense and worried before big matches. You are asked whether you think you will win. You can use this situation to put pressure on your opponent and take it off yourself. You could reply that you think it will be difficult and that you would be lucky if you did win because your opponent is such a good player and he is playing so well. As long as you remain consistent with your story the focus will switch to your opponent and he will have to handle the pressure. It will certainly give him something to think and possibly worry about.

Exploiting your opponent's attitude during play

It would seem sensible to try to upset your opponent's attitude in the area of tactics and fitness. It might frustrate him if you play a game which is not of his liking. He may be a fast one-pace player whom you frustrate by slowing the game down and by playing building shots that give him nothing to attack. He may then become irritated and begin to lose his concentration or become impatient and make unforced errors.

Exploiting your opponent's attitude between rallies

I remember a player some years ago who used to stare menacingly at his opponent just prior to serving or to receiving a serve with the deliberate intention of dominating the opponent. Some players would find this unsettling. Another used to announce the score calmly and deliberately as though he intended to take a grip on the game and turn on a special performance.

It would be acceptable to keep the pressure on between rallies. After a hard rally allow little time for your opponent to compose himself – just pick up the shuttle and get on with the game. Alternatively you might take your time between rallies to compose yourself and irritate an opponent who wants to get on with the game. It is not, however, acceptable to waste time deliberately, though this can be difficult to prove.

WHAT DO YOU DO WITH PLAYERS WHO TRY TO EXPLOIT YOUR ATTITUDE?

You must first recognise what your opponent is trying to do. In my experience very few players resort to trying to upset another player when they feel that they are in control of the game so you will have obviously got them worried about the way the game is going. Some players try all sorts of tricks to upset others. They will talk, make comments, fool around, question line decisions, keep trying to change the shuttle, forget the score, or even make up a score in their favour.

A good way of dealing with this is by being completely expressionless and letting them get on with their act. You could even smile at them when you hit or pass the shuttle to them to serve for the next rally, and just prior to their serve or your serve. I remember one club singles game in which a player called a shuttle out which was a good 35 cm in. On being questioned by his opponent he refused to accept that the shuttle had landed in the court. He then proceeded to serve and served high. His opponent who had a sense of humour as well as a sense of fair play just stood there, watched the shuttle land well in the court, smiled and called, 'Out'. The server shouted and complained but the receiver simply said, 'It was out' and picked up the shuttle to serve. Then he walked to the net and said, 'We can play the game fairly or we can both cheat and call every shuttle out, in which case there is no point in playing on any further. What do you want to do?' The cheat agreed not to cheat and they got on with the game. I should add that, being a club night, they could not obtain an umpire.

There are various forms of cheating. Your main policy is not to allow the cheat to upset you as that is what he will want to do. Instead deal with the incident calmly and if necessary ask for an umpire. You might have to accept that you will have lost that rally but you can make sure that you do not lose your self-control.

If such players succeed in upsetting you then you really have not done your homework and prepared properly. Think of what they do as just another type of game plan and prepare for it. When other players go beyond the bounds of what is reasonable then there are the Laws of Badminton for you to apply. Make sure that you know them thoroughly!

CONFIDENCE, CHARACTER AND THE WILL TO WIN

I have left these to the last because they are a consequence of developing appropriate attitudes in all areas of the game. Competition is the true test of your attitudes. However, when a contest is a close one and your skill, fitness and attitudes are equalled by your opponent then you have to call on something extra. In some way you have to intensify your efforts. This is where the discipline you have developed in your practice and training will pay off. Through hard work you have reached high standards and you know that you are capable of playing well and have the ability to cope with any situation that arises. This is what confidence is, that you know that you are up to the task. With it any doubts are usually removed and you can concentrate on the task of winning. Character and the will to win come through from the work you do, and are unique qualities possessed by certain players. If you possess them you will know it just as you will recognise it in players that you meet on court. They are a combination of mental toughness and spirit that will enable you to intensify your resolution and lift yourself to an extra dimension of effort. With them you will raise your standards, and get totally absorbed in trying to beat your opponent(s) and win.

'When the going gets tough the tough get going.' Does that apply to you?

chapter 16

Improve Your Defence

When you defend you should still play in accordance with the **principle of attack**, i.e. *whenever you hit the shuttle try to create a situation that will increase your chances of eventually winning or reduce your opponent's chances of winning the rally*. You should also make sure that in using your strokes as tactical moves they are used as building shots or attempted winning shots. It is usual to talk specifically about defence when your opponent is smashing in an attempt to hit a winning shot.

PASSIVE AND ACTIVE DEFENCE

There are two forms of defence, *passive* and *active*. (*See* Fig 78.)

Passive Defence

You will use passive defence when you 'sit back' in a catcher's position and let the shuttle come closer to your body as you absorb the force. It is similar to catching a ball kicked or thrown hard at you in a competitive game; for example a wicket keeper in cricket, a catcher in baseball or a goalkeeper in football. Many top players use passive defence, e.g. Li Yongbo the brilliant Chinese doubles player who excels at this. The use of passive defence makes nonsense of the recommendation that you should always take the shuttle early. If you follow this outdated rule, preached by so many traditionalists, you will hinder your ability to defend well and play good building shots. In passive defence the rule is '*Take the shuttle later rather than earlier.*'

Active Defence

You use active defence when you step forwards to take the shuttle early and so reduce your opponent's recovery time as you counter-hit his smash at speed.

It is important to understand the difference between these two forms of defence so you can practise them more effectively and defend to your advantage. There are times when it is better to take the shuttle late just as there are times when it is better to take the shuttle early. You will defend better and make fewer errors if you know when to use one or the other.

HOW SHALL I LEARN PASSIVE AND ACTIVE DEFENCE?

You probably already use both more frequently than you may be aware of. What you need to do is to distinguish between them and for this there are two things that you must do.

FIRST: you should accept that there are two ways of defending, i.e. passive and active defence.

SECOND: you should adopt a particular attitude of mind for each type of defence. For passive defence you should adopt a 'taking in', receptive attitude as you allow the shuttle to come towards you and prepare to hit it. For active defence you should adopt a 'going at' attitude to the shuttle as you move towards it to hit it.

A brief explanation will make this clearer. Imagine that you are positioned in the middle of a large sphere. You 'sit back' on your thighs in balance, alert like a 'catcher', with your racket held in front of you, facing your opponent and watching him very closely. If you stretch out your arm with your racket you will just touch the surface of the sphere (*see* Fig 78). That is how big it is. All the space included within it is your hitting zone, the space within which you hit the shuttle. Your sphere is situated in the centre of your court. On the other

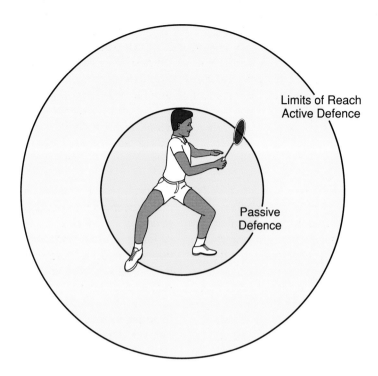

Fig 78
Hitting Zones for Active and Passive Defence

side of the court is your opponent who smashes the shuttle to you. You allow it to pass through the surface of your sphere and travel into your hitting zone, closer towards you. As it gets nearer you simply lob it up to his rearcourt, block it to his forecourt or push it to his midcourt. Your opponent is given more time to recover to cover your replies just as you have more time to play them.

Now imagine the same scenario. This time you do not allow the shuttle to travel very far into your hitting zone. As it travels towards your sphere you prepare to hit it. As the shuttle touches the surface of your sphere you extend your arm forwards to hit it from just inside your hitting zone. You block to the forecourt, lob it to the rearcourt or push or drive it to the midcourt. Your opponent should have less time to cover your replies just as you will have less time to play them.

If you think about this for a moment you will hopefully agree that there are many occasions in the game when you want more time to play your shots and it suits your purpose to allow your oppo-

nents time to recover.

For example you want them to travel into the midcourt so that you can lob it back over their heads to the rearcourt. Or you want to deceive them into thinking that you will play a lob when you intend to play a net reply. You want them to commit themselves to responding to a certain shot before you play it. This you can only do when you have time to 'pretend' to play a particular shot and your opponents are give time to be deceived. Taking the shuttle late will give you this time.

On other occasions it will suit your purpose to give your opponents less time to recover. You must therefore take the shuttle early, which will also give you less time to play your shot. The benefits will be that your opponents may not be in position to cover your shot and will have less time to react to the shot that you play.

If you want to improve your defence you should use both passive and active defence to outwit and exploit your opponents.

HOW SHALL I PRACTISE MY PASSIVE AND ACTIVE DEFENCE?

All you require is a partner with a good smash. Refer to chapter 5 (pages 32–4) for advice on practice stages. Position yourself in the midcourt, serve a high doubles serve and ask your partner to smash the shuttle towards you so that you can practise forehand defence and backhand defence.

Passive Defence

First, practise just getting the feeling of the action and allow the shuttle to come close to your body while you sit back in balance on your thighs. Sit back further as you hit the shuttle. On no account should you allow your body weight to move forwards as you hit the shuttle. Try different stroke-moves, e.g. block, push and lob. Do this for forehand and backhand shots.

When you can do this practise accuracy and consistency in continuous rally practices.

Active Defence

First, practise stepping forwards with your racket foot to block the shuttle. Do not try to hit the shuttle anywhere but simply place your racket face in line with the shuttle to meet it. The most important action is to step forwards on your racket foot.

When you feel comfortable stepping forwards then do so and play a particular stroke-move. Block, drive or lob the shuttle.

HOW CAN I DEVELOP THIS TO MAKE IT MORE GAME-LIKE?

There are two further practice stages you should do now. You should add a travel phase to the practice so that you have to travel away from the centre to hit the shuttle; you should add some uncertainty so that you do not know where your partner will hit the smash.

Use passive defence with a travel phase: Ask your partner to smash the shuttle wide to your forehand side. Now simply travel to the forehand side, in which case you would move your imaginary 'sphere' with you and defend from a new position. You may have to defend from a half or full lunge position within your hitting zone. *See* plate 29, page 103. Repeat this on the backhand side although now you may use your non-racket foot to step sideways in a half or full lunge.

Use active defence with a travel phase: Repeat as for passive defence. The exception is that if the shuttle is in front of you on your backhand side you will usually step across and forwards to the court side on your racket foot.

Now add some uncertainty to the practice

Ask your smasher to smash to anywhere while you practise both types of defence. Agree how the practice will be done if you block the shuttle. Will your smasher travel forwards and play a net reply for you to lob high for him to smash again or will you start again with a high serve?

Practise your defence in conditioned games and informal competition:

Conditioned games

- Play a game and restrict yourself to using passive defence only in reply to a smash.
- Play a game and restrict yourself to using active defence only in reply to a smash.
- Play a game and use forehand passive defence and backhand active defence in reply to a smash.
- Play a game and use backhand passive defence and forehand active defence in reply to a smash.

Informal Competition

Use passive defence for the first game regardless of whether or not you win and use active defence for the second game. If you play a third game use both types of defence to play your building shots and attempted winning shots as you decide will be effective in the situation.

chapter 17

Learn to Deceive Your Opponent

You should learn how to deceive your opponent to increase your chances of winning a rally. The main purpose of deception is to gain a tactical advantage and you can do this in two ways: you can make your opponent anticipate your shot wrongly and send him the wrong way; or you can make him pause and wait to move until you hit the shuttle. In both instances your opponent should be late getting into position to hit the shuttle or unable to reach it at all.

HOW TO SEND YOUR OPPONENT THE WRONG WAY

Your intention here will be to make your opponent move forwards so that you can hit the shuttle behind him; make him move backwards so that you can hit the shuttle in front of him; or make him move to the left so that you can hit it to the right and vice versa. To do this requires some form of pretence from you.

Play Pretends

When you deceive an opponent you would usually pretend to do one thing and then do another. For example, I could pretend that I am going to smash at you. So you get ready and brace yourself to receive the smash. Instead I play a check smash, a dropshot to the forecourt, which you are not ready for and you may be late getting to the shuttle, if at all.

Body Language

You have to use 'body language' to deceive an opponent. If you pretend to play a particular shot, e.g. a net reply, then you will want your opponent to think 'Oh, he looks as if he is going to play a net reply.' He can only do this by reading your 'body language' which suggests you are going to play a particular shot. If he interprets your body language as you expect then you will succeed, you will deceive him.

It is important, therefore, that you keep your pretence very simple or you won't deceive anyone. If your body language is unclear or too complex your opponent may not be able to interpret it and you will be less likely to deceive him. Likewise you have to give your opponent time to 'read' your body language and to respond as you intended.

YOUR OPPONENT'S RESPONSE

Your opponent's response will depend on two factors:

(a) his reaction time, which is to do with how quickly he can transmit information through his nervous system to his muscles, and (b) his speed of movement, which is determined by how quickly he can contract his muscles to enable him to respond in travelling to the shuttle.

You cannot do much about his speed of travelling but you can do a lot about the information that he sends to his muscles through his nervous system. You simply give him false information so that he anticipates your shot wrongly and goes the wrong way.

Make your opponent wait to see what shot you actually play before he responds

You may have played opponents who use deception and have such good technique that it's difficult to know what shot they will play until they actually hit the shuttle. For example, the player who takes up a *smash position* in the rearcourt. He starts to 'throw' his racket head at the shuttle and until he actually hits the shuttle you do not know whether he intends to hit a clear, smash or dropshot. You have to wait to see. Such players are successful because their preparation is the same for all their overhead strokes. The same would apply for the sidearm and underarm strokes.

The main point here is that you should not give your opponents any 'clues' about your intentions. They will 'read' the clues from your body language.

For example if you prepare for an overhead stroke and drop your elbow when you do a dropshot, or remain more square on when you do a clear, or turn completely sideways when you smash, then any intelligent opponent will notice these 'clues' and be able to anticipate your shot.

To prevent this you should practise to make sure that your preparation is similar for particular groups of strokes.

HOW DO I LEARN AND IMPROVE MY DECEPTION?

It helps to learn deception if you adopt the right attitude towards it. You should enjoy outwitting your opponents, to trick them and cause them to delay or make the wrong response. You should also appreciate that there is a tactical basis to deception. You should not use it just for the sake of it, which is pure indulgence; you should use it to gain a tactical advantage.

To be deceptive you will need a good standard of racket and body skill. You should learn to control the speed of your racket head; to speed it up or check the speed at any time during your stroke-cycle. You should learn to control the racket face so that you can direct the shuttle where you please with a change of the racket face position at any time before impact with the shuttle. Refer to chapter 7 for racket skill practices.

Finally you should practise using deception as much as possible in conditioned games, informal and formal competition. It may help to look at some of the ways that you can be deceptive.

Some ways in which you can be deceptive

● Always prepare as if you will play the most attacking shot (stroke-move) in any situation. This poses a threat to your opponent who should always get ready to cover that shot. You will then be free to play other shots.
● Try to keep your preparation identical for similar groups of strokes, e.g. overhead strokes. This will prevent early anticipation and may actually cause your opponent to experience some doubt and uncertainty about your intentions.
● Always have your racket prepared to make your stroke as you approach the shuttle. In this way you can put the actual stroke 'on hold' and tempt your opponent to anticipate your shot.
● Try some of the deception and tactics used in other sports. If you watch football, basketball, rugby, hockey, netball and martial arts you will see many examples of feints and body sway to send the opponent the wrong way. There are many instances in badminton when you can do this, for example when you defend, play net replies, or serve. You could sway or step in one direction and hit the shuttle in the other direction.

Finally remember you can only deceive an opponent if, when you pretend to do one thing, he actually believes your pretence and has given time to respond to it. The best advice I can offer here, is to keep your deception *simple*.

chapter 18

Learn to Analyse and Assess Your Performance in Competition

Know yourself and know your opponent and you can increase your chances of winning.

WHY SHOULD I LEARN TO ANALYSE AND ASSESS MY PERFORMANCE IN COMPETITION?

To become a better player you must play in formal competition which, providing you give 100 per cent effort to trying to win, is the only true test of your progress. It is here that you learn what parts of your game are developing and in what part there are still weaknesses to be worked on. You will also learn about your opponents and the parts of the game they are strong or weak in. With this information you can work out tactics and learn when you can take risks. But you will only learn this if you make a deliberate effort to assess how you played and how your opponent played after each match. It makes good sense to analyse and assess yourself and your opponent as it is how strong or weak you both are against each other that will decide how well or poorly you play against each other. To do this you need information which you can analyse to learn about each other's performance in your singles and doubles matches.

It is difficult to assess your game accurately when you have to rely on your memory. You may be good at remembering lots of details about a game, or you may only remember superficial details or the highlights. Even if you do have a fantastic memory and can recall the game in complete detail you must still learn how to work it out and analyse all the information in order to learn from it and use it to help you to become a better player.

HOW SHOULD I RECORD INFORMATION AND ANALYSE MY PERFORMANCE?

The ideal method is to video your game and use a computer programme to give instant analysis and advice. This is now being done as part of research in games analysis in several British universities but it is unlikely that you will have access to this kind of equipment.

Here are some simple and effective methods of recording the game, aided by a questionnaire to help you extract the information you need in order to analyse and assess your performance. You should find that using the questionnaire will help you to remember more about your game and it should also help to make you more aware of how you and your opponents are playing. The more you use the questionnaire the better you will become at analysing the game while you are playing, and at changing your tactics when necessary during it.

Try this Procedure

- Play your match and use two simple methods to record information, your memory and/or video tape.
- Extract the information that you want by asking specific questions. For example you might ask, 'How many of my backhand clears were successful as building shots and how many were unsuccessful?' If you are using your memory this might prove difficult but if you think hard about it you might decide that you hit about ten backhand clears – five were a good length and moved your opponent to the rearcourt. About 50 per cent were successful. If you are using a video you could watch it and make a more accurate estimate.
- Apply the questions to your opponent's play so that you can identify his strengths and weaknesses as well as your own.

WHAT QUESTIONS SHALL I ASK TO OBTAIN INFORMATION?

You should ask questions about the different aspects of your performance and your opponent's performance. These include:

- technical skill
- tactical skill – building shots and attempted winning shots
- fitness
- attitude.

Here is a sample questionnaire. Let's imagine that you have just played a game or you are watching your game on video. Sit down, focus on the game in your memory or on the video, concentrate and begin to answer the following questions.

QUESTIONNAIRE

All the questions below will relate to your own performance. You should also ask them of your opponent's performance. If you want a detailed analysis then you should answer all the questions. If you only want to analyse and examine certain parts of your performance or your opponent's performance then only apply the questions concerned with those parts.

1 Serving – the opening tactical move

Apply these questions to all the serves: low, high, flick and drive.

- Where did you serve from?
- When did you use it most?
- Where did you aim it to – the centre or to the forehand or backhand side of your opponent?
- How did you position yourself after your serve?
- What replies did you expect to receive?
- Was your serve accurate?
- Were you consistent?
- Did you vary it in any way?
- Did you have any particular habits (body language) or weaknesses that would help him to anticipate your serve?
- In what situations did you use your serve as a building shot or an attempted winning shot?

2 Receiving the serve

Apply these questions to all the serves.

- Where did you stand to receive serve?
- Were you able to explode from the spot?
- What replies did you make to a low serve (a) from your forehand side, (b) from your backhand side?
- What replies did you make from the flick or drive serve to your forehand side and to your backhand side?
- What replies did you make from the high serve?
- Were there any replies you found difficult to make to any of the serves?
- Which replies did you play as building shots or attempted winning shots?
- Did you have any particular habits or weaknesses that would help him to anticipate your reply?
- Were you accurate and consistent with your replies? If not, which replies did you perform badly or make most errors on?
- What replies did you think might be effective against him?

3 Rearcourt Stroke-Moves

- Did you use your clear effectively as a building shot: (a) your forehand clear and (b) your backhand clear?
- Did you use your smash effectively as a building shot and attempted winning shot?
- Did you use your dropshot effectively as a building shot/attempted winning shot?
- Were you accurate and consistent when you clear, smash or drop? If not, which did you perform badly or make the most errors on?
- What replies did you expect your opponent to make?
- Did you recover quickly into position to cover the probable replies? If not, decide from what shots you do not recover quickly?
- What shots did you make the most errors in?

4 Midcourt Stroke-Moves

- What shots did you play from a high position (forehand and backhand side in the sides or centre)?
- What shots did you play from a low position on the forehand and backhand sides?
- What stroke-moves did you think he might expect from you?

- What stroke-moves did you think might be effective against him?
- Did you recover quickly after your stroke?
- What sorts of replies did you expect to receive from the different shots?
- Did you travel into the right position to cover the probable replies?
- What shots did you make the most errors in?

5 Forecourt Stroke-Moves

- What stroke-moves did you play from near the ground, just below net level and above net level?
- What shots were effective in different forecourt situations?
- Did you recover quickly after a particular stroke?
- What replies did you expect and prepare for?
- Did you cover all the probable replies?
- What shots did you make the most errors in?

6 Racket Skill

- Did you have good control over your racket head and face?
- Could you change grip quickly under pressure?
- Were there any situations when you felt that your racket skill was weak?
- Were there any situations when you felt that your racket skill was strong?

7 Body Skill

- Were there any situations in which you felt that any aspects of your body skill were weak and your opponent could take advantage?
- Which body skill components were weak in these situations?

8 Deception

- Did you use deception?
- In what situations did you use deception?
- What strokes did you use to deceive your opponent?
- Was your deception effective?

- Did you have any habits (body language) that will help your opponent to recognise your deception and anticipate your shot?

9 Attitude

- Did you adopt the appropriate mental attitude during the game?
- Were there any occasions when you adopted an inappropriate mental attitude?
- What did you think caused you to adopt an inappropriate attitude?
- Did your opponent benefit from your attitude in any way?
- Did you try to exploit any weaknesses in your opponent's attitude?

10 Fitness

- Did you have sufficient endurance to play long hard rallies at a fast pace?
- Did you recover quickly between rallies?
- Could you play very fast rallies and travel quickly on the court?
- Did you recover quickly after a very fast rally?
- Did you need a long time to recover between rallies?
- What was your state after a long hard rally if (a) you won it, (b) you lost it?
- Did you tire quickly?
- How did your tiredness affect your play:
  (a) slow down your speed in reaction or travelling;
  (b) ability in travelling backwards, forwards, changing direction, recovering quickly.
- Were there any ways in which your opponent exploited your fitness?
- What were your main fitness weaknesses?
- What were your main fitness strengths?

HOW SHALL I USE ALL THIS INFORMATION I HAVE GATHERED TO ASSESS MY PERFORMANCE?

There are a number of different ways you can use this information. First, however, there are two important questions that you must answer:

What have I learned about my performance and my opponent's performance?

What do I need to do to become a better player?
Only when you have answered these two questions can you actually assess your performance and work effectively to improve it. You need to sift through all your answers and make a summary of all the information that you have gathered.

I have devised a simple ***Performance Analysis Report Form*** for you to copy and use, unless you want to devise your own. It can be used for singles or doubles matches. Complete this form.

Now you have completed the analysis report form you can consider some of the further benefits of doing this analysis.

Create a file on each of your opponents
You can use the questionnaire not only to gather information about opponents you have played but also about future opponents. If you observe or video them you can study their game and plan and work towards eventually beating them. The more you practise analysing and studying your own and your opponents' performances the better you will become at doing so and the more you will increase your chances of winning. You will be able to devise practice situations in which you can improve your own performance, learn how to exploit your opponents' weaknesses, cope with their strengths and plan your tactics accordingly.

Practise and train to improve your perform-ance
Now you have an accurate assessment of your strengths and weaknesses you can work to improve your game. You can assess your fitness training programme and decide whether you are doing the right training or need to adapt and improve it. You will recognise areas in which you may need to get back to the practice court – you may need to do some standard technical skill practices or some individual specific skill practices (*see* page 20). In this way your practice will become more meaningful because it will be directly related to the situation you have experienced in formal competition.

Practise mental rehearsal of your game
Included in the performance analysis report form is a section on 'How would I play him next time?' Your analysis should have given you a good picture of your opponent's game which you can use for mental rehearsal. This is a method used successfully by athletes in many sports to help them imagine themselves competing in a competition. The idea is that you sit quietly, concentrate and imagine yourself playing a particular opponent. Picture yourself serving, your opponent's reply and the subsequent rallies. In this way you will 'see' the game developing and become familiar with your opponent. Some players find that this helps when they actually meet their opponent on court. They feel more prepared and it helps them to 'read' the game and cope with their opponent.

PERFORMANCE ANALYSIS REPORT FORM

NAME   TOURNAMENT

OPPONENT(S)   ROUND
NAME(S)
                                    DATE

WHAT DID I LEARN?

About My Game

About My Opponent's Game

WHAT WORK DO I NEED TO DO?

HOW WOULD I PLAY HIM (THEM) NEXT TIME?

CHAPTER 19

Prepare and Compete to Win at Singles

The singles game is for the solo artist. It is for players who feel at ease and enjoy being alone on the court; who like being independent and responsible for their own actions and want to control their opponent's or create their own opportunities. Above all it is for players who relish the ups and downs of a good one-to-one battle. If this is how you like to play then the singles game is for you. The purpose of this chapter is to help you to become a better singles player.

Your primary aim in singles is to beat your opponent. All your efforts should be directed towards this, but you should also have a secondary aim. When the game is over, no matter whether you have won or lost, you should also want to know whether your performance has improved and your game is progressing. You should be able to learn much from each game as formal competition is the only true test of your performance and a measure of your progress as a player.

To achieve your primary aim is relatively simple. You must win more rallies than your opponent by working to ensure that your opponent doesn't return the shuttle back over the net; which he will not do if you hit the shuttle to the floor or if he makes a forced or unforced error.

To achieve your secondary aim you will have to analyse the game to find out how you have played. You should analyse and assess your own and your opponent's performance, decide where your play was satisfactory, where you were weak and whether you are making progress. With this knowledge you can continue with your training and practise to eliminate identified weaknesses and maintain your strengths.

All players try to achieve the primary aim but few players, in my experience, give sufficient thought or effort to the secondary aim. Yet it is only by trying to achieve your secondary aim that you will increase your chances of winning. This chapter should help you to focus your attention on and help you to achieve both.

As a start here is a list of the main qualities that I try to develop in the singles players I coach. I feel that if players can improve in these areas they will become better players and increase their chances of winning. All the qualities simply illustrate some aspect of your technical and tactical skill, fitness and attitude.

THE QUALITIES OF A GOOD PLAYER

TECHNICAL SKILL

- Has good body skill and moves around the court lightly.
- Plays all his strokes easily and fluently.
- Makes fewer errors and is consistently more accurate.

TACTICAL SKILL

- Makes fewer errors.
- Seems to have more time to get into position to hit the shuttle.
- Seems to have less space to cover and always seems to be in the right position to cover his opponent's replies.
- Can deceive his opponent when necessary.
- Plays the right shot at the right time, intentionally and consistently, i.e. uses his strokes effectively as tactical moves to play building shots and attempted winning shots.
- Can adopt a strategy to exploit the opponent's

weaknesses, create openings and take his chances when they arise.
- Can adapt his game to cope with and beat different types of opponent.

FITNESS

- Can play for longer periods of time at a faster pace before getting tired.

MENTAL ATTITUDE

- Has a good competitive attitude and can remain calm under pressure.

PREPARATION

- Knows how to practise and train effectively.
- Knows how to analyse the game and assess his performance in it.
- Knows how to prepare for competition.

How do I acquire these qualities?

You should be aware of the qualities you want to have and then try to build them. Before you begin let me remind you that this book contains information on how to develop many of these features. If you have been reading through the book you should know how to develop them. If you have not read the other parts then I will simply refer you to the chapter or pages where you can find the information. Where this is not so then the information you need will be included in this chapter.

TECHNICAL SKILL

How do I develop good body skill and move around the court lightly?

- Read chapters 8 and 12.

How do I perform all my strokes easily and fluently?

Information on this is contained in several chapters with each chapter having a slightly different emphasis. Choose which chapter(s) you want to read.

- Read chapter 5 to learn how to practise properly to improve your strokes.

- Read chapter 7 if your racket skill needs improving.
- Read chapter 9 and refer to the particular stroke that needs improving. You can find out where this is by looking at the reference list of strokes in chapter 6.
- Read chapter 11 if you want to devise your own practices.
- Read chapter 10 to learn how to analyse and correct your technical faults.
- Read chapter 12 if you want to practise under pressure.

How do I learn to make fewer errors and become more accurate?

If your technical skill is weak, e.g. poor racket control or incomplete stroke cycle then you may need to correct your stroke by eliminating any technical faults you may have.

- Read up on your stroke in chapter 9.
- Read chapter 10 to learn how to correct your faults.

If your stroke action is satisfactory then you can practise to become more accurate.

- Read chapter 5, pages 32–4 and follow the procedure outlined in the practice stages.
- Read chapter 12 to learn how to practise under pressure.

TACTICAL SKILL

How do I learn to make fewer tactical errors?

This requires a combination of your technical and tactical skill. Sometimes, however, no matter how accurate you are in practice, you can still make errors in a game. This can be caused by the pressure of the match; you may be trying too hard; you may be getting tired; feeling frustrated; or losing confidence and you go for quick winners or try impossible shots. You may even be following another one of those suspect traditional rules, 'hit to the corners' and in doing so leave yourself no margin for error. Whatever the cause you may make errors and hit the shuttle into the net or out of court. You can also make tactical errors through not 'reading' a situation correctly and playing the wrong shot for the situation. One way to reduce

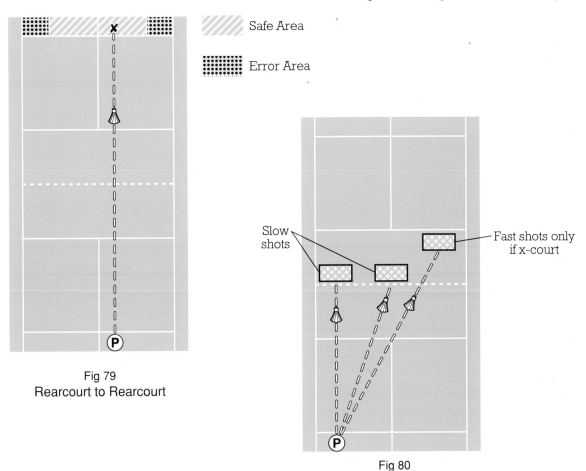

Safe Area

Error Area

Fig 79
Rearcourt to Rearcourt

Slow shots

Fast shots only if x-court

Fig 80
Rearcourt to Forecourt

these errors is through percentage play which also includes safety play.

Percentage Play

The intention here is to play a safe shot, give no advantage to your opponent and reduce the possibility of making an error. You can reduce your percentage of errors and increase your percentage of successful shots by playing your building shots to various areas of the court. Here are a few examples.

HITTING TO THE REARCOURT. *See* Fig 79.
This will apply for clears from the rearcourt and lobs from the midcourt or forecourt.

● Do not hit too close to the sidelines as this is the error area.
● Hit the shuttle to the safe area.

If your accuracy is good you can reduce your error area and hit closer to the sidelines; if not then play percentage shots to the safe area.

HITTING TO THE FORECOURT. *See* Fig 80.
This will apply mainly to drops from the rearcourt and pushes and blocks from the midcourt. When you play a percentage shot to the forecourt you must consider where you hit the shuttle and whether you hit it there quickly or slowly. The general rule is to play a percentage shot and hit straight or to the centre with fast and slow shots and across the court, the furthest distance away from you, with fast shots only.

How can I make more time to get into position to hit the shuttle?
This requires a combination of your technical and tactical skill.

- Read chapter 8, pages 51–2 to improve your quickness off the mark.
- Read chapter 12, pages 123–4 'multifeed practice', to develop your reaction speed.

In addition it will help if you know what replies your opponent is likely to play in a particular situation. This will help you to anticipate his shot and get into position earlier to return it. You should know what replies are logically possible from a given situation but you need to know which replies your opponent can actually make. To do this you must watch and analyse his game. Then you should devise a tactical practice so that you can learn to recognise and anticipate certain shots and get into position to return them.

- Read chapter 18 and learn how to analyse your opponent's game.
- Read chapter 5 about how to practise and/or chapter 11 on how to devise your own tactical practice.

Finally you can make time as follows, particularly when you are under pressure.

- Hit the shuttle very high to the rearcourt when you clear from your rearcourt or lob from your forecourt. You should hit it high and deep enough to have time to **walk** back to your midcourt before your opponent actually hits the shuttle from deep in his rearcourt. As you do this watch the opponent and not the shuttle. Practise walking in practices with your partner and then try it in conditioned games. You will be surprised how easy it is to do.

How can I make sure that I am in the right position to cover my opponent's replies?

You should know what your opponent's probable replies will be in a given situation.

- Read chapter 18 to analyse your opponent's game.

If you are not yet sure or meet a new opponent then you take up a position which will allow you to cover all the probable replies in that situation. Most coaches and writers describe this as **dividing the angle of possible returns**. *See* Fig 81 *below*.

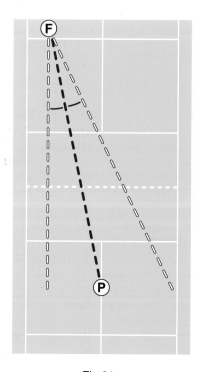

Fig 81

Your task should be to divide the angle of the possible returns from a high position in the rearcourt. Your opponent can smash, to your centre and left or right sides, dropshot to your centre and right and left sides in front of you and clear to your centre and right and left sides behind you. You have to position yourself to cover all those shots but particularly the strongest threat, the smash, as that is the shot he will most likely use to attempt a winner.

You can also make sure that you do not make your task more difficult by playing a shot that gives you insufficient time to get into position to cover your opponent's replies. For example if you are jumping backwards to reach a shuttle in your rearcourt and you hit a horizontal cross-court smash with your opponent waiting in position, then do not be surprised if he blocks the shuttle over the net into your forecourt while you are still trying to recover. Use your intelligence to play a building shot, a good high clear, so you can make time to get into position, rather than an attempted winning shot which will allow you insufficient time to get into position.

● Do not play a particular shot if you cannot cover the replies.

How can I learn how and when to deceive my opponent?

● Read chapter 17 to learn about the benefits of deception and how to deceive your opponents.

When you use deception will depend on the game situation and your opponent's likely responses. For example if you meet an opponent who continually anticipates your net reply then you might use it to catch him out. You should look as if you are about to play a net reply and as he travels forward flick the shuttle past him over his head or to the sides. If you have developed your deception you should be able to do this quite easily. It will help if you can practise using this in different situations in preparation for a particular opponent. To do this you must know your opponent, which means studying and analysing their game.

● Read chapter 18.

How can I learn how to play the right shot at the right time effectively and consistently, i.e. to use my strokes as tactical moves?

Too many players are quite weak in this area because they play without purpose. They chase around the court hitting clears, smashes, drops, lobs, net replies and other strokes as if by habit rather than design. They are stroke players rather than badminton singles players. Much of this sort of aimless play comes from poor coaching in which players do meaningless routines and aren't taught to think. If you want to be a good singles player then you have to be smarter than this. You have to use your strokes *solely* as *building shots* to create situations in which you can *attempt winning shots*. No more no less!

● Read chapter 1 to learn about the basic tactical moves and how to use them as building shots and attempted winning shots.
  When you understand how to use them then you must learn when to use them. This will vary with different opponents. Study your opponents and analyse their game so that you can plan when to use your building shots and attempt winning shots. Devise tactical practices and practise doing this in tactical situations.
● Read chapter 18 to learn how to analyse your opponent's game.
● Read chapter 11 to learn how to devise your own specific tactical practices.

What strategies can I adopt to exploit my opponent's weaknesses and create openings for possible winning shots?

There are a number of general strategies that you can use. Which ones you use will depend on how your opponent plays. To strengthen your position you should analyse his play before, during or after playing him.

● Read chapter 18 to learn how to analyse your opponents.

Try these Strategies:

Strategy 1: Play to Get the Reply You Want
There are several methods that you can achieve this:

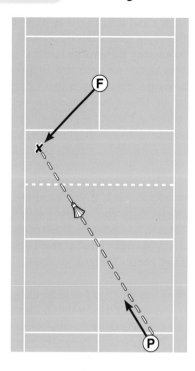

Fig 82

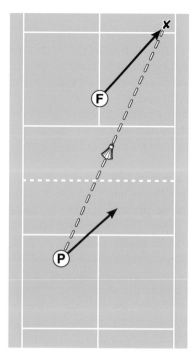

Fig 83

METHOD 1: Play to his weaknesses

1st EXAMPLE: If he always plays a dropshot from his backhand rearcourt when the shuttle is behind him, then make sure that he has to do just that. Open up his backhand corner first with a fast drop to his forehand forecourt. Then hit his reply quickly to his backhand rearcourt and travel forwards to cover any reply to the forecourt. *See* Figs 82 and 83.

2nd EXAMPLE: If he always blocks straight in reply to your smash to his backhand then make sure that you smash to his backhand and then travel quickly forwards to deal with his reply.

METHOD 2: Play to his strengths

Before you do this you must be sure that you can cope with his strengths.

EXAMPLE: He may have a strong forehand round the head smash from his backhand side which he always hits cross-court if he is in position to do so. Your task is to give him time to get into position by hitting the shuttle higher than usual and then get ready for his cross-court smash. What shot you play in reply will depend on what he does after his smash. I will let you work that out.

METHOD 3: 'Invite' a reply

Invite him to play a reply to a certain part of the court by restricting some of the space and leaving him obvious space to hit the shuttle into. *See* Fig 84(a) in which you play a net reply and then position yourself more in the forecourt, so 'inviting' him to hit into the open space in the rearcourt. Alternatively you could play a dropshot and then stay near the rearcourt to invite a reply to the open space in the forecourt. *See* Fig 84(b).

Play games: the best way to learn this is to play games.

Strategy 2: Force an Error or a Weak Reply

Your intention here is to make life difficult for him and try to force him into making an error. Obviously it helps if you really do know your opponent's weaknesses as you can then use the most effective method from the start. If you do not you will have to try them out in the game and find what works best.

METHOD 1: Hit the shuttle to the space furthest away from him

Some players are slow at travelling across the

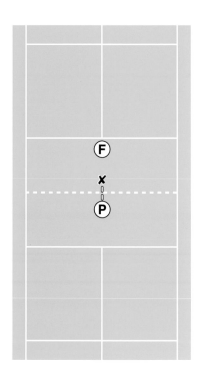

Fig 84(a) *left*
Invite the reply to the rearcourt

Fig 84(b) *right*
Invite the reply to the forecourt

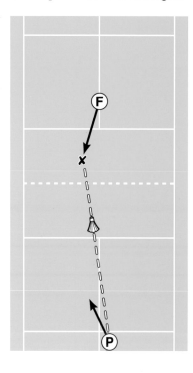

court, or recovering after playing a stroke, or running forwards, or running backwards. If this is the case with your opponent then hit the shuttle to one corner and hit the reply to the corner diagonally opposite. *See* Fig 85.

METHOD 2: Hit the shuttle back to the place he is leaving.

Some players recover and travel back into position so quickly that they can often be caught out if you hit the shuttle back to the space they have just

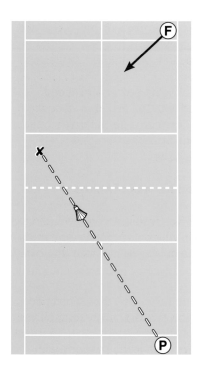

Fig 85 *left*
Hit the shuttle to the furthest place from the opponent

Fig 86 *right*
Hit the shuttle back to the place he is leaving

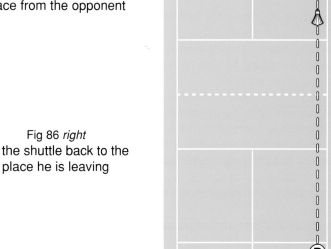

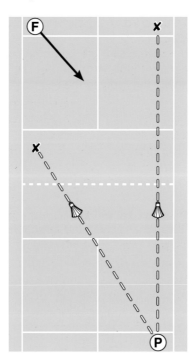

Fig 87

left. They may find that they are travelling too quickly to stop and change direction easily and that they have travelled too far to get back into position in time to hit the shuttle. Try hitting a clear and if your opponent replies with a clear, hit a fast attacking clear back to the same place as he travels forwards at speed. At the least you should get a weaker reply. *See* Fig 86.

METHOD 3: Hit the shuttle to his sides
Some players are not very agile and find it difficult to change direction at speed to the right side or left side. You can exploit this by hitting the shuttle to their right or left side.
EXAMPLE Imagine that your opponent has hit a cross-court clear from his forehand rearcourt to your forehand rearcourt and travels back to the midcourt to cover your replies. You can choose to hit a straight attacking clear to his backhand rearcourt or a cross-court dropshot to his forehand fore-court, whichever will be most effective. *See* Fig 87.

Strategy 3: Upset his tempo and the rhythm of his game
Some players like to settle down into a rhythm and

maintain a steady tempo. Your task will be to change that tempo and disturb that rhythm. You can do this in several ways.

- Vary the pace of your replies: mix fast attack clears with high clears.
- Vary your direction: play angled replies and straight replies.
- Vary your attack: play power and sliced smashes mixed with fast and slow dropshots. Hit the shuttle down on different trajectories.
- Speed the game up with fast rallies.
- Slow the game down

Strategy 4: Exploit his lack of fitness

- Read chapter 13 on fitness and you will find out various ways in which an unfit player can be exploited. Here are some methods you can start with.

METHOD 1: Play long rallies at a quite hard pace
If you are fit then you can test out and exploit your opponent's lack of aerobic endurance. Your task here is to play at a pace that you can cope with and

yet might push up your opponent's heart rate and place such demands on him that he cannot obtain sufficient oxygen for his needs and has to slow down. Then, after each rally, allow him insufficient recovery time between rallies and begin the next rally as soon as possible.

METHOD 2: Increase the pace of the rallies
As he tires increase the pace of the rallies so that he has to work anaerobically. Give him little recovery time between rallies.

METHOD 3: Exploit his lack of flexibility and strength

- Try to make him play shots from deep positions in the forecourt so that he has to attempt deep lunges. Hit his replies back to the rearcourt so that he has to lean backwards or jump to hit the shuttle. Lunging and jumping are very hard work on the legs and if he lacks strength and flexibility he will tire, slow down and may make errors or weak replies.
- Force him to change direction at speed which will also test his strength and flexibility.

Strategy 5: Exploit his mental attitude

- Read chapter 15 to read about mental attitude and how to exploit your opponent's attitude.

How can I adapt my game to cope with and beat different types of opponent?

The previous questions and my answers will give you some idea of how to do this. If you haven't read these then may I suggest that you do so before or after you read this section.

Here are a few examples of different types of opponent and how you might adapt your game to cope with them.

The fast attacking player

This player keeps up a high rate of play, meets the shuttle early and gives you little time to recover from your shots. His shots comprise fast drops, steep angled smashes, power smashes, fast attack clears and kills and tumblers at the net. He is usually very fit and extremely difficult to beat. He applies constant pressure.

METHOD: Upset his rhythm, slow him down, give him time to think and exploit any weaknesses

- Slow the rallies down by hitting high defensive clears to the centre of his rearcourt if you are under pressure. For this you need a good defence and good body skill to travel quickly into position to hit the shuttle or to cover his shots.
- Play the unexpected move and mix straight replies with angled replies.
- Try to catch him out by hitting the shuttle back to the space that he is leaving.
- Vary the pace by taking the speed off the shuttle and playing pushes to the midcourt and forecourt.
- Use your deception to delay his anticipation, to create doubt and upset his rhythm.
- Give him no chance to hit cross-court shots by playing your returns to the centre of his rearcourt or forecourt/midcourt areas.

The Runner

This is the type of player who enjoys long rallies and plays mainly building shots to the rearcourt and forecourt with the occasional attempt to hit a winner. He likes to manoeuvre you out of position and force you into making errors.

METHOD: Restrict his game so that he cannot open up the court and outmanoeuvre you

- Hit down as much as possible using your power smash and sliced smash.
- Play attack clears to the centre of his rearcourt so that he must hit from his centre which will not give him much of an angle to manoeuvre you around the court so easily.
- In the forecourt play tumblers and spinners to restrict his game to the net or to force a weak reply which you can smash.

In general his game is very simple and predictable. Try not to get caught up in long rallies unless you choose to but use the appropriate building shots and attempt a winning hit whenever possible.

There are other styles of player, e.g. the strong power player and the touch player, which you can deal with if you use the information in this chapter.

FITNESS
How can I play for long periods of time at a faster pace before getting tired?

- Read chapter 12 and train to get fit.

ATTITUDE
How can I develop a good competitive attitude and remain calm under pressure?

- Read chapter 15.

PREPARATION AND COMPETITION
How can I learn how to practise and train effectively?

- Read chapter 5 to learn how to practise: chapters 7, 8, 10 and 12 for what to practise.
- Read chapter 12 to learn how to train effectively for competition.

How do I learn to analyse the game and my performance in it?

- Read chapter 18.

Where can I learn how to prepare for competition?

Read chapter 2 which will give you some idea of what is involved in preparing for competition. As formal competition is the test of your progress towards becoming a better player the procedure to do that is quite simple. *See* Fig 88.

- Play a game to win.
- Analyse and assess your performance and that of your opponent. Read chapter 18.

- Decide what you have learned from the assessment. Chapter 18.
- Decide what features of your game need working on. Chapter 18.
- Devise specific practices or revise basic conventional practices. Read chapter 11.
- Train to maintain or develop your fitness. Read chapter 13.
- Play conditioned games in informal competition. Read chapter 5 for an explanation of conditioned games and then try some from the list below:
- Play in formal competition and repeat the procedure.

Examples of conditioned games:

GAME 1: All shots played from the forecourt must be returned to the forecourt. This will help to improve your net play.

GAME 2: No smashes allowed except from the forecourt. This game will help to improve your building shots, deception and attitude at having a go for the winner when the chance arises.

GAME 3: No replies allowed to the midcourt. This means that you will use drops and clears only and improve your accuracy in playing building shots to the rearcourt and midcourt and using your deception.

GAME 4: You must walk back into position after a lob or clear to the rearcourt. Here the emphasis is on helping you to make time to get back into position.

GAME 5: No lobs allowed in reply to the smash. This game will help to improve your defence.

GAME 6: Backhand clears only from your backhand rearcourt. This will help you to develop your backhand play. You could apply the rule to round the head shots only.

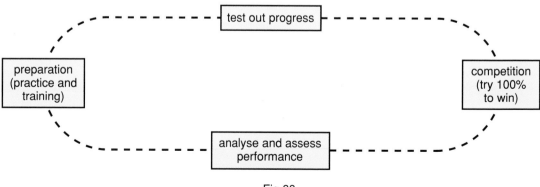

Fig 88

CHAPTER 20

Prepare and Compete to Win at Level and Mixed Doubles

oubles is a fascinating and exciting team game. When you watch top-level doubles matches it appears as such rapidly interchanging positions of the players that you may often wonder how they can know where to move to so easily and which shots to cover. In fact positional play in doubles is quite easy to follow once you understand your role and function in doubles. This will apply whether you are playing level doubles or mixed doubles.

Obviously to play good doubles you will also need all the basic skills in order to operate effectively as a team member. It is your tactical play however that is the most important feature of dou-

bles and for this you should know and understand:

a) your positional play in attack and defence
b) the roles and functions you may have to perform in those positions.

Only by doing so will you be able to prepare and compete to win effectively.

In this chapter therefore I will mainly focus on these two areas and include other aspects of level and mixed doubles team play when necessary. As you will also need to develop all the other qualities of a good doubles player, such as your technical skill, fitness and attitude, I will refer you to the

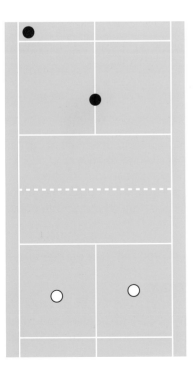

Fig 89 *left*
Rearcourt front and back
attacking formation and sides
defence

Fig 90 *right*
Forecourt front and back
attacking formation.
Lady is the front player

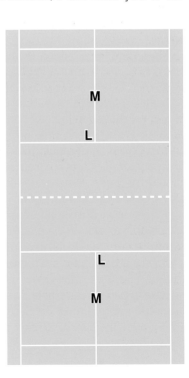

chapter or pages of this book where you can learn about them.

WHAT ROLE DO YOU ADOPT IN YOUR TEAM?

There are two main roles you can adopt when your side is on the attack. You can be the *front player* or the *back player*, as in the rearcourt front and back attacking formation in level doubles. See Fig 89. In mixed doubles the lady will usually take on the front player role and the man the back player role as in the forecourt *front and back attacking formation*. *See* Fig 90.

In *defence* you would both adopt a similar role side by side in the midcourt both facing and both equidistant from the hitter. *See* Fig 89 where the defenders are in *sides defence*.

WHAT FUNCTIONS DO YOU FULFIL IN YOUR TEAM?

There are two main functions that you can fulfil as a team player. You can function as a *hit-player* or as a *set-up player*. Your job as a hit player is to attempt to hit winners and to keep the pressure on your opponents; your job as a set-up player is to create opportunities for your hit-player to attempt winning shots. You may be one or the other type of player; or you might be one of those talented players who can fulfil both functions with equal ease.

Most effective doubles teams usually contain one player who is mainly the hit-player or the set-up player. Either one will take on the role of back or front player. If your partner is a back set-up player positioned in the rearcourt or midcourt he should try to create an opening for you as the front hit-player to attempt winning hits from the midcourt or forecourt. If you are a front set-up player you should try to create openings for your back hit-player to attempt a winning hit.

Whatever your role and function, you should still be able to take on the other role and functions to some extent should the need arise. For example if you are a back hit-player and find that you are caught at the front in the forecourt then you should be able to play a set-up shot (building shot) if you cannot attempt a winner. Similarly in sides defence a hit-player may have to play a set-up shot to regain the attack.

Why is it necessary to describe players as hit- and set-up players and front and back players?

It isn't necessary but it is useful to do so as it can help in practice and in forming a doubles team. PRACTICE: You can use all the standard attack and defence practices in doubles and devise specific practices to develop your strengths as a hit-player or set-up player and as a front or back player. You can also devise practices to make you competent, at the least, if you have to take on another role and function. And most important you can devise practices to strengthen you as a team. In these ways you can make your practice time more meaningful.

FORMING A DOUBLES TEAM

It is always difficult to find the right sort of partner to form a team with. When you do it is often more a case of good luck than careful choice. Now you should find the task rather easier. If you consider the role and function that you like to adopt then you can think about what sort of partner would be suitable.

Consider the partners that would not be suitable in a team.

- Two back players.
- Two front players.
- Two set-up players: no one would be trying to take risks and attempt a winner.

Consider the partners that would be suitable in a team.

- A front player and a back player, one as the hit-player and one as the set-up player.
- Two hit-players: one front and one back.
- Two all-court players who could play front or back and hit- or set-up functions with equal ease.

What type of team do you and your partner form?

PLAYING AS A TEAM

Team work is about playing for each other. It helps therefore if you fully understand the roles and functions that you and your partner fulfil; and how your partner will play as a front or back hit- or set-up player and how you can help him to play well.

The back hit-player

This player likes to play fast, run and jump, smash and drive hard, anticipate early and take chances. When he is on form he can be a great asset but when he is off form (which can happen at any time during a game) he can be reckless, make errors, get caught out of position and become a handicap to the team. If you are his partner then you must accept that this is likely to happen. It will not help him if you become irritated, discouraged or complain as he will be likely to lose more confidence and be scared to go for his shots. It will not help him if he tries to play safe as it is not in his nature to do so.

Your task is to show that you are not bothered by his lack of form and encourage him to keep going for his shots. In the meantime you must concentrate on your play and maintain your form which you will do if you understand and accept your partner's poor form. If you can do this then your partner will be more likely to come through his bad patch and begin to play well again. There are many benefits from discussing such a policy before you begin a game so your partner will not get too concerned about letting you down with errors and being caught out of position.

The front hit-player

This player usually has quick reflexes with a fast racket hand and can hit hard with the minimum of movement. He should be able to hit the shuttle just off the top of the net at speed. He is agile, quick off the mark and can recover quickly after playing a shot. He is adventurous and likes to take risks; he goes for his shots. His job is to keep the pressure on your opponents by always looking for the chance to go for the winner. He also will be prone to a hit-player's possible loss of form.

The back set-up player

This player usually has a range of strokes from high and low positions in the rearcourt and midcourt. He should be able to vary the speed, direction and trajectory of the shuttle. He needs good racket control and should be able to vary his attack mixing smashes, drop shots and attack clears (particularly in ladies' doubles and mixed doubles). He should be patient and prepared to work to create openings. Imagination and deception are features of his play.

Most important is that he should be ready to cover any replies to his front hit-player's adventurous attacks especially if he doesn't recover quickly enough having gone for a winner.

The front set-up player

This player should have good racket control and touch as he will need to take the speed off the shuttle and play angled blocks, soft pushes, net replies and be skilful at playing strokes just below net height. He should be quite skilful at using deception. He is usually quick and alert and able to attempt a winning shot if the chance arises. He will play building shots mainly to force your opponents to lift, allowing his back hit-player to attempt a winner. He requires patience, concentration and good positional and tactical sense to enable him to 'read' the game and anticipate your opponents' replies.

HOW CAN I BECOME BETTER AT PERFORMING MY ROLE AND FUNCTIONS IN THE TEAM AND HOW CAN WE IMPROVE OUR TEAM WORK?

Obviously you improve by doing tactical practices and playing in informal and formal competition. In addition you will need to develop some, if not all, of the qualities which good players show in performing their roles and functions. These are listed below with the chapters you can refer to if you want to develop a specific quality. Read the list and see how you compare.

TECHNICAL SKILL

● Speed in using your racket and travelling to the shuttle and back into position to cover the probable replies. Refer to chapters 7, 8 and 12.

● Consistency in hitting the shuttle accurately. Refer to chapters 7, 9 and 11.

● Ease and fluency of movement on the court. Refer to chapter 8.

● Makes fewer errors. Refer to chapters 10, 11 and 12.

● Solid in defence and can turn defence into attack. Refer to chapter 16.

TACTICAL SKILL

Most of these qualities will be covered in this chapter.

- Moves quickly into the right position in attack and defence.
- Plays the right shot at the right time.
- Plays more percentage shots.
- Has more time to play his shots.
- Knows how to apply pressure.
- Knows how to 'read' the game and anticipates the opponents' shots. Read chapter 18.
- Knows how to make effective use of his team's strengths and how to exploit the opponents' weaknesses. Read chapter 18 to learn how to analyse the game.

FITNESS

Refer to chapters 12 and 13.

- Reacts quickly to the opponents' shots.
- Plays fast for long periods of time.
- Recovers quickly after hard rallies.

ATTITUDE

Refer to chapter 15 and also this chapter.

- Plays for his partner.
- Shows good concentration, determination, adventurousness, perseverance, patience and calmness under pressure.
- Prepared to take chances when they arise – goes for his shots.

Many of these qualities will be developed as you practise to improve your team work in attack and defence. I will begin with your positional play in the various attacking and defensive formations and how you might develop your skills as a front or back hit- or set-up player in these positions.

HOW DO WE KNOW IF WE ARE IN THE RIGHT POSITIONS?

This is quite easy to work out but not always easy to do at speed during play; which is why you should practise positional play.

The general rule is: *start from the hitter and then ask three questions*.

The answers will help you to get into the correct positions. Refer to Figs 91(a) and 91(b).

In Fig 91(a) the hitter is in the rearcourt ready to smash the shuttle.

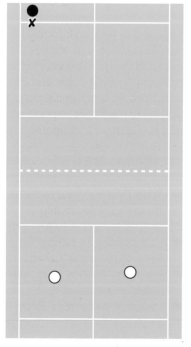

Fig 91(a)

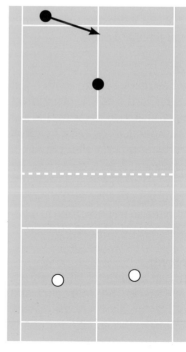

Fig 91(b)

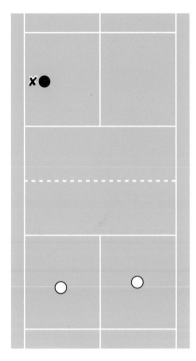

Fig 92(a)

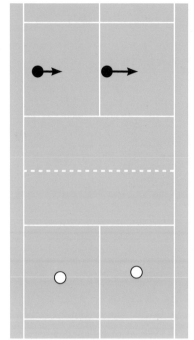

Fig 92(b)

Question 1 *Where do the opponents stand?*
The opponents get ready to cover his probable shots (his replies to their shot). These could be a smash, drop or clear. So they take up a position in the centre midcourt to cover the strongest threat – the smash.

Question 2 *Where does the hitter's partner stand?*
See Fig 91(b). The hitter's partner gets ready to cover the opponents' replies not covered by the hitter. These could be shots to the forecourt, midcourt or rearcourt. The hitter is already in the rearcourt so the hitter's partner gets into position to cover the replies to the forecourt and also the midcourt.

Question 3 *Where does the hitter move to after playing his shot (a smash)?*
The hitter's partner is already in position to cover some replies so the hitter travels into position to cover the remaining possible replies. He travels towards the centre line in the midcourt behind his front player. *See* Fig 91(b).

Here are a few more examples:
Example 1 *The hitter is at the side of the midcourt*

with the shuttle just about net height. See Fig 92 (a).

Question 1 *Where do the opponents stand?*
They stand in the midcourt ready to play their shots to the sides or centre of their forecourt and midcourt and lobs to their rearcourt.

Question 2 *Where does the hitter's partner stand?*
He stands in position in the midcourt ready to cover any replies to his forecourt, midcourt or rearcourt. *See* Fig 92 (b).

Question 3 *Where does the hitter move to after playing his shot?*
He travels to the centre of his midcourt to cover any replies to his side of the court and his partner does likewise. *See* Fig 92(b).

Example 2 *The hitter is in the forecourt with the shuttle below net height. See* Fig 93.

Question 1 *Where do the opponents stand?*
One opponent travels forward to the forecourt to cover any shots to the forecourt. His partner positions himself in the centre midcourt to cover any shots to the midcourt or rearcourt. *See* Fig 93.

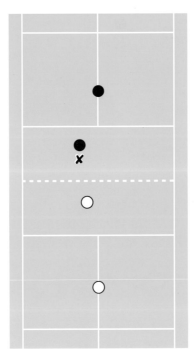

Fig 93

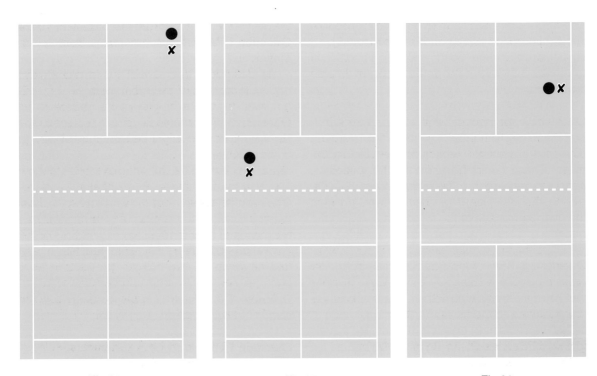

Fig 94
Hitter ready to reply from the
rearcourt

Fig 95
Hitter ready to reply from near
the ground in the forecourt

Fig 96
Hitter ready to reply from low in
the midcourt

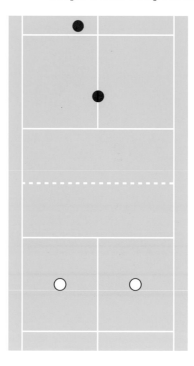

Fig 97

Question 2 *Where does the hitter's partner stand?*
He stands in the centre midcourt ready to cover any replies to the midcourt or rearcourt.

Question 3 *Where does the hitter move to after playing his shot?*
This will depend on what shot he plays and what replies his opponents can make from his shot. If he plays a net reply then he remains in the forecourt. If he pushes down to the midcourt he will also stay in the forecourt as the front player. If he pushes the shuttle to net height in the midcourt he will withdraw to this midcourt. If he lobs he will withdraw to the midcourt to defend.

If you ask the three questions above you can work out your positions for any situation in the game. Try some for yourself. Here are three game situations with the hitter in position. Fill in the positions of the other players. *See* Figs 94, 95, 96.

HOW SHALL WE PLAY AS A TEAM IN ATTACK AND DEFENCE?
Although there are a number of moves and replies logically possible in any situation you should se-lect those which suit your style of play. If you are attacking with a front hit-player and a back set-up player you will use different stroke-moves from a pair with a back hit-player and a front set-up player.

As defenders you should try to adapt your replies to the type of attack that you meet. You will not want to give a hit-player the chance to hit winners, and you should feel less threatened by a set-up player who might be less forceful though more creative.

I have provided the following examples to show you how to use different forms of attack and de-fence in different situations. I will also explain how to exploit the positional play of your opponents – for example, how to reverse the positions of the front and back players in a team. And, just in case that happens to you, how to get back to your stronger positions as front and back players.

Many of the situations apply to mixed doubles and I will emphasise this when such is the case.

Example 1 Rearcourt front and back attacking formation and sides defence
THE ATTACKERS
In this formation you, as back player, are in posi-tion to hit the shuttle. Your front player is positioned

Plate 31 – *above*
Front Man

Plate 32 – *left*
Front Lady in Mixed Doubles

to cover the reply. *See* Fig 97. He can function as a set-up player or a hit-player depending on which function he prefers. It is assumed that he can perform as a hit-player should the need arise. If he operates as set-up player you must operate as the hit-player. In mixed doubles the lady as front player will operate as a hit- and set-up player, as will the man as the back player.

In the rearcourt situation shown in Fig 97, you may have to vary your smash and use a dropshot to obtain a reply which will enable you to attack from nearer the net. Your front player should be ready to intercept, blocking the opponents' replies and angling them down to the forecourt and midcourt whenever possible. Any early interception before the opponents have fully recovered will help you, as back player, to maintain the attack.

If your front player is a hit-player, you will again have to vary your smash and drop, particularly the steepness of the smash and drop – to force your opponents to hit up towards your front player rather than at him or her, e.g. in mixed doubles. The flatter smash from the rearcourt is usually an advantage to your opponents. The shuttle can be angled away from the front player with a quick block, or hit quickly to skim the net and fall into the midcourt. Your front player will cover any reply to the forecourt with his racket held up, ready to hit down whenever possible. *See* plates 31 and 32.

If he cannot hit down he will play a tumbler to force a mis-hit or a weak lift for you to play a building shot to enable him to attack and attempt a winner. In the midcourt, he must be ready and able to leap sideways to smash, drive or push the shuttle. If he is unable to hit the shuttle hard, he will tap it downwards towards the centre midcourt or to the centre forecourt, each time recovering very quickly to travel into position to threaten and attack all replies to the forecourt. His task is 'hit and move', 'hit and move'.

THE DEFENDERS

In general you should be ready to defend against all types of attack. Here are two types.

1 *Defending against a back set-up player and a front hit-player*

You should appreciate that the back player will try to create chances for his front player to attempt a winner. Your main task will be to keep the shuttle away from the front hit-player unless you get the chance to force a lift from the front player. You should be alert to receiving steep smashes and fast dropshots, check smashes and the occasional attack clear. If you cannot counter-attack with drives or fast pushes to the midcourt then try to keep the back player pinned down deep in his rearcourt.

● Hit your lobs high and deep to the rearcourt as building shots to give you time to recover into good defensive positions. *See* Fig 98.

If your opponents hit a flatter (horizontal) smash then counter-attack. *See* Fig 99. Hit the shuttle down the lines past the front player, or whip it cross-court out of reach of the front player and away from the back player. Additionally the quick cross-court block away from the front player will often obtain a lifted reply.

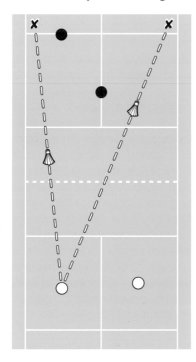

Fig 98

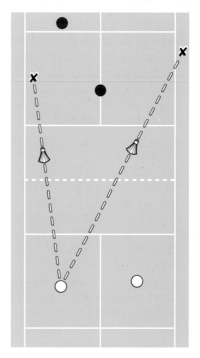

Fig 99

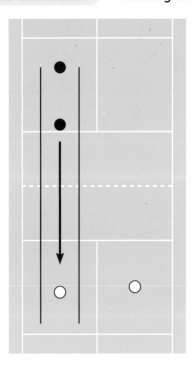

Fig 100

The opposing front player, if a hit-player, will pose a constant threat in the midcourt and fore-court. He will attempt to hit the shuttle at you or between you to maintain the pressure until he gets the chance to attempt a winner. You must be very alert and ready to counter-hit at speed. You need quick reflexes and should be ready to travel quickly to the forecourt to reply to a set-up shot from the front player if he cannot attempt a winner.

2 *Defending against a back hit-player and a front set-up player*
Your main task here is to give the back player few chances to attack. You must keep a good length on your lobs to reduce the speed of the smash on arrival of the shuttle to your midcourt. Try to keep the back player on the move and make him work hard to get into a balanced hitting position.

● Play deep lobs and occasionally whip the shuttle in a flatter lob away from him to the opposite rearcourt corner or back to the corner he is leaving, particularly to his backhand corner.
● Counter-attack his less forceful smashes with

pushes and drives past the front player to draw the back player forwards out of position.

Example 2 Channel Attack and Sides Defence
The Attack
Channel attack positions are adopted when the shuttle is inside the midcourt/rearcourt area and when the back player's smash is stronger than the straight defender's defence. It is assumed that the defender can only make straight replies in which case both attackers stay on the same side of the court as if in a channel focused on one defender. *See* Fig 100.

Your intention here is to focus on one defender, preferably the weaker one, and attack him until he weakens under pressure. As attackers you should keep the pressure on and hit fast and hard at the defender's body until you get a weak reply and then go for the kill, i.e. hit a winner at the opponent or to the floor.

The Defence
Only one defender is in action here, though his partner must be ready to take part in the rally should the attackers hit the shuttle towards him. The defender under attack should attempt to lob the shuttle high to the rearcourt or counter-hit at speed. He cannot afford to hit a soft reply. This may be possible by moving back into a deeper defensive position in order to take the shuttle later. In which case if the front attacker plays a shot to the vacant space in the forecourt the defenders must be ready to sprint forwards to make a reply.

Example 3 Wedge Attack and Sides Defence
This is a similar situation to channel attack except that now it is assumed that the defender's defence is stronger than the attacker's smash, and he can play cross-court replies. The front attacker, there-fore, positions himself in the centre midcourt to cover the cross-court reply. *See* Fig 101. The attackers focus on the one defender whose main task is to hit a deep lob to the rearcourt, or whip the shuttle cross-court away from the back attacker or push the shuttle straight to the forecourt or midcourt to obtain a lift (*See* Fig 102).

Try to weaken the attack by reversing the attackers
You can, as defenders, try to bring the back player

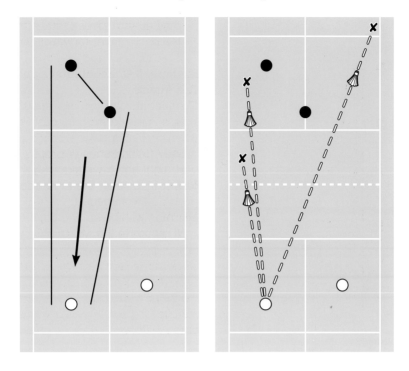

Fig 101   Fig 102

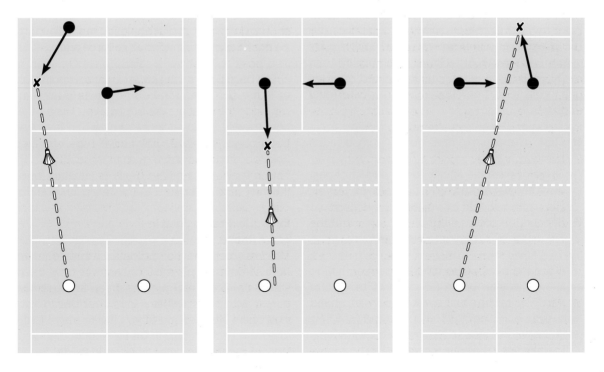

Fig 103 (a)   Fig 103 (b)   Fig 103 (c)

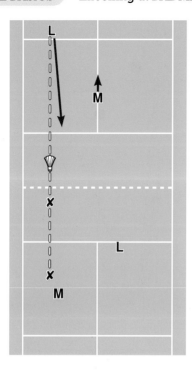

Fig 104
Lady (L) smashes or drops
straight and travels quickly
forwards to cover the replies to
the forecourt.
Her man withdraws and covers
all replies to the MC or RC.

to the front and send the front player to the back. This is a typical strategy in mixed doubles when one team tries to send the opposing lady to the back. At the world-class levels of mixed doubles this is not such a problem as with strong ladies, the ladies and men often reverse their positions by choice in the game. At the lower levels of play it can really weaken the strengths of a mixed doubles pair if you can do this. Here is how you do it in level doubles.

● First manoeuvre the team into a sides position.
Drive or push the shuttle to the midcourt past the front player and towards the back player. His partner should move into a sides position.
● Second, manoeuvre the back player into the net, or the front player to the rearcourt.

When the back player plays his reply, hit the shuttle to his side of the forecourt to bring him forwards; or, hit the shuttle over his partner's head to the rearcourt. See Figs 103 (a), (b) and (c). Their positions will be reversed as a result of two moves.

The attackers maintain the attack but now have the problem of trying to regain their stronger positions.

Try to regain your stronger attacking positions
If you have had your positions reversed then here is how you regain them.

● The current front player plays a building shot to the forecourt or midcourt to force a lob.

His back player then smashes or drops straight or to the centre and travels forwards to take any replies to the forecourt as front player. His partner now travels backwards to take up his favoured back player position. They have regained their positions in one move, e.g. a smash or drop. This is typical of a mixed doubles situation when the lady is manoeuvred to the rearcourt. See Fig 104.

Example 4 Sides Attack
The Attack
This is a typical attacking situation if your team are both all-court hit-players. You each occupy a section of the court and play as if you are a singles player with responsibility for all replies to your side of the court. If one of you has to travel to the forecourt or rearcourt to hit the shuttle then your partner would take up a position in the midcourt. Your positions then change from sides attack to front and back attack (see Figs 105 (a) (b)).

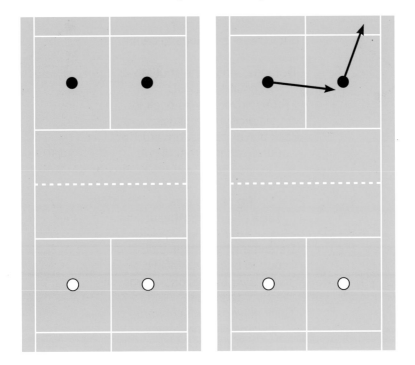

Fig 105 (a)   Fig 105 (b)

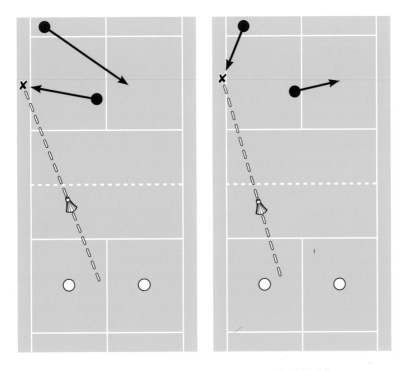

Fig 106 (a)   Fig 106 (b)

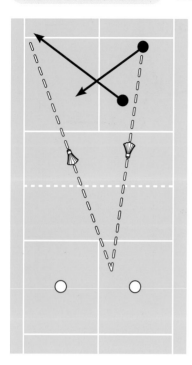

Fig 107 (a) *left*
Back player smashes to centre MC.
Defender whips the shuttle x–court to MC/RC.
Front player travels back to intercept and attack.
Back player comes forwards to operate as the front player.

Fig 107 (b) *right*
Back player smashes at defender.
Defender whips the shuttle x-court to backhand MC/RC.
Front player travels backwards to smash.
Back player sprints forwards towards channel attack position in FC.

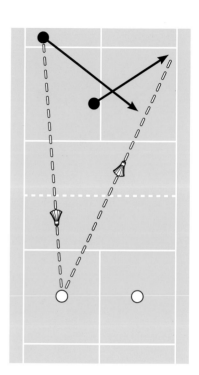

You usually take up the sides attack positions when the defenders hit the shuttle to your midcourt (*see* Figs 106 (a) and (b)). Once in that situation you should keep the pressure on your opponents with fast shuttles which skim the net and are aimed at your opponents' bodies or the space between them. In this way you will try to obtain a weak reply from which you can attempt a winner.

The Defence

As defenders you will be under pressure but in a situation where you also can apply pressure and counter-attack. You can engage in a 'slugging' match with your opponents until one side lobs the shuttle to the rearcourt or plays a reply to the forecourt. If you or your partner do this make sure that you try to reverse the favoured positions of the back player and front player.

Example 5 All-Court Attack

You should adopt an all-court attacking game when you are both equally skilful in functioning as front and back hit- or set-up players. You will only set up a chance for your partner if you are unable to function as a hit-player in the situation.

There is much reversing of positions in this type of attack as there will always be one of you trying to anticipate replies and attack the shuttle while your partner immediately adjusts his position to cover you (*see* Figs 107 (a) and (b)). You should both allow each other to be adventurous which is a dominant feature of your play. As you use speed mainly to put pressure on your opponents, there will be little margin for error.

Much of the dominance of the all-court attacking players comes from having control of the midcourt; hence the sides attack formation is used as much as possible. So unless you have pinned down your opponents in channel or wedge attack you will usually travel to the rearcourt or forecourt to hit the shuttle and recover to sides attack in the midcourt (*see* Figs 108 (a)–(d)).

From rearcourt front and back attack to sides attack (*see* Figs 108(a) and (b)).

From forecourt front and back attack to sides attack (*see* Figs 108(c) and (d)).

The Defence

As defenders you should not get caught in a fast slugging rally unless you can match the speed of the all-court attackers. You should try to control the pace of the shuttle and upset the rhythm and timing of the attackers by changing the pace and direction of the shuttle.

As the attackers continually work towards the

From rearcourt front and back attack to sides attack (*see* Figs 108(a) and (b)).

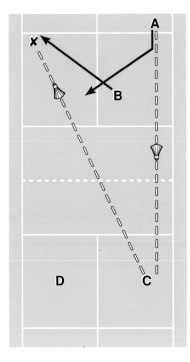

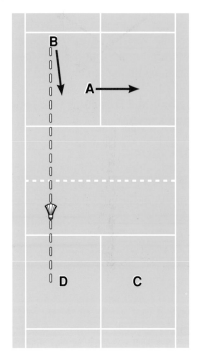

Fig 108 (a) *left*
Player A in backhand RC and
player B in MC.
A smashes to C and
approaches MC.
C whips the shuttle to forehand
RC.
B travels back to smash while
A adjusts to front player
position in MC.

Fig 108 (b) *right*
B smashes and travel forwards
to sides attack while A adjusts
his position to sides attack,
level with B.

From forecourt front and back attack to sides attack (*see* Figs 108(c) and (d)).

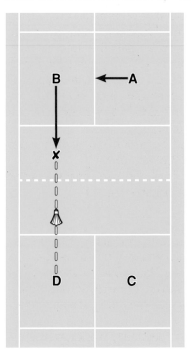

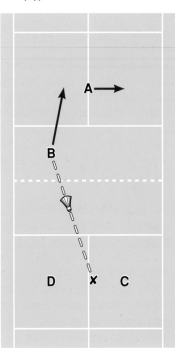

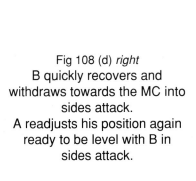

Fig 108 (c) *left*
The defender blocks the
shuttle to B's FC.
B leaps forwards to attack and
hits the shuttle between the
defenders while A adjust his
sides position to cover B
from the centre MC.

Fig 108 (d) *right*
B quickly recovers and
withdraws towards the MC into
sides attack.
A readjusts his position again
ready to be level with B in
sides attack.

midcourt to maintain control, you can catch them out by hitting the shuttle back to the space they are leaving. They tend to travel to a space, hit the shuttle and leave the space at speed. You can wrongfoot them and catch them slightly off balance by hitting the shuttle to those spaces.

Example 6 Forecourt Front and Back Attack and Defence

The Attack

In this situation you are in the forecourt with the shuttle *just below net height*. Your partner is positioned in the midcourt as the back player. Your opponents are positioned similarly. See Fig 109(a). To some extent the situation is evenly balanced between you and your opponents. Neither side has yet gained the attack nor is either side defending.

Such a situation occurs when you open the rally with a low serve, or when you are engaged in a forecourt rally with the opposing front player with your back players in the midcourt covering any shots that get past you. For example Figs 109 (a)

and (b) illustrate the low serve and two types of reply to the serve.

This is a cat and mouse' situation as you each play building shots to gain the attack. You will require accuracy, control and deception to force your opponents to lift the shuttle. The building shots that you play to the forecourt and midcourt will be determined partly by the relative strengths and weaknesses of your opponents. In Fig 109 (b), for example, if B is usually a front hit-player now positioned in the midcourt as the back player, and C is a front hit-player in his usual position in the forecourt, then B might be wary about hitting the shuttle to the forecourt where C can attack it. It might be better to drive the shuttle past C to the midcourt towards D, and for A to drop back level with B to sides attack (*see* Fig 110). This move would allow B to travel to the forecourt as the hit-player if a forecourt situation should develop. Alternatively B might decide to whip the shuttle to the right or left corner of the opponents' rearcourt and manoeuvre D into the rearcourt. This shot would be appropriate if D was a front set-up player and not so much of a threat in the rearcourt. Such a

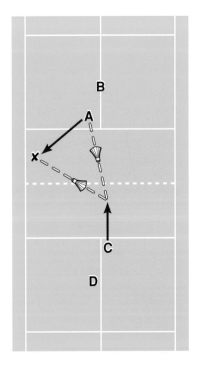

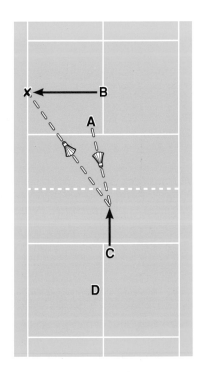

Fig 109 (a) *left*
A serves low to C who plays a net reply to A's FC. They play a net rally; each threatens the other's reply to force a lift to the FC or MC which can be hit down.

The back players on each team are positioned in the MC and continually adjust their positions relative to the shuttle position in the FC.

Fig 109 (b) *right*
A serves low to C who pushes the shuttle down to the MC away from B.
C is now ready in the FC to intercept and attack any replies to the FC or MC.
A is ready to cover any C's shots to the FC.
D is ready to cover any shots that get past C.

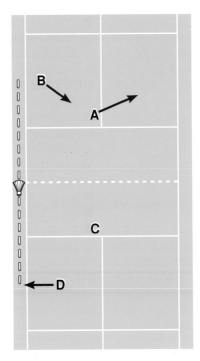

Fig 110

move would reverse the positions of the opponents and allow A and B more chance to gain the attack.

General Advice on Attacking Play
Back hit-player

● Maintain pressure with your smash and occasional check smashes to the centre until you or your front player get the chance to smash from nearer the net.
● Use your smashes mainly as building shots from the rearcourt. Mix power smashes with sliced smashes.
● Reduce the chance of error by hitting percentage smashes towards the centre or the centre side of your opponents.
● From nearer the net attempt a winning smash or force a weak reply by smashing at your opponent or to the centre or sides of the opponent.
● Smash steeply to the sides of the court to prevent the defenders hitting the shuttle past your front player.
● Recover quickly and get into position to cover

the probable replies and any replies that get past your front player. This is a typical mixed doubles situation with the lady at the front.

Back set-up player

● Maintain pressure with power and sliced smashes, fast and slow dropshots and in ladies' doubles use the attack clear to the centre.
● Hit the shuttle down steeply to make your opponents play it from low positions and hit it up towards your front hit-player.
● Hit angled smashes cross-court towards the defenders' left side so that your front player can cover any straight replies on his forehand side. You should practise this move with your partner before you use it in a game.
● Vary the pace of your smash and aim at differ ent parts of the defenders' body, e.g. head, chest, knees, as well as to his forehand and backhand sides.
● Be prepared to cover the midcourt for shuttles that get past your front player.
● Attempt a winning hit only if you are nearer the net by hitting the shuttle at your opponents'

bodies or to the centre or sides.

Front hit-player

● Be ready to intercept and hit hard at your opponents' bodies or to the spaces if it is possible to hit steeply downwards. Attempt winning hits whenever possible.
● Recover quickly to cover any replies.
● Play a building shot when you cannot attempt a winning hit.

Front set-up player

● Be ready to intercept and block your opponents' replies and angle them down to the forecourt or to an opponent's weaker side whenever possible. An early interception will reduce your opponents' recovery time and could help you to maintain the attack.

● Attempt a winning hit if a good chance arises by hitting the shuttle at your opponent's chest, weaker side, or at the floor.

DOUBLES PRACTICES

I will not provide you with a list of doubles practices as you should be familiar with many of them. It is important to understand, however, that all practices in level and mixed doubles should be designed to improve:

● your role as a front or back player
● your function as a hit- or set-up player
● your positional play as a team in attack and defence.

Before you begin any doubles practice make sure that you know what the purpose of the practice is and in what ways it will help you to improve.

Recommended Reading

Aldridge, John and Pilgrim, Norman
 Prevention and Rehabilitation of Injury,
 National Coaching Foundation,

Dick, Frank W., *Sports Training Principles*,
 Lepus Books, 1980.

Downey, J. and Brodie, D., *Get Fit For Badminton*,
 Pelham Books, 1980.

Downey, Jake, *Winning Badminton Singles*,
 A. & C. Black, 1982.

Downey, Jake, *Winning Badminton Doubles*,
 A. & C. Black, 1984.

Gleeson, Geof (ed.), 'Increasing Joint Range
 Movement in Young Athletes', ch 10, in
 The Growing Child in Competitive Sport,
 Hodder and Stoughton, 1986.

Grosogono, Vivian, *Children and Sport
 (Fitness, Injuries and Diet)*, National Coaching
 Foundation,

Grosogono, Vivian, *Sports Injuries, a Self-Help
 Guide,* John Murray Publishers Ltd, 1984.

Inge, K. and Bruckner, P., *Food for Sport*,
 Heinemann, 1986.

Fadcliffe, James C. R. and Farentinos, Robert C.
 Plyometrics (Explosive Power Training),
 Human Kinetics, 1985.

Peterson, Lars and Renstrom, Per, *Sports Injuries
 (their prevention and treatment)*,
 Martin Dunitz, 1986.

Read, Malcolm with Wade, Paul, *Sports Injuries*,
 Breslich and Foss, 1984.

Sharp, Craig, *Developing Endurance*,
 National Coaching Foundation

Way, Peter (ed.), *Food for Action*,
 Pelham Books, 1987.

Wirhed, Rolf, *Athletic Ability and the Anatomy of
 Motion,* Wolfe Medical Publications, 1984.

Wootton, Steve, *Nutrition and Sports
 Performance*, National Coaching Foundation,

Wootton, Steve, *Nutrition for Sport*,
 Simon and Schuster, 1988.